Bat-Galim Shaer

Expecting My Child
A Mother's Longing

Bat-Galim Shaer

Expecting My Child
A Mother's Longing

Translated by David Swidler

Bat-Galim Shaer

Expecting My Child

Managing Editor: Hila Ratzabi
Cover Design: Nechama Spielman
Cover Art: Bat-Galim Shaer
Photography: Michal Giladi

© All Rights Reserved to the author and ACUM for the song It's Pleasant Now by Illi Botner
© All Rights Reserved to the author and ACUM for the song Open Your Heart by David D'Or
© All Rights Reserved to the author and ACUM for the song A Great Light by Amir Dadon
© All Rights Reserved to the author and ACUM for the song Yomuledet by Bari Saharoff
© All Rights Reserved to the author and ACUM for the song Walking to Caesarea by Hanna Senesz
© All Rights Reserved to the author and ACUM for the song Yisrael by Avigdor Kahalani
© All Rights Reserved to the author and ACUM for the song Now Closely by Iddan Reichel
© All Rights Reserved to the author and ACUM for the song My Life by Smadar Shir
© All Rights Reserved to the author and ACUM for the song Everyone's Abba by Elad Shaer

The editors thank the author for allowing us to use photos from her private collection. The editors did everything in their capacity to identify the copyright holders for all material (including photographs) taken from outside sources. We apologize for any omission or error, and if such are brought to our attention we will work to correct them in subsequent editions.

Duplication, copying, reproduction, recording, digital storage, broadcast, or recording by electronic optic, mechanical, or other means may of any part of the material in this book is prohibited. Commercial use of any kind of the material included in this book is prohibited without the express written consent of the publisher.

© All Rights Reserved 2018

To my five daughters, my life's joy:
Shirel, Tahel, Meitar, Hallel, and Maor

All matters are bridges, the bridges that are all things
Intertwined branches, tied together, overlapping wings
Each with a window through which to peer, openings.
Thus bodies, too, bridge limb to limb, together-holding,
Attractive force among tears ever-flowing.
Linking plains to river, valleys to mountains rising.
Stone-to-stone meeting as brows, bosoms touching –
Horns locked, words issuing from lips... magnets and chords:
In the cleft of my breasts resting... nights of breaking waves' longing, rushing heard.
Ever-beneath, abyssal waters, and above – the birds.

> (Translated from "Lasa'if Sela' 'Eitam," *The Complete Works of Uri Zvi Greenberg*. All rights reserved to the poet's estate.)

Foreword

> In three ways does a person express his profound sorrow: The man on the lowest level weeps;
> The man on a middling level remains silent;
> And the man on the highest level of all knows how to transform his sorrow into music and song.
>
> – Rabbi Shlomo of Radomsk

As I write this we mark three years without Gil-ad, may Hashem avenge his blood. We lost our only son among five daughters. The loss caused me the most extreme emotional upheaval; our world became dark.

I confess that these three methods – weeping, silence, and musical song – all blend together in my grief. My deep pain vacillates all the time among the three, with no fixed order.

Perhaps, contrary to expectations, and in contrast to the writing process, I find myself now in the silent mode. Words don't really have the capacity to convey the coping, the pain, and day-to-day existence without you, Gil-ad.

Most of this personal journal was written in real time, except those eighteen (*chai*) days, whose sequence of events I reconstructed several months later. It begins the day of the kidnapping and ends three years after our loss, with greater focus on the first year's sequence of events. With trembling hands I tried to put things in some kind of order, to assimilate both the horrific upheaval of the tragedy and the jam-packed chronology that crowded into our lives. Real therapy, if you will. In practical terms the journal layers within its pages two intertwined acts: factual narrative and the evolution of my insight. In other words, it presents the facts as they happened, alongside personal insights that empowered me and enable me to keep living as best I can.

The cover design is my artwork.

For years I've expressed my hidden inner world through oil colors on canvas. The painting I chose, I made parallel to the writing of this book, but not intentionally so. It's no coincidence, however, that both the painting and the book express the same meaning for me.

My desire to reflect the best in *Am Yisrael*, our unique power as a wonderful people, is what led me to shine a spotlight on a nation that amazed me with its collective singing of the song of G-d [*Shirel*, an anagram of *Yisrael* – ed.] in the summer of 5774, from the launch of Operation Brother's Keeper and into its continuation that same summer, Operation Protective Edge. That spotlight formed an integral part of the purpose of this journal and the insights it contains. We felt our loss was not merely a private one, and exceeded the boundaries of private grief. As I noted, an entire people felt solidarity with us and revealed its finest qualities, returned to its essence and showed its most beautiful face.

The *chai* days can be condensed into three Hebrew words: *nora, nora* and *hod*. Terrible, and terrible splendor.

I wanted to put these feelings and qualities into writing.

Each night before I go to sleep I take inventory.

With my gaze I caress my children asleep in their beds. I say thank you to Hashem for the privilege of having them.

Each night I verify that the sheep have returned home. I love to count them, to note each one, to be extra sure that each one is where they should be at that moment.

I call to wish a good night to those who chose to spend the night away from home.

I love to watch them as they sleep, seeing the pure softness that lights their faces. In my heart I expect their relaxed breathing to calm my choked breathing, a calm that has never found a place here.

Thursday Evening, 15 Sivan 5774, June 13, 2014

It was almost one in the morning.

I finished my Shabbat preparations, the cooking, the cleaning – routine things; my routine is such that I can remember what I was doing at that moment, where my thoughts wandered at that time, what was occupying my mind...

Of course I didn't imagine what could happen. Sometimes reality surpasses all delusion.

For years I've maintained the practice of finishing Shabbat preparations on Thursday to clear Friday for quality time with my husband, for leisure or errands. That week we'd made an appointment at a ceramics showroom for Friday morning, to make some progress on the construction we'd been doing for a long time.

Drained from a hectic day, I lay in bed. In my half-awake state I ask my husband Ofir where Gil-ad was, since he'd already told us he was on the way home.

With half-closed eyes, as the day's hassles try to make room for sleep to give me strength, Ofir answers he's on the way.

"On the way? When did he leave?" I ask.

Ofir answers that he spoke with Gil-ad at nine, when Gil-ad said he'd leave for home at about ten.

Three hours had passed.

"Call him," I requested laconically. "I did. He's not answering."

Something inside me wouldn't rest – Gil-ad wasn't answering? Weird. Gil-ad always answers or sends a text.

"We should check with one of his friends before we fall asleep that he actually left and didn't change his plans," I say, positioning myself for sleep.

"It's one in the morning – are you sure? He should be here any moment."

"His friends in yeshiva are awake, it's ok," I respond, wanting to know whether he's on the way or decided to stay at the yeshiva.

One call to friends removes the small doubt and creates other, larger ones.

His friends report that Gil-ad in fact left the yeshiva at ten. The time elapsed since then is worrisome but still reasonable; nevertheless we both launch out of bed, trying to locate Gil-ad at some road junction – maybe he got stuck on the way.

We dress in a hurry and get into the car. We drive to the Shilat Junction, the only way to get to Talmon from Jerusalem and Gush Etzion.

I'm not a hysterical mother, but something didn't sit right.

Under normal circumstances, the unexpected lurks behind the expected; just how unexpected we would discover in the coming hours, days, and weeks.

Our oldest daughter Shirel, still awake, opens a phone chat. Something doesn't sit right with her, either. Maybe he changed course? Did he go to Jerusalem? His friends in yeshiva also sense something amiss.

Gil-ad is very responsible, and always gives updates when his plans change.

The one who doesn't apprise us of changes in plan is the Creator of the world.

Had I only known, I would have petitioned the Heavenly Court itself for Gil-ad, begging, praying, tearing up the heavens... but being human, what I knew then I didn't know before, and what I know now, I didn't know then. Maybe we have to stop thinking life is a given, and seize the opportunity every day to ask the Creator to protect our children and us.

During the drive to Shilat Junction, Shirel reports that Gil-ad had left with a classmate, Naftali Fraenkel, and he wasn't answering his phone either. And at Naftali's house?

We didn't know Naftali and his family, but a call to Information told us there were five families named Fraenkel in Nof Ayalon. Friends got us the right number, but the Fraenkels didn't answer. It was almost two a.m. Gil-ad wasn't at any of the junctions and the fact that the boys weren't answering and not staying with any friends, as far as we could tell, led us straight to the police station in Modiin.

For the first time in my life I wrench from my mouth the words "My child is missing," trying to give the policeman before me the sense that this is a real incident. The same sense we would try all night to convey to various people that we needed to take action. At the station they take our report seriously, reporting that they had opened an incident file, and send a police car to the Fraenkel home – maybe the boys decided to sleep that night in Nof Ayalon.

At three in the morning the police report: negative, the boys aren't there. The Fraenkel family wakes up to a painful reality of uncertainty about their son Naftali.

The boys' absence and the fact that both are unreachable on their cellphones lead the police to perform triangulation on the devices – by electronic means, the last known location of the phones can be identified, perhaps leading to the boys' whereabouts.

At four a.m. we are told that the triangulation pointed directly to the Yehuda Junction near Hevron, far away from our home in Talmon and in the opposite direction of their intended course. The report intensifies our worries about the boys' fate, a worry that thickens gradually; a worry accompanied by great optimism; a worry that unfortunately became the most painful reality.

Ofir calls the Binyamin and Gush Etzion hotlines and realizes that the reports have not yet reached all the right channels, meaning the system had not yet internalized the significance of the incident. It's a chilling feeling – every moment counts, and our son's life and that of Naftali (we didn't yet know about Eyal at that point) are hanging by a thread.

Normally we're regular people, everyday citizens. We don't have any special connections and have never needed any. At the moment we felt pain over that lack. Who could we call in the middle of the night that would take the matter seriously?

Phone call after phone call, a total of fifty-four calls to the hotline, police, and army. Two hours of eternity, two hours that, it later would become clear, were the easiest part of the journey we would be forced to endure.

At six in the morning Ofir lets me know that the army and Shabak are now in the picture; apparently you have to know with whom to be kidnapped, because Naftali's father works for the police and now things start to move.

We decide to split up. After long hours of waiting at the police station in Modiin, Ofir goes with Avi Fraenkel, Naftali's father, to the Gush Etzion area to ensure that the search is getting into high gear, and I get on a school bus going from Shilat Junction to our community to get home to our daughters. I sit a few seats away from the unfamiliar driver, attempting to remain alone with my thoughts. Tears stream down my cheeks. I refuse to believe the possibility that Gil-ad has been kidnapped is real. My worries grow stronger, conquering a place inside me.

Powerlessness and tears.

The driver looks at me and tries to calm me down: "Lady, there's no need to worry. Lots of women get on when I get to the village from Shilat, it's OK."

The words bring a smile to my lips, and I share my inconceivable worries with him: my son didn't come home and I'm beside myself with worry.

The words are not wasted. It turns out the driver will share my worries with all the teachers and students on his bus that morning. My daughters will be on that bus, and I haven't told them a thing; fortunately, they hear nothing.

Friday, 15 Sivan, June 13
Kidnapping Day 1

I come back home.

The decision not to worry the girls, not to tell them anything yet was a joint one between Ofir and me.

We were so optimistic when we heard the army and Shabak were now in the picture. There's no doubt, I believe, that our powerful army will find the boys and return them home intact even before Shabbat starts. I muster an outward smile and wake the girls for another routine day.

The girls get ready and get on the school bus as I contact the faculty and administration. I inform them we didn't think it right to worry the girls, who still know nothing, a fact that prompted an alert teacher to inform me, in turn, that not everything is in our control, and that a driver is sharing his primary-source info. Fortunately, as I mentioned, his chattering doesn't reach the girls, who go through a relatively calm, routine day at school, under the principal's watchful eye.

Meanwhile, at home, we're experiencing a most confused morning. Neighbors come and go as the news spreads. Friends are asked to make an effort to find Gil-ad, and as 9 a.m. approaches we approve an official announcement in the town: "Gil-ad did not return home from yeshiva. Anyone who knows something about his whereabouts is asked to help. The parents request that his peers be woken to see if they can provide any information."

But there's nothing new.

We're ready for Shabbat, the food is in the fridge, the floor is washed – but the important part is missing...

A neighbor comes in, gives hugs, and infuses me with inspiration and strength without her even knowing, and without my knowing how much I'll need that over the next eighteen days. "Speak to him," she says. "Gil-ad can hear you. Give him strength; he needs you strong..."

And I, so practical by nature, thirsty for every word of encouragement, say to myself perhaps I'll try it – what do I have to lose?

She continues: "Think positive and it will be positive. Gil-ad can feel you; send positive energy his way." She puts my wishes into written words, a *segulah* for finding the boys:

> I believe with perfect faith that in G-d's treasure house of unconditional gifts, and through His great power and truly infinite heavenly grace, wonderful deliverance is occurring for me in the matter of finding my son Gil-ad whole and healthy in body and spirit... (borrow joy from the desired future and cry out inside...). Thank you!

Again and again, the words "think positive and it will be positive... Gil-ad can hear you and feel you everywhere" resonate in me, and I resolve to be with Gil-ad, to project strength and optimism, to be strong for him. I believe he can hear me, so if I stay strong he will hold up well. At that moment I decide not to allow any space for negative thoughts in this story. Negative thoughts will be the end of me. The fear of what's happening right now to Gil-ad, the fear of what they're doing to him, will just drive me crazy.

The choice to think positively is, to me, nothing less than to be or not to be.

Today, in retrospect, I realize my choice then helped me immensely in standing on my own two feet and surviving those horrible, heart-heavy hours of uncertainty, through all the eighteen days – the *chai* days, as we called the search period, the numeric value of the letters representing the word *chai* – "life."

I remember going to sleep exhausted from the double effort of blocking out negative thoughts and only thinking positive ones. I tried to strengthen myself with "logical" arguments, for example that the kidnapping had to be for purposes of negotiation; Gil-ad is strong and can take care of himself; he knows we're doing everything for him, and that will give him strength; he's not alone, there are three of them; the kidnappers have interests in mind other than killing them, or they'd have shot the boys right there at the roadside; and others...

My thoughts vacillate between the horrific worst case and maximum optimism. A high-ranking neighbor in the army tries to convince me the nightmare will be over any minute now, Gil-ad will come into the house with a smile and tell me he fell asleep somewhere. "It's happened to my son occasionally," he reassures me, as I think to myself: not my Gil-ad. Gil-ad would never just fall asleep in some random place and let the whole world start searching for him. But maybe, I wish, he could be right. I try to grasp every sliver of hope.

People come and go; the house door stays open. Neighbors come in to give hugs, to see how they can help. The town rabbi enters, and I start shaking. I'm afraid to see his face, lest he bring unhappy news I don't want to hear. The whole day I swing between hope and despair. On one hand I'm afraid of news they've found the bodies, while I'm also full of hope and faith this nightmare will end well by Shabbat.

At about 11 a.m. a neighbor shows me a Facebook page put up by friends looking for help in the search for Gil-ad. Reality is starting to penetrate – everyone is looking for my Gil-ad; the incident has spread beyond the borders of this little town, of the Mekor Hayim yeshiva where he studied.

By the afternoon there would already be a gag order on the names of the missing boys, but by then social media and text apps would be carrying their full names and a call for the public to join in prayers for the three missing boys.

Journalists started coming to our town Friday morning. The town spokesman went out to greet them, and a resident representative met them with welcoming words and set out a table full of refreshments, but no entry was granted to journalists that day, and not on Shabbat. Only on Saturday night would the gates open to journalists, who over the course of the *chai* days would make Talmon their home – a place they never would have imagined they'd come to, and certainly not calling it home; a place they would find new friends, and where, later, they would fight among themselves over who would continue to broadcast from here to the rest of the nation.

Dozens of reporters were asked to concentrate themselves in one spot to prevent invasions of privacy – other residents' and ours, the Shaer family.

The only journalist to whom this did not apply was Emily Amrusi, a *Yisrael HaYom* reporter. She lives in the town. A neighbor. A friend. Of her professional dilemmas at that moment I would learn only months later.

In the afternoon the Rosh Yeshiva of Mekor Hayim, Rav Singer, visits. The rabbi is an admired personality and an inspiring educator. He gives hugs and provides encouragement: "In this week's Torah portion, *Parashat Sh'lach*, we're told about the spies sent to reconnoiter the land, to see whether it's good or bad, and to look at the nation dwelling there, whether they are strong or weak. 'You shall see the land, what it is, and the people dwelling upon it, whether they are strong or limp, whether sparse or numerous' (Numbers 13:18).

"In this *parasha* there appears the most important verse in the Torah!" says the rabbi. Remarking on the ambiguity of the Hebrew phraseology, he notes another possible meaning: "The strong is the limp! In other words, one who can let go, relax, is truly strong. Now is the time to let go. There are things that don't depend on you. Everyone is making a tremendous effort, and you have to make an effort to let go. Let those who can, do – do your part by letting G-d do His."

Wow. I'm a woman who doesn't really know how to let go. Now? How do you do that? Let go... Oh, Father, You've found the least suitable person for this struggle...

In Talmon, the local emergency squadron had gotten into gear first thing in the morning, providing updates for residents and attempting to keep abreast of the situation. Like us, they didn't imagine what we would face in the days and weeks ahead, but the brain only thinks of how to help; thoughts that would be put into practice with each passing day.

Toward afternoon Ofir returns from Gush Etzion. Partway there he met another Talmon resident sent to drive for him, since he hadn't slept in more than thirty hours. Ofir tells me he sat with Avi Fraenkel in the security forces' situation room, but when they realized they couldn't contribute a thing they decided to return to their respective families.

I remember Ofir coming into our room, and I looked at him; his eyes said everything.

We internalize that we're in the midst of a maelstrom bigger than we are – just how much bigger we didn't yet realize – and in that maelstrom, we were starting to swim...

We decide to bring the girls home not on the school bus, and to tell them Gil-ad didn't come home, but everyone's looking for him. I share the worry with them, trying to be as restrained as possible to avoid emotional scars. "Gil-ad didn't come home from yeshiva. Everyone is very worried and looking for him and his friend from the yeshiva who disappeared with him. The army is in the picture and with Hashem's help they'll find them soon."

I specifically choose not to use the word "kidnapped." Such a harsh word, a word that would enter our house only when our four-year-old came home from preschool a week later and asked me, "Imma, is it true Gil-ad was kidnapped?"

I'll answer her, "Yes... you know what that is?" Little Maor will shake her head, and I'll explain it. I'll explain that kidnapping is when someone is taken against his will, and that Gil-ad is being kept against his will, because he really wants to go home, and the Arabs who took him won't let him go home...

Through the day an army liaison staff establishes itself in our front yard, including Ofer, Roni, and Yotam, reservists called up overnight and who became part of the fabric of our lives over several weeks. They left wives, children, and a girlfriend at home to join us on this journey into the unknown. Uniformed men who live lives different from ours, see the world differently, but only in appearances. Their heart, it turns out, is a big Jewish heart. The barriers between us fall during our time together, and our hearts bond in an extraordinary way.

The hours pass. Shabbat is imminent. Suddenly a message appears on WhatsApp: "the boys were freed in an amazing military operation." The details appear precise; the report sounds credible.

But it only appears true. The liaison staff informs us the message is wrong.

Relatives, like others all over the country, get the message, which fills them with emotion. "The information is wrong," we inform them, but they're still in their false euphoria. "You're out of touch," they tell us, "everyone knows already."

The pain, against the backdrop of disappointment and chaos, is unbearable. But what about other relatives? What about neighbors? What about the rest of Israel?

For the first time, and unfortunately not the last, I comprehend the power of the cellular device, how such a helpful tool can become so destructive; how a communications network designed to connect and share information, to encourage prayer and provide support in times of crisis, can cause loss of life with false rumors.

Caution is so critical when it comes to sharing rumors.

At 5 p.m. all the news broadcasts open with coverage of searches for the three missing boys. Only then do we first hear there's another, a third missing boy, Eyal Yifrah of Elad.

Recognition is penetrating deeper and deeper. It's no longer just a story of the Shaer family and the Talmon community.

By the time Shabbat begins the episode becomes a nationwide phenomenon.

By Saturday night it has reached Jews around the world.

My optimism cracks a little before Shabbat. Does it make sense for them not to find the boys? Maybe, though, I tell myself, it's a good sign they haven't found any bodies. If they'd killed the boys, they'd have dumped the bodies. They must want them alive. I repeat to myself: "Don't let the negative thoughts in."

The neighbors ask whether we want a quiet, private Shabbat, and what to tell the rest of the families in Talmon. I smile to myself: a quiet Shabbat? Since last night quiet has been way beyond us, with the liaison staff sitting in our yard. Nevertheless, we decide to come together as a family this Shabbat, to eat two meals with just us and open up the third meal to all the town residents, with the hope it will be a thanksgiving feast to celebrate Gil-ad's, Eyal's, and Naftali's return home.

Prime Minister Binyamin Netanyahu calls before Shabbat and promises to do everything, everything to return the boys home whole. I appreciate that he called and thank him for telephoning.

Shabbat is starting; I go to my room to get ready in its honor. I remember the surprised look on the faces of the liaison staff when I came down into the living room dressed up and ready for Shabbat. The fact that you have to accept Shabbat, receive it, stop everything but keep praying but from a good place, is a gift. The home has to keep functioning. The girls need Shabbat, Ofir and I need Shabbat, and the restraint must continue.

A few minutes before Shabbat a man calls, introducing himself as a "Kabbalist." I don't recognize his name, but he promises the boys will come home by the time Shabbat is over. I draw strength from him. It will be the first and last time I pay any attention to such pronouncements.

I light Shabbat candles with the utmost concentration and intention. Before Shabbat I managed to hear that an entire people is accepting Shabbat a few minutes early; that an entire people is lighting candles with a single plea, a single prayer: the boys' safe return home. Women all over the country separated *challah* while thinking about them.

We start Shabbat with a tremendous embrace by the community of Talmon, by all of Israel, an encouraging, empowering hug.

Happy is the nation with these as its children.

First Shabbat, Parashat Sh'lach, 16 Sivan, June 14
Kidnapping Day 2

A quiet family Shabbat. I make every effort to minimize, if possible prevent, any traumatic harm to the girls. Friday evening we held a prayer service in our home with close neighbors. The Shabbat meals were uneventful. We update the girls with what we know, which is very little.

The liaison staff makes good on its promise to be invisible. Its members manage to provide calm through their presence, with continual updates – including knowing when not to give updates. As time passed, we would form amazing friendships with the people at our sides who gave us much more than a shoulder to cry on and emotional support through the insane days and nights. Every hour of the day or night they were available to us, ready to listen and trying to provide what solutions they could.

We try to keep the atmosphere calm, not to let negative thoughts in.

Only at night do Ofir and I allow ourselves to cry together, to release the emotional burden, the intolerable tension, the profound anxiety. Ofir promises me the family will remain strong and united. We try to give each other strength.

At 5 a.m. on Shabbat I awake into a nightmare and struggle to believe nothing has changed. Ofir goes off to the synagogue services. When he returns he finds me immersed in conversation with several neighbors. I wonder to myself what I want more: to be alone or together? In any case I remain restless.

Ofir sits with us and suddenly shares with everyone present, for no apparent reason, the story of his grandfather's deliverance – a Holocaust survivor. His grandfather stood among a line of people taken out for execution by firing squad by a ditch. He was at the end of the line. When they reached him there were no more bullets in the magazine, so he survived. He was loaded onto a train to an extermination camp, jumped off into the fields, and managed to elude the Nazis' claws. Later he married Ofir's grandmother, also a survivor, and they immigrated to Israel together. The story moved us all and strengthened us.

A young uniformed soldier comes into our house, a member of the liaison staff. I look at him; he seems familiar.

Several moments pass before I recognize him: he was a student of mine at the public high school in Shoham. It's only been a few years. A brief exchange clarifies that it is, in fact, he.

For a moment I'm flummoxed that he can't remember me: "I'm your teacher Bat-Galim." The next moment I realize something and stop being flummoxed – how could he remember me? My head-covering is different, my non-made-up face and swollen eyes from lack of sleep and crying have done their share. "I'm Gil-ad's mother," I continue to introduce myself. It takes me a few more seconds to realize what I've set off inside him, and the boy turns pale. You could see the shock in his face. The story he's investigating was suddenly connected to a face, to names, to memories from his high school years. To this day I don't know which was more dominant, the shock or the awkwardness.

Later on another soldier enters, this time from the *BaMachaneh* magazine, also a Shoham high school alumnus, from the same grade. He chooses to introduce himself. Good wishes, regards, and blessings for us all, from him and on behalf of the Shoham community, and wishes for a quick, positive end to the episode.

Shabbat, 4:00 p.m., and no news.

The feeling that the uncertainty would end well within just a few hours was still strong and still gave me strength.

Evening, the Third Meal

Many of the town residents gathered in our yard – young and old, friends of Gil-ad, and ours – for a group sing in a large circle. The songs take on immense significance. Each word feels carved in stone, etching marks of pain, but with a prayer of longing, faith, absolute dependence on the Creator of the World. As if the songs were written for that very moment:

"Though I walk in the death-shadow valley I shall fear no evil, for You are with me; Your rod and staff console me..."

"My brothers I seek; tell me, please, where they are grazing..."

Oh, *Ta-te*...

Rani Sagi, an educator and close friend who made sure to come to our house as soon as he found out what was happening, facilitates a discussion among those sitting in the circle. "Will you hear my words, my distant one," he opens, choosing the words of the poet Rachel (Bluwstein). "Friends and family are here to talk about Gil-ad, believing that words, the loving, reinforcing fruit of our hearts' thoughts, can reach him, and he hears us, listening," he continues. "'Hashem is your shadow at your right hand' – if a shadow shields you, how much more so does G-d shield you; from here we send you strength, Gil-ad. We speak to you in the second person because you're here, with us."

I also gather myself and speak to him:

> My beloved Gil-adush, I'm opening up and speaking to you, believing you're receiving and listening, drawing strength

from me. I want you to know I love you, that you're dear to the family, to friends, to the community, to the entire people of Israel. We're here with you, absolutely, embracing and strengthening you from afar.

Of course you know we're doing everything to find you and bring you back home safe, you, Eyal, and Naftali. I'm trying to be strong for you, to give you strength. We get that strength from the whole amazing community and from the whole people, and I hope that energy is flowing to you.

You always knew how to manage. I know your smarts will stand you in good stead, and I trust your tremendous abilities and wits. The army is doing everything to find you all, and with Hashem's help it will all be done as soon as possible. We're worried about you here and praying for your return, and the return of Eyal and Naftali quickly and safely.

In my mind's eye I see consecutive images of you in deep darkness, a closed room, a narrow, sealed pit. I turn in my thoughts to you, down there, in the depths. Shades of gray and black paint my heart. Where are you now? How alone do you feel? Is it hard? Are you in pain?

In the coming weeks I will notice changes in the way the shades stand out in my imagination. Since I found out you were killed, shades of blue surround your image, and as I look up at the heavens your smile doesn't leave my memory.

I try with all my might not to let my imagination run wild, happy I've never watched horror films in my life. I feel pained that you, Gil-ad, have seen horror films; I lament the historical accounts you've read of soldiers held captive. Where do your thoughts go in such moments? How much fear do you feel?

How exposed have you been to the unending possibilities of evil? Rabbi Nachman of Breslov wrote:

> A person is located where his thoughts are focused; make sure your thoughts are in the place you want to be.

What do we put in our heads – what do we fill our thoughts with? How do we build our internal, spiritual world? I've spoken with you a lot about that, Gil-ad. Be strong. I'm praying with all my might. All of you, be strong.

The liaison staff are touched, moved by what they see and hear. The songs and communal togetherness inject us with the necessary determination to keep our thoughts from going where we don't want to be.

Shabbat ends. No news.

I can't believe the Shabak and IDF – the strongest army in the Middle East – haven't found the boys. I was sure within a few hours we'd get back to routine, and never considered at that moment how far away we were from that, and how far you would be taken from our lives – even a year later.

After Shabbat ends the neighbors ask whether we'd prefer to curl up and maintain our privacy, or were we prepared to let the people of Israel – knocking on the door, wanting to embrace and strengthen – into our space. Without hesitation, and with a powerful inner sense, we answered together: if the people of Israel are knocking on the door, we're opening it.

At the time we didn't realize the full depth of that decision's significance; we didn't get what it meant to open the door to our humble home; we didn't grasp the price opening that door would exact from us nor the strength we would receive from it. So the door was opened, and the future would prove how right that decision was – and we would bless it with all our might.

In those moments when our door was opened to *Am Yisrael*, the entire town was opening its gates to the many journalists thronging there since Friday. Town residents set up a proper place outside our house. A few hours pass and the media personalities realize that in Talmon they won't need to fight one another for prime time or an exclusive picture. Here the discourse is different. Here we share information, involving and respecting one another. Here we welcome guests no matter where they come from. Here they can feel at home.

That first Saturday night we receive a report of a mass rally at the *Kotel*, and of hundreds of local prayer gatherings in communities around the country. We would see the moving footage later.

It's close to midnight. It's been two whole days since the night they were kidnapped. We had already established preliminary contact with the Fraenkel family that night. The existence of a third captive boy, Eyal Yifrach, we found out about only before Shabbat, and the thought won't leave us alone. We decide to call his family first. What will we say to them?

Iris answers; Uri joins in. On the other end we hear strong people, full of faith. They sound optimistic and that gives us strength. "Eyal is strong and mature; they'll get through this together valiantly and come home safe, with Hashem's help," they seek to encourage us. We're moved by this amazing couple and try to find comfort in the words of our partners on this odyssey, the duration of which we had yet to imagine.

Sunday, 17 Sivan, 15 June
Kidnapping Day 3

The feeling that the whole nation is behind us reinforces us moment by moment. The stream of visitors doubles and triples. Throngs of people flow to our house just to be with us, to provide support and hug us. We don't know most of them.

The parade of VIPs also begins. Members of Knesset, ministers, and figures from across the political and social spectrum rush to us. Some admit it's their first time in Judea and Samaria. Artists, authors, and intellectuals don't forgo their contribution and presence. They try to support, sing, generate discourse that unites and strengthens, and the humane side in everyone is revealed in all its beauty and splendor. People who think differently from one another, who hold clashing opinions, people who habitually criticize one another and attack others' positions, are revealed as people who want the best. They bring to expression their primary drive to do good.

So much care and concern comes out in *Am Yisrael*. Such love exists in this nation. We discover more and more of it each day.

People visit us with a hug and baskets of baked goods and other foods. Food manufacturers and supermarket chains deliver large quantities of food, drinks, dairy products, and disposables. Later, a neighbor will tell me a dairy company's truck couldn't get onto our narrow street. The driver just unloaded his merchandise on a neighbor's lawn and asked for help in distributing it. All the children on the street enjoyed fine yogurts and puddings that day.

A beverage company truck brings soft drinks and leases a huge refrigerator that is placed in a neighbor's yard for all the people visiting from near and far.

Someone donates large fans to help bring relief to those visiting in the oppressive heat. Giant umbrellas go up in the yard. It's not an easy sight for me. Those shades are usually seen at the homes of people sitting Shiva, whereas we're sitting waiting for our son to come home.

We consciously don't let anyone photograph or film inside the house, a decision I will in the future come to regret on occasion. I don't want the camera to disrupt the special atmosphere that's been created there. I prefer to experience things as they are, without the camera's eye, which I think distracts from the present and causes people to act unnaturally.

The way the people of Talmon are coping with the situation surprises us anew each day. Residents take off from work to be available for anything they might be asked to do. To participate. Committees of volunteers form for every purpose. They think of everything: taking care of the girls; help with food prep and daily chores; spokespeople to speak to the media; contacts with VIPs; and much more.

All the residents on our street open their homes, for bathroom use or a refreshing drink. One neighbor called our oldest daughter, Shirel, and offered his car for whenever she felt like taking a break. They were always trying to determine what would help us. They never stopped asking: what would make this easier?

To this day I'm stunned by the fact that I didn't know what to answer, but the people of the community, with their healthy, spot-on sense, knew better than I, and their help can't be measured in gold. They even recruited Hadas Harel, a healer from the town of Neriah, for the purpose. Every evening, at the end of a grueling day, she waited patiently for me with a calming body treatment, as if trying with her delicate touch to draw away a bit of the anxieties and worry that wouldn't leave my body and soul alone.

The people around us thought of everything. They managed to clear our schedule and heads so we could focus on one thing: bringing Gil-ad home.

The only ones not allowed to enter or home were journalists and photographers, except for one, a neighbor. As I mentioned, Emily Amrusi was with us from the first moment, as a friend.

She's with us much of the time, and tries to keep a journal of sorts to share with *Am Yisrael* what's going on, who we are. For the first two days I'm suspicious. I ask to see every word she writes. Very quickly I realize she's a friend more than a journalist, and let her write with a free hand.

The significance of the statement I would hear thousands of times later on, for months afterward, "I know you well, but you don't know me," I would appreciate only much later, when I had found time to read all those articles coming from our house during those days.

Over the course of the day we are told that one of the boys managed to phone the police, and that his call apparently didn't get proper attention. Only later would we discover those were the final moments of his life, their lives. I'm sure it was my Gil-ad. His sense of responsibility, the intuition with which he was blessed, point to him without a doubt. Within a few hours the doubt becomes complete certainty: it was indeed Gil-ad; the matter is under investigation.

Waves of motherly love and pride fill me up. What was in that conversation? We're so curious; we want to hear it.

What abilities you have within, my child. I'm sure you'll get through this mess safely, because you know how to manage and take care of yourself!

Oh, *Ta-te*, we so need your help...

Evening

Singer Aharon Razel comes to embrace and give strength with music and songs. The encounter begins with us at home, and grows into a tide of people moving toward the synagogue plaza, trying to break open the heavens in tremendous song.

There's chaos in the house with people coming and going, and I decide to join in the last part of the evening's events. I emerge in house clothes, tired from the day's toil, physically and emotionally. The many hours without sleep, the unceasing worry, show on my face.

I join the circle of women hugging and singing in the plaza. The intensity of prayer and pain is visible to all. The singing is infectious; the atmosphere, one of a kind. Suddenly my eye spots a camera lens, of a photographer about to shoot. They caught me, I think to myself. I signal to the photographer, gently, that I really don't feel like having my picture taken right now, and am moved by his humanity as I see him lower the camera and gesture to his colleague: "She asks not to be photographed." That's how my connection was with the media at that time – human, supportive, and mutually respectful.

The suspicion and mistrust on both sides were replaced by appreciation and the dispelling of stereotypes, ours toward them and theirs toward us. At first we refused to cooperate with their cameras, and at first they refused to believe it was possible to conduct respectful discourse with "settlers." But when the barriers came down, the sky was the limit.

One of the reporters joins the dancing. A Talmon resident who pulled him into the circle told him after a few laps he could "go back to work." "Forget it, I'm praying with you now," answered the reporter with deep emotion. He stayed in the circle, hugging us until the prayers ended.

A resident saw him crying on the side afterward.

Monday, 18 Sivan, June 16
Kidnapping Day 4

I went to sleep optimistic two nights in a row. How do you fall asleep? Just by collapsing. No nightmares, no dreams.

That's what happens when you're awake all the time...

The real challenge at this time is staying vigilant. Think positive. Our natural inclination is toward negative thoughts. Unpleasant scenarios. But as I said, you can't let those in. Not now. It weakens you and drives you crazy.

Think positive, and it will be positive.

Think positive and make it reach Gil-ad, the boys.

Send out positive vibes. That's what he needs now. It's what we need now.

For two days I got up crying; I woke up to the impossible. Monday morning I awoke to a surreal situation. In the morning WhatsApp is buzzing with news that they found the boys' bodies. The liaison staff again protects us, telling us it's a false report.

I find it hard to make peace with the report. Why would anyone spread such a lie on the internet? Maybe they want to protect me? Maybe they haven't had a chance to update someone important so they're waiting to release the official announcement? I refuse to accept the denial and tell the staff I don't believe them; I know what I'm feeling.

They look at me, pained, and insist it's a false report.

Again a communications network becomes an intentional miscommunication network. Frankenstein's monster. The same cruel dilemma as always: a tool with immense potential to benefit humanity, at the same time so potentially and profoundly damaging. Are we aware enough of the power of social networks? Do we sufficiently understand the advantages and disadvantages? Have we internalized the necessary level of caution before we share unsubstantiated information?

The town's spokespeople deny the rumor, and hours pass before everyone realizes it was false.

Ta-te, I don't have the strength... my batteries are drained.

Am Yisrael continues to come en masse, supporting and embracing us. Another text message from a student long ago, another message from a current one.

That day, in the afternoon, Mrs. Sarah Netanyahu comes to us. We suddenly became aware of the human side of public figures. They're all human. Mrs. Netanyahu is full of compassion, and offers us practical advice from her professional experience as a psychologist. She promises the prime minister will do everything to return the boys home safely.

The Minister of Internal Security Yitzchak Aharonovich also arrives. He takes us into a side room. He promises the police will take responsibility for the failure with the phone call. That the matter is under investigation. At that stage we decide to leave the issue alone so that efforts can be fully dedicated to the search for the boys, and the matter can be examined after the boys come home. We feel this isn't the right time. Knowledge of the phone call, which we've yet to hear, and of the snafu in handling it, will yet echo inside us again and again.

At least we don't have pangs of conscience or guilty feelings.

Today, looking back, I know nothing would have helped: the boys were murdered minutes after they got in the car. It wouldn't have helped if the police had acted quicker. It wouldn't have helped if they'd answered the call quicker.

We couldn't save their lives.

We harbor no anger or accusations toward anyone. It's the harshest decree, and we have to live with it.

Nevertheless, it's clear the State would have saved much money and time had they gotten to the car in time, and the right conclusions must be reached so that such a situation doesn't happen again, G-d forbid.

But we're beyond such help now.

The police did in fact reach the proper conclusions and improve its emergency response procedures.

Does it guarantee against human error? I'm not so sure. Only those who do nothing don't make mistakes. We have to train our children to call the police in any case. Imma isn't always available, and her conversations aren't recorded.

That afternoon representatives of the town organize a tour for the journalists. Many of them are in Talmon for the first time in their lives, with a good number never having crossed the Green Line. The youth center holds a meeting of all youth movement coordinators of the Matteh Binyamin Council. It turns out all Council sessions have been moved to Talmon for the time being.

The youth give the reporters a tour, taking them along the paths and showing them the wonderful activities taking place at Shulamit Heiman's Corner, a place for soldiers to take a break, in memory of a Talmon native who had died of cancer two years earlier. The Corner serves the many soldiers in the area and is run by the youth and women of the town.

In the afternoon Rabbanit Yemima Mizrachi comes to support me. Such a wonderful woman, so special. "What will be?" I ask her. "What are you feeling?" she asks, and explains: "I trust a mother's feelings." "I don't feel anything," I answer. "I don't know myself right now." Moments of weakness in her presence, and now I can't keep the tears inside. Together we pray for the swift return of the boys home.

That afternoon we also get a visit from Esther Pollard, the wife of Jonathan, and with her Asher Mivtzari, one of the principal activists campaigning for his release. They share what they're feeling, describe their activities, and the support Jonathan gets from *Am Yisrael* that gives him resolve.

The head of the Jewish Agency, Natan Sharansky, also comes, and tells of his experiences in the Soviet gulag. "In the end," he says, trying to give encouragement, "it all passes and seems like a single day. With the perspective of time, Gil-ad will come back and recover, *B'ezrat Hashem*."

A little over a year later a recording will be publicized with the story of the day before Scharansky was imprisoned and received a phone call of encouragement from Rabbis Eli Sadan and Tzvi Tau. They asked him to remember that *Am Yisrael* was with him and would do everything to free him. During those years in captivity, the jailers and KGB tried to weaken him by telling him everyone had forgotten about him, that he had nothing to fight for, but he never forgot that phone call and knew a whole nation was behind him. That's what gave him strength and implanted in him the certainty that there was a light at the end of the tunnel.

That's also what I thought at the time would give Gil-ad strength. Gil-ad knows we'll do everything to free him. He also knows and feels a whole nation is behind him. That's the message I try to convey to him via the cameras, certain that his captors will use those images. I'm sure he's alive and watching them.

That week a Knesset lawmaker uploads a post to Facebook with preliminary information indicating it was Gil-ad who made the phone call from the kidnappers' car. Until then neither the public nor the kidnappers knew. The MK had visited our home and we talked freely about it. She asked me if it was Gil-ad. "He's not a kid, but a real man, physically and emotionally strong, and I wouldn't be surprised it was he who mustered the courage and resourcefulness to report the kidnapping," I told her with pride. Not for a moment did I consider she might use what she heard from me. Right after her Facebook post goes up I call her, and ask if she's willing, in exchange for such a gossip scoop, to have my son get beaten. If the kidnappers find out it was Gil-ad who made the call they'll have no mercy. She's embarrassed and tries to apologize. She stammers something about not being the first one to release the information. You can't undo what's done.

When Iris Yifrach tells the media that Eyal is the strongest and oldest of the three, I immediately call her and warn her to be careful with what we say so the kidnappers don't misuse what information they get. "Why do you want them to know he's the biggest? You want him to get beaten the most?" That was my mode during that period. Gil-ad was always on my mind. My brain wouldn't let me rest: what are the kidnappers doing with the information they get? How are they trying to manipulate the boys? And other such questions.

Monday Evening

Friends in Talmon press us to speak to the media: "Racheli Fraenkel spoke yesterday; you have to go out there today. *Am Yisrael* wants to know the faces behind the prayers, who are the parents of these boys... if you want the people to stay with you have to be exposed to the camera." Emily, as well, armed with her media experience, pressures us and recommends not to delay any longer. I relent.

A good friend who was with me at the time tells me to go shower, dress up, and put on makeup before the filming.

"Are you sure?" I hesitate. "How will that be interpreted? Dressed up properly? With cosmetics? In times of trouble?"

Gil-ad's picture leaps into my vision... the kidnappers will certainly use these images to pressure my beloved son. I can't grant them any possibility to use this to manipulate him; Gil-ad will see we're strong, and he'll steel his resolve.

That thought kept me going throughout the ensuing *chai* days. It put words in my mouth and enabled me to cope with the filming and the exposure. I see Gil-ad's image standing before me, watching us from the wrong side of the camera.

I make my first appearance to the media, in the square near our house, where the reporters and cameramen are waiting, and am surprised by the number of people waiting to hear what I have to say.

> We're in the midst of a difficult period. I want to embrace *Am Yisrael* with a tremendous hug, a hug of appreciation, of prayer. We feel your tremendous embrace. It strengthens us; it gives us resolve; and all that positive energy I pass on to Gil-ad. Gil-ad is a strong kid; I'm sure Naftali and Eyal are strong...
> I want to request of Am Yisrael to continue praying for the boys, for the soldiers and security forces who are doing everything with amazing dedication. With this togetherness, with these prayers, we will breach the heavens quickly. We know that from the prime minister down to the last soldier, everyone is doing everything possible to bring back our beloved boys, and I want to encourage everyone and say thank you.

Appreciation envelops me the whole time. An entire nation enlists to find three boys who left for home and never arrived. No other place in the world is like this... the solidarity of everyone – from the cabinet to each and every soldier and citizen – can't be taken for granted, and it empowers us. This is the mutual responsibility of a whole nation anxious to find its children. A whole nation in Israel and abroad, as we will gradually learn.

Happy is the nation that these are its children.

From that day I ask the public praying for the boys to add a prayer for the welfare of the soldiers and security personnel searching for them, and I plead to the Creator that none of the soldiers or searchers come to harm when looking for them.

Late at Night

The World Cup is on.

A friend brings a report of an announcement prepared by Minister of Communications Gilad Erdan and Minister of Sport Limor Livnat, broadcast at the start of the game to all viewers in Israel:

> Before we go to the game broadcast, we do not forget for a moment. The Broadcast Authority and Channel One share the worry and pain of the families of the missing: Naftali Fraenkel, Gil-ad Shaer, and Eyal Yifrach. We all hope to see them soon. Our hearts are with you.

Later we will see pictures of Israeli fans at the World Cup. They made signs calling for freeing the boys safe and sound, and waved them during the game.

It's already close to midnight. Sleep appears nowhere on the horizon. The sounds of sawing come from the yard; I go out and don't believe my eyes.

Two of the neighbors' kids, Gil-ad's age, are mowing the lawn and pruning the hedges at the entrance.

By their side stand Yissachar Heiman and Yaakov Dolev, two dear neighbors who took charge of the operational side of things. It turns out you need significant logistical planning for such situations. I feel embarrassed.

"You didn't mention it was all-inclusive," I smile. "This is already awkward. You're already taking care of the food, the girls, the guests – what's the garden got to do with it? Gil-ad will be very happy to know you're helping him with this, since he hates to prune, but still, I feel awkward and it's late..." They smile back: "The house isn't big enough for all the people coming, and you'll feel better when the garden is all set."

They were so right. I would bless them repeatedly over the coming days, which grew far longer than anticipated.

A neighbor from the town of Neriah, Rabbi Michael Rekhel, would arrive later on and take upon himself the gardening care with his students from the Elisha junior college. Wonderful boys.

Tuesday, 19 Sivan, June 17
Kidnapping Day 5

We decide to initiate a joint meeting in Nof Ayalon with the Fraenkel and Yifrach families.

Morning. Ten o'clock. We leave our home and town for the first time since the night of the kidnapping, with a police escort, to Nof Ayalon – to the home of Racheli and Avi Fraenkel. The three families meet for the first time. We didn't count on this becoming an enduring, profound, and extended relationship. Three sets of parents in the same careening roller coaster car, getting to know one another.

We finally meet the people behind the names.

The conversation opens with a round of introductions. Each family presents itself.

Before we start to wallow in the difficulty and anxiety eating away at our hearts, before we start discussing solutions and what to do, we have a short talk about one question: what gives me strength at this time? We try to give strength to one another and discover wonderful, strong, faithful families. Then we move on to practical matters.

The media outside want us to come out with a joint announcement, and the last part of the meeting is dedicated to formulating the message we will deliver to them. The fact that we all completely agree with the main points stuns us.

The announcement includes a thank you to the citizens, security personnel, and government for their absolute dedication, and for the intensive searches; an expression of confidence in our leadership and security forces; and a request from the public to keep praying for the boys to return home safely.

I hug Racheli and Iris, and feel how the three of us share one beating heart.

In the afternoon I go out to my yard and see a group of seniors sitting around a table studying Gemara. Some of them look familiar. "Where are you from?" I try to clarify.

"We're the parents of girls who studied at the Renanim Amit high school in Raanana more than ten years ago. Every week we learn *Daf Yomi* together. We decided this week we should hold the learning here, with you, at your place, for the boys' welfare and safe return home."

Perhaps it was only during this period that I truly grasped the immense power of my chosen career in teaching. What a tremendous embrace I got from my students then; what reinforcement and encouragement. The phrase, "and create many disciples" gives meaning, puts all the difficult moments in teaching in different terms, and reminds me repeatedly how right I was to choose it.

Gil-ad would say to me with a half smile, when he saw the many hours of work I'd dedicate at home before or after delivering a lesson, the tests and homework I'd grade, that it makes no financial sense to be a teacher. So you were right, my Gil-adush, it really isn't the most economically rewarding profession, but the gratification and satisfaction are priceless.

Evening Descends

Ofir goes out to talk to the press. It's hard for him; he's afraid he might break in the middle of speaking.

They tell us we're broadcasting strength, but I have to tell you that strength comes from you.

We're waiting for the children, for Gil-ad, for Naftali, for Eyal, who are all of our children. All of *Am Yisrael* has committed itself to this, and we feel we already want to see them here. We feel the connection with all the communities, the entire public. Representatives from across the political spectrum were here with us, and they are all united in this. We're getting phone calls from all parts of *Am Yisrael*. We're getting support from communities around the world who are praying for our children.

Keep praying and supporting one another, supporting the security forces and the government of Israel, who are acting night and day for our children's sake.

We know the government of Israel, the prime minister, the IDF, and the security forces are doing the utmost and we wish to strengthen them.

We trust Gil-ad, who has strong faith and great abilities. I wait for the moment when I can wrap you in my *Tallit* for the Priestly Blessing, to protect you.

I pray to the Creator that we see him back at our sides soon. Thank you very much.

At night a neighbor tells us that while we were away during the day a charming young man named Binyamin Winter visited, a resident of Beit-El. This was his story: on that special morning, he, a career military officer, was on the way to get married that evening to his beloved, but his heart felt he could not go to the bridal canopy without stopping by to share his intention to pray for the boys' welfare and return, since, as he cited, "the prayer of a bridegroom is heard and accepted," as we all hope.

Later his newlywed bride, Shani Cohen-Winter, would tell us that the day after the wedding her groom was called back to his unit. With simplicity and natural faith, she added, "There are three kidnapped boys, three families no longer whole; this isn't the time to think about yourself." I was moved by her generosity and how well matched she and her husband were in breadth of heart.

A few days later the inspiring couple would return to console us in our mourning. Later again, we would meet them with their charming baby daughter, and then with another baby boy. A young couple whose unique story symbolizes our life here in our land.

Happy is the people with these as children.

Wednesday, 20 Sivan, June 18
Kidnapping Day 6

This morning we're invited to the Minister of Defense's office at the Kirya in Tel Aviv. The meeting means very much to us, and we want it to be productive. The gap between the effort invested in searching and the results is quite difficult for us to bear. We want to take advantage of this meeting and not leave it with the sense it took place only for publicity purposes.

How do you begin to think about what you need? What is it important to clarify? Good friends equip us with a list of questions and subjects important for us to raise in the discussion. We come to the meeting prepared.

The shock in the presence of a family managing to function and think during such a complicated time is visible on the faces of those in the room. It's not really us. It's our good friends who step up to help with everything we need, and assist us in thinking and formulating what to say. We're goal-oriented. We have one task: free Gil-ad; free the boys. G-d sends us the right people to help. This time they have to think.

We come home and I see all the reporters waiting for an update. Before I hold forth on the meeting with the Minister of Defense, I don't hold back – I ask them to put down their cameras and turn off the microphone. I see questioning looks on their faces, but they nevertheless grant my request.

"Tell me, how are you? Are the neighbors taking care of you? Have you had a chance to sleep and eat?" I ask. I feel proud of the people of Talmon who have opened their hearts and homes to take care of the media people each day, to provide them with food, drink, and shade over their heads.

Then the cameras and microphones are activated: "We had a meeting that focused on the issues, during which we were given the impression that the system is doing everything for our children. We hope to see them home soon."

Over the course of the day many citizens come by, among them Nobel laureate Professor Yisrael (Robert) Aumann. We sit with him and show him a photo of him with Gil-ad that Ofir took at the professor's office at the university three years earlier.

As part of the preparations for his Bar Mitzvah Gil-ad chose to explore the significance of the verse from Proverbs 3:6, "In all your ways, know Him." We wanted to give Gil-ad a glimpse into the ability to see the Creator in all aspects of life, and of the integration of Torah and practical life. We therefore selected a number of personalities who convey that integration in their careers, and Ofir and Gil-ad met them for long, fascinating conversations. One of the personalities we chose to meet was Professor Aumann.

Together we recalled that meeting, during which Gil-ad asked Professor Aumann questions he'd prepared in advance – about his childhood, about his family, about his studies, and about his winning the Nobel Prize. This second meeting is moving, and deep in my heart I'm waiting for Gil-ad to come back already for another photo with Professor Aumann.

Another accomplished person who comes to support us that day, whom Gil-ad and Ofir had also met before the Bar Mitzvah, is the rabbi and author Haim Sabato. His riveting personality was and is an inspiration to us.

Minister of Finance Yair Lapid also comes to our home that day. He tells us with emotion that he hadn't prayed since his son's Bar Mitzvah. "Six years I didn't set foot in a synagogue," he says. "When the story of your sons came out, I turned the house upside-down looking for my grandfather's *siddur*. I sat and I prayed."

Four p.m. Police representatives come to our house so we could hear a recording of Gil-ad's phone call. They warn us it won't be easy, but it's clear to us we won't relinquish this chance to hear it under any circumstances. We want to hear it and know everything possible about Gil-ad, easy or hard.

We gather in Gil-ad's room, which is near the entrance to the house, and has therefore become the place we have welcomed VIPs and conducted private conversations over the last few days. The recording device is in the middle of the room, and police representatives are there with us and the liaison staff. There's a package of tissues on the desk. Silence.

Ofir and I are excited, holding hands. Trying to encourage each other.

Gil-ad's voice can be heard, whispering, but clear. The rest is not clear to our ears. Background noises. Muffled sounds. We are told the findings are not unequivocal. That it's hard to know from the recording what exactly happened. They explain that the muffled sounds are from a gun with a silencer. We hear the kidnappers say, "Heads down," and the assumption is those were warning shots. They tell us anything is possible, and since there's no proof they harmed or killed the boys, the working assumption is they're alive.

And that's what they're looking for. Living boys. But also not. They're recruiting the finest minds and bodies to find them as fast as possible.

Ofir listens to the recording again, closes his eyes and tries to concentrate. At the end he opens his eyes and says to those in the room, "One thing I do know – my son is a hero and that's what I'm going to sleep with tonight."

We remain optimistic. Today I realize just how strong that optimism was.

The same day a national initiative is launched from Talmon: "Fly the flag for unity in Israel! We call on the public to fly the flag of Israel on houses and cars. It strengthens the IDF and our sense of shared purpose. It restores Jewish national pride and expresses support for the efforts to search for our boys. Give them strength."

The Talmon youth go out to road junctions and distribute Israeli flags to drivers and passersby.

Thursday, 21 Sivan, June 19
Kidnapping Day 7

Everything is so hard, but some moments are even harder.

It's hardest in the morning. To wake up to the worst of all. Time crawls by.

A whole night has passed and nothing new. I'm learning this is the toughest part of my day.

We wake up after a short sleep to another morning with no new information. Our frustration is immense: we were told searches are taking place during the day and focused military operations are happening at night that are supposed to help the search for the boys progress significantly, usually based on intelligence information. That news also strengthens in us the sense that the boys are alive.

It's an especially difficult morning, after a short, restless night, during which it was hinted that there will soon be a special operation aimed at a specific building in which they're sure the boys are being kept. "Pray for something good," they told us, as if we're not praying every moment. We're pouring out our pleas before the Creator of the Universe that no soldier come to harm during these searches and operations.

We wake up early after only a few hours' fitful sleep. The clock shows it's not yet five, but our heart isn't at rest and won't let us stay in bed. My soul is aggrieved they didn't wake us up in the middle of the night to tell us good news. I go down with an inquiring face to the liaison staff, who are always waiting for us with calm, radiant faces. Their eyes indicate there's nothing new, and their hearts feel the pangs with us anew each morning.

Oh, G-d, I don't have the strength!

I pray for us to be over this already, that we hear good news.

You've chosen the least suitable person for this struggle.

I'm a practical woman; I want to see immediate results. Beyond the suffering of anticipation and anxiety, the waiting and the tension are just shattering, just unbearable.

During the morning Avi Freund calls from Kfar Etzion. He's the one who drove Gil-ad with Naftali Fraenkel from Kibbutz Kfar Etzion to the hitchhiking post in Alon Shevut. He wants to speak to us, the parents. The memory of that conversation's details will weaken later on, but a little over a year later I'll come back to it, and realize for a moment that he was the last person to encounter Gil-ad and Naftali.

He recounts that about half an hour before the kidnapping he left Kfar Etzion to go shopping at the Gush Etzion Junction. The boys asked for a ride to the bus station at the junction, about a five-minute drive. The hitchhiking station there is big and well-lit; they were loaded with bags and hurried to get out of his car because they saw a car at the stop that might get them farther along – they didn't even have the chance to close his car door properly. Nevertheless, he stressed, they didn't neglect to wish him a *Shabbat Shalom* and thank him.

It was about twenty-five minutes before they got into the wrong car.

Avi didn't make the connection between his trip and the kidnapping until Shabbat afternoon; as part of the searches, a town resident showed him a photo of the missing boys and he recognized two of them. After the chills and shock came the investigators.

At the time another boy, from Kfar Etzion, was standing with them at the Alon Shevut stop. That other boy was in a bit of a rush, and when a car came by, Eyal Yifrach, who was there first, let him go instead. That boy's life was saved. His mother came during those few days to give hugs and strengthen us, slowly realizing the magnitude of the miracle that happened to her son.

Eleven a.m.
The families are invited to the President's house. A convoy of police vehicles escorts us there. Who would imagine that in a single week we'd meet the whole country's leadership with such intensity?

Gil-adush, you would have loved this. You would have known how to leverage these encounters. How could it be that the most important person of all isn't here with us?

Later, Emily would remind me I wanted to memorialize these moments on camera to show Gil-ad when he comes back, like other such moments during that time that I wanted to document for him. The president comes out – Shimon Peres – and meets us in the reception room. He asks us questions warmly, with interest, embraces, strengthening and empowering us with his words. We pose for more photos; we make another statement to the press. When will we finally be able to make a happy announcement that this whole thing is over?

As we're driving Ofir remembers it's the birthday of Deputy Commissioner Eitan Madmoni, the police officer escorting us along with military officials. Ofir doesn't wait – he calls the neighbors with a request to throw a surprise party for Madmoni. Madmoni was much more than a police representative for us. With sensitivity and calm he escorted us on our trips, always providing updates and guidance.

When we get home we see the neighbors had taken Ofir's surprise celebration request with all due seriousness. The journalists fell over themselves in competition over who could paint a more positive portrait of the town and its people. They posted touching photos and social media statuses. One, Doron Herman of Channel 10, kept a personal Facebook journal during those *chai* days:

> Thursday, our sixth day in Talmon. Eitan Madmoni, a police official appointed to handle contact with the Shaer family, and who can since be found here all the time, has his birthday today. He didn't tell anyone, but somehow it became known. And then out of nowhere came a cake and balloons, and for a few moments this sad place was full of joy tinged with tears. Another magical human moment testifying to the noble spirit of Talmon's people. It's important for me as a journalist to bring you these little stories from time to time. They are so humane, beautiful, and simple. Come back, our brothers!!!

That week Emily would hear surprising statements from both sides of the divide. On one hand, "You know, the settlers aren't as bad as we thought," and on the other, "The media aren't as bad as we thought."

One people. One fate.

Afternoon

The dearest of people comes to visit: Rabbi David Grossman, rabbi of Migdal HaEmek. In talking with him we recall Ofir and Gil-ad's trip to see him as guests in the institutions he runs there. Rabbi Grossman, known as a rabbi who excels at integrating Torah study and acts of kindness, was also part of Gil-ad's pre-Bar Mitzvah journey. The rabbi stuns us by bringing along a photo we didn't recognize of him and Gil-ad hugging during that visit.

Together we remember the conversation the rabbi had with Gil-ad and

Ofir, which lasted close to an hour and discussed the meaning of life and what it means to take on the yoke of *mitzvot*. The discussion was extremely meaningful to Gil-ad and was etched profoundly into his memory.

That same Thursday the people of the Dolev-Talmonim bloc want to organize a support and prayer rally for the boys' return.

It's six p.m.; hundreds of people pack the benches of Talmon's central synagogue as many more crowd out past the doors. The place looks too small to hold everyone.

Ashkenazi Chief Rabbi David Lau, Sephardi Chief Rabbi Yitzchak Yosef, and Rabbi David Grossman honor us with their presence. The penitential prayer liturgy integrates Sephardic and Ashkenazic rites. The sound of the shofars thunders into the sky. Everyone feels the emotion: the prayers tear open the heavens.

We ask that what human voices can't accomplish, the sound of the shofar can.

We didn't know then that the decree was already determined, and all the prayers were like an afterthought, and to this day we don't know what those voices created, up there in the heavens, and which decrees they sweetened. And I'm certain those prayers were heard, and I'm certain they made an impact, in some way, for the good.

Prayers do not return unanswered.

We realize that prayer is not a one-dimensional encounter that happens at the synagogue three times a day, but is a living, breathing entity present in each thought, contact, conversation, or free-form speech to the Master of the World. It intensifies in the face of this incredible circumstance: each person is trying to determine how to help, how to do good, how to bring the boys' return closer.

A client of Ofir's asks him one day, "I think about you all the time – is that praying?"

A Tel Aviv man we don't know calls one morning during the *chai* days and wants to share that for some time he's been trying to find his way, trying and debating, and in the midst of this intense time he gains clarity, and decides to strengthen his religious observance. He started putting on *tefillin*.

A Haredi woman from Jerusalem tells me, months after the search, of the great change her family underwent during that time. "We live in Meah Shearim. We decided to open our doors and host secular Jews on *shabbatot*. That summer wrought such a transformation in our family! I never knew I was capable of such things until then."

A young fellow from Haifa tells Ofir on the phone that he feels he became a better person during that period. He doesn't give details of what made him feel that. He just became a better person.

Wow.

Friday, 22 Sivan, June 20
Kidnapping Day 8

It's all so hard, but some moments are harder than others.

It's hardest in the morning. It's hardest of all Friday morning.

I can't believe a week has passed without Gil-ad in the house. My soul is consumed by worry. I get up more disintegrated than ever; I share with Ofir my feeling that I don't have the strength to get through another Shabbat without Gil-ad. The whole crazy week we just had, we just rolled with the days, waiting each moment for the doubt and anxiety to be removed, but were still able to live in the present, to keep ourselves afloat in the day-to-day, the here and now. That's how we would survive another day.

Each morning I get up weaker than before and ask the Creator that this be the last day of tension and anticipation, and the first day of joy at Gil-ad's return.

I have enough strength for only one more day, *Ta-te*... please bring this to a happy conclusion quickly.

We chase time, exhausting ourselves with the constant thought of what else we can do to find the boys.

Am Yisrael has gone above and beyond; the government is acting and the Knesset supports its efforts; the security apparatus is up to its neck in search operations; but the result is nil. Gil-ad, Naftali, and Eyal aren't home.

I can't handle that thought.

As I said, the first Friday found us confused, shocked, with nerve-wracking anticipation. Grasping hope with our nails. Swinging like a pendulum between waiting for the worst news of all and real hope of hearing Gil-ad's familiar footsteps, of seeing his shining face again, striding toward us and concluding with a smile, "Sorry I didn't answer the phone."

And it's already been a week.

The weekend brings a sense of alignment: an alignment between us, as humans at the week's end, and Hashem as the Day of Rest approaches. G-d attempted to order Creation on the sixth day, by creating humanity on this day, after making the basis for their existence, and a moment before granting them rest.

In our routine, things that get pushed off from one day to the next during the week wind up on Friday, as the house seems to organize itself for Shabbat. But now we can't conclude anything with the search for Gil-ad still going on, and there's no way we can have order inside without him.

Frustration increases each moment, each hour. The powerlessness of a parent who wants so much to help his child.

Under normal circumstances we're raising an independent, opinionated generation. We get the sense even our little four-year-old daughter Maor doesn't really need us anymore. She makes play dates with her friends on her own, decides what to wear, what to eat, and how to spend the afternoon. But now an enormous need arises. Gil-ad the child, the teen, needs us, his parents, very much. He depends on us, but our abilities fall short of saving him. Our powerlessness as parents is too hard to bear. What's become of us!

"Oh, G-d," I murmur, "I have no strength left. I can't take another Shabbat without Gil-ad!

Please, bring back the boys, today, now, before Shabbat, healthy and whole."

The youth of Talmon travel to Tel Aviv and hold a mass challah-taking event in Rabin Square with the general public. I see the pictures on my phone and my heart expands a little.

Noon

We're invited to the residence of the prime minister and his wife in Jerusalem. At the start of the meeting the prime minister says, "The nation is giving you strength, and you give strength to them in return." The atmosphere is warm and heartfelt. The prime minister promises he'll do everything to bring the boys home safe. We feel that the prime minister and his wife are in solidarity with our anxiety and pain as parents.

"Mr. Prime Minister," I say to him quietly, privately, "Can you guarantee me my son will come home alive?" He looks at me quietly and says, "We're doing everything we can."

"We greatly appreciate what you're doing, but bottom line, my son isn't home."

"The entire system has been enlisted," he says.

"I know, and I appreciate that very much, but maybe we have to think outside the box?" I ask delicately.

"We're thinking and trying," he answers empathetically.

I come out of the meeting weak. What did you want, anyway?, I think a few days later. How could the prime minister guarantee you Gil-ad would come home safe? But all I wanted during that time was to hear that promise.

When we get home another warm embrace by the neighboring communities is waiting for us. The children of Dolev are giving out cakes baked by the girls training in the culinary program at Dolev High School next to Talmon. The children of Neriah and Charsha are going door-to-door giving out bottles of wine. They're trying to give support, to remind the people of Talmon we're not alone in this struggle.

And they're not the only ones.

That morning a young soldier from Gittit in the Jordan Valley comes to our door, carrying a basket full of peppers and dates grown locally, a gift from the people of her village. In their way, they wanted to express their solidarity with us in our difficult time. I'm sure in a few days this uniformed soldier will finish her military service. To my surprise, I hear a completely different story: she holds a senior position in the standing army and is already a mother to three small children.

"Shalom," she says with a smile. "I want to share my feelings with you these last few days, and what's been happening to me this week whenever I wear this uniform. Until a couple of weeks ago I wore it with mixed feelings. We don't always get treated right by everyone. In some places it's not easy to walk around in an IDF uniform. But in the last week pride has been restored to this uniform. In the last week we've succeeded in functioning properly as an army," she smiles again, and I smile back.

"We go where we need to go, restoring order and security, feeling proud to be part of the people's army. An army that protects its citizens, that gives the country security. I'm here to embrace you and say I'm proud of this uniform, proud to be part of the army, and proud to be a citizen of the State of Israel."

Wow.

It's almost Shabbat; I need more strength and I get it.

Just like in storybooks, with perfect timing, two hours later a dear neighbor knocks on the door. He's a career soldier whose son is in preschool with our youngest daughter Maor; that week the son told her his father was participating in the search for Gil-ad and his friends. The teacher, who witnessed the conversation, recounted what was said: "You know my father isn't home because he's looking for Gil-ad?" And Maor answered, "If he finds him, tell him to bring him to me as fast as he can, because I miss him so much."

A blood bond.

Roi, the soldier father looking for my son, lost his mother, Rachela Druck (may Hashem avenge her blood) in a terrorist attack on a bus more than twenty years ago. He wanted to share his brief time off with us before going back to his wife and family, whom he hasn't seen all week. "I don't know how this story will end, BatGalim," he addresses me, "but I feel there are national phenomena going on here that are bigger than us. Already, because of your son, because of Naftali and Eyal, we've saved many lives. We've found illegal money and weapons, we've arrested dozens of suspects trying to harm civilians; we've saved lives."

I listen with an awkward smile and answer, "It really is moving, but I want my son here at home.

I'm worried about him. I'm not interested in national phenomena right now. I want Gil-ad back."

He looks at me, perplexed. "You're a mother, and you're entitled to ask for that, but there's much more going on here than just your private story.

"The time you spend waiting for your son at home isn't passing in vain. We don't really understand what's happening here, but there are really significant, immense things are occurring," he says through tears.

I gaze at this fine young man, a soldier with real dedication.

Happy is the nation with these as its children, I think to myself. What a special person, who thinks of all of Israel. Ofir and I part with him with a Shabbat Shalom.

As he leaves, I turn to our Abba in heaven. "Master of the World, I don't understand a thing about Your considerations. This is how much

You need my Gil-ad there? Is there no other way to redeem *Am Yisrael* and achieve atonement – this is the only way? To imprison three pure boys in horrible captivity? OK," as if I'm appeased, "if You need my Gil-ad one more Shabbat, I'll try to hold out a little longer. "Gil-adush," I address my only son. "Let's muster our strength for one more Shabbat. But that's it, Abba," I beg, "no longer; I want him home."

I whisper to my Gil-adush that we'll get through this together just as we got through the past week. "You have it in you," I try to send him the most positive message possible. "Just one more Shabbat," I mumble, not dreaming for a moment that he was already smiling at me from above, looking in pain at his suffering parents and praying, perhaps even more than we were, for this to be behind us.

A few minutes before Shabbat, D., commander of the liaison unit, passes us a moving handwritten note:

> Ofir, Bat-Galim, and the entire beloved Shaer family,
> As Shabbat begins, alongside the operational and intelligence efforts,
> I pray with you and all of Am Yisrael that our boys come home.
> Bless me with peace, O angels of peace,
>
> Yours, D., unit commander

And that's how I start Shabbat: receiving an infusion of energy from the soldiers, from *Am Yisrael* thronging to us all week, from all over the country, to hug and support, and he doesn't realize how important his presence in our house was the whole time.

Happy is the nation with these as its soldiers; happy is the nation with these as its children.

Second Shabbat, Parashat Korach, 23 Sivan, June 21
Kidnapping Day 9

Rabbi Yehoshua Schapira and Rabbi Yaakov Meidan and their wives come to Talmon to embrace the community. They give discourses, conduct conversations, and the community feels significantly strengthened. We opt to spend Shabbat with only family. To spend time with the girls, who all week were scattered in every direction, hugged by their friends.

The neighbors try to ascertain what gives us strength. They keep asking: How can we make it easier? What support do you need? Prayer gives strength, and song is prayer. All week long we held gatherings in our yard where people could open their hearts and join in. Shabbat afternoon there are plans for a town-wide gathering at the big amphitheater. Hundreds of Talmon residents, women, men, and children, come to be with us in song and prayer. Just to be with us, something so basic and not to be taken for granted.

Saturday Night

The flow of visitors recommences. A big circle forms in our living room. That's how we sit here during this time; we open as big a circle as possible and try to involve everyone who comes. Most of the people don't know one another; we don't know most of them. Despite everything, people have wonderful, riveting conversations.

With stories and songs we escort Shabbat's departure, trying to renew our strength for the new week, praying that it bring good news.

Rabbi Shmuel Eliyahu, the Rabbi of Tzfat, is also counted among those providing spiritual help. He tells us of a large rally for the three boys, numbering 3,000 participants, taking place on the beach in Tel Aviv, attended by all walks of life. At the Kotel there was a children's prayer service.

Rabbi Gross moves us with the double miracle his grandchildren experienced. Several months ago they were poisoned by an illegal spray used by an exterminator. Four children were affected; two survived. The family came back to life. Everyone present saw the half-full portion of the glass and anticipated that our story, too, would end well.

A Hasidic entertainer comes to sing away Shabbat, with heartfelt pleasantness that touches our souls. The songs flow as if by themselves. Talmon residents hear the songs and come to fill their hearts. People come from near and far.

Concurrent with that, Odelia Berlin holds a gathering for women, with singing and dancing, and I join them for the second part of the program: a slow-moving circle of women and girls, around and around, each revolution filling the space with more song, more prayer. The words are charged with a revitalizing, magnetizing force. I think of Honi the Circle-Maker who drew a circle and stood in side it, saying to G-d: "I'm not moving from this spot until You make rain fall." The divine response was less than welcoming: first the rains were too weak to matter; then too powerful, but Honi didn't move until he got was he asked for; drops fell exactly in the quantity and strength needed.

And I, what can I say to You, Creator of the World? Another circle, and another, my heart is full of prayer, and my entire being makes one, single request: bring my only son back whom You took. I don't want to leave this song and prayer circle until my request is fulfilled, like Honi

69

the Circle-Maker who drew his line and didn't move until he got what he wished.

Alongside the pain and worry, the constant restlessness and the frustrating feeling of sinking ever downward, we also get to experience moments of exaltation.

The tireless youth of Talmon set up a study tent in our yard in which Torah classes take place around the clock. Twenty-four hours a day there are teenage boys and girls, young men and women, as well as adults, focused on one desire: "Come Home, Brothers."

I feel new heights in my connection with the Creator.

I have a strong feeling the *Shechinah*, the divine presence, is with us in the house. My soul grapples with new, unfamiliar feelings that surround me.

What does G-d want from me, I ask myself over and over. His presence at every moment is palpable. Palpable yet crushing – the hug is too tight.

How do you maintain that? Where do I take all this togetherness? How do we make sure the people stay united not in times of pain and distress? Those questions will yet occupy me for a long time. The prayers ascend to heights I don't recognize. Crying and prayer become routine. My tears flow as in the verse, "Pour out like water your heart in the presence of Hashem's face" (Lamentations 2:19). Prayers I mumbled in distraction have now taken on a new form, etching lines within me the likes of which I've never known. The divine presence is as real as my tears.

Abba, "Whence will come my help; my help is from Hashem, the Maker of Heaven and Earth" (Psalms 121:1-2).

During this time the idea to hold a rally in Rabin Square a week later began to develop. It's clear to Ofir that all the diverse sectors of our society have to be represented there, and we can't leave out even one. The issue of women singing comes up. Ofir refuses to budge, insisting on finding a solution that will allow the entire public to participate. Finally, one of the leading rabbis of the Religious Zionist movement agrees a woman may perform – the main thing is the increase of unity and love in Israel.

It's something so necessary.

Sunday, 24 Sivan, June 22
Kidnapping Day 10

The media keeps asking for photos of Gil-ad. Gil-ad loved to have his picture taken so we have quite a few, but he almost never stood alone in the frame.

Right at the beginning of this episode we decided not to allow pictures of our daughters, Gil-ad's sisters. We were determined to maintain their privacy, which had already been severely compromised. We want them to grow through the years to become themselves, not "the sister of."

I ask a good friend of Shirel to pick other photos from the computer to give to the press. Who's got the time for this? The thing is, a picture that other people like might not look so good to me. In the end I decided to go through them myself. Sometimes it was too late: many pictures slipped through via Facebook or through people who lacked the sensitivity, but everyone had good intentions.

The stream of visitors continues uninterrupted. Thousands come to see us, creating a single human fabric: Israelis, foreigners, Jews and non-Jews, the young, the old, secular, religious, Right, Left, soldiers, Torah scholars – each of them emissaries of kindness and goodwill.

Afternoon; the house is full.

Ruti Gillis enters. She lost her husband Dr. Shmuel Gillis in a shooting attack in Gush Etzion. In his memory she set up a "hot spot," a corner with refreshments for soldiers at the Gush Etzion Junction. Ruti introduces herself and tries to share with us her impression of the wonderful dedication and concern flooding through *Am Yisrael* right now. Every day, ten thousand cakes are delivered to her corner. The families of the Gush, she relates, are covering the soldiers and searchers with affection. Shoulder to shoulder, they all contribute to support the soldiers in their critical mission. The soldiers give up sleep and trips home, devoted to their mission, which they see as sacred.

As she's still sitting on my right, a precious Jew comes in from the U.S. and sits to my left. He says he just landed yesterday; his community in the States wants to show their support, their embrace. By yesterday they had collected about $10,000 in contributions to the Gush Junction hot spot. I smile in disbelief. "Please, let me introduce you two." To my right and left, in my house with perfect timing, the donor and the operator meet.

One of the visitors who left a lasting impression also brought us more strength: Avri Gilad. We're sitting in a big circle in the yard: rabbis, public figures, neighbors, and others. Avri joins the circle just as someone is expounding Torah teachings to strengthen us. He keeps talking; I remember what he said, but mostly that he didn't know when to stop.

After him Avri asks to speak:

> The three families are broadcasting on a precise frequency that differs from what the people are used to. The frequency you've generated penetrates all the heart's chambers, reaching the divine within all of us. Our nation is searching for its path, looking for someone who can show them exactly where to go. The people are used to hearing a hysterical frequency of "Me! Me!" of now, now; of gimme, gimme, of entitlement. Not that I

have a mission in the world. But from the three families and the circles surrounding them we get a clear message that man has a mission in the world; that he must give of himself and add to the world. That mission is not suspended in difficult moments. Israeli society assumes that even if you have a role, you get an exemption when the going gets tough. You broadcast to us how to continue carrying that role even in the worst moments, the capacity to continue shouldering the burden even when it's unbearably hard. And it's unbearable!

Avri studies the teachings of Yemima Avital, and tries to share with us some of her insights into time:

> We divide time into three: past, present, and future. Yemima argues that in fact there are only two dimensions to time: the present, in which we physically are, with the world in our *vision*; and imagination, in which we *envision* what will be or was.
> "Most of the time people are in the second state – living in imagination, anticipating what will happen, for things to change, for some future event to arrive. Envisioning and waiting... sometimes the visualizing takes hold of the past, of what was. Few people see things as they are, focusing on the present, where they are, and make full use of the present."

Wow.

"When you're locked into envisioning you miss out," Avri concludes.

We live most of our lives in the dream-world of anticipation, living in the gap between what we want and what we have. Of course we need both modes; the main question is the balance between presence and anticipation. Between reality and imagination.

In our impossible reality, that of the three families, the only way to cope with the anticipation is to be in the here and now. Focusing on the present. Anticipation just makes things harder, and it won't help us when we're trying to function in the present, in the everyday.

His words found me where I already was. Each morning I ask Hashem for the strength for one more day, just one more day. With a longing in my heart that at the end of day everything be for the best.

Each day we address the very present, and that doesn't let in thoughts that would weaken us. It gives us strength.

Do we succeed in realizing the potential of the present, in living the moment, taking pleasure from it and full advantage of it? Do we have the skill to differentiate confidently among our quotidian tasks and duties, such that when we're at work, we're focused on work; when we're with the children, we're focused wholly on the children, et cetera? What a waste that we live in unrealized anticipation so far from reality!

During that time of anticipation we're rediscovering Gil-ad.

A remedial education teacher in a neighboring town sends over some things she wrote. She shares a story with us that she's kept to herself for several years:

> It was an exhausting afternoon. Student after student. A knock on the door. I open it. There stands a cute kid, like many others, about ten-years-old. He strides forward into the room. It's a small room. Just a little space for individual instruction where I've been working for a few years at the Shachar Institute for Remedial Instruction. Kids who need extra tutoring, or those with learning disabilities from various schools in the Modiin area register with the Institute.

I don't know this boy, but I'm not surprised; the Ariel School in Talmon is big.

The boy says hello. I ask what he wants. "You're Chani?" I confirm.

"Can I get help with my studies?" I ask what help he needs. He doesn't really answer. I ask if his parents called me, if they made an appointment. He whispers a no. I repeat that if he needs help with school, he should ask Abba or Imma to call me and set up a meeting so he can register with me.

He stands there awkwardly, thinks for a moment, and then states with confidence that he needs help with homework. Since he insists, I try to diagnose his level of disability. It takes me just a few moments to determine I have no idea what his difficulty might be. He's intelligent and competent in the material. He certainly doesn't need remedial tutoring. I try to clarify again: "Why did you come here? Who brought you? I don't think you need to be here," I insist.

Because I didn't consent to accept him, he came clean: "I'll tell you why. I have a friend whose teacher sends him here and there's no way he'll agree to go, because it's for dummies. So I decided to go to so he'll come too." I'm stunned into silence, hesitant. I wonder where he's from, and I don't recognize him; I don't know everyone here. I want to ask his name so I don't end up talking to a kid without his parents knowing. "You're a good kid. You can ask your parents and I'll admit you happily." He smiles and says, "It's fine – I was here, and now I can tell him I was here. It won't be a lie." Then he left. A kid. A few days ago I encountered him again, a cute kid in the newspaper. Smiling, arms around friends. My heart stopped. I know him. It's that kid. That boy. It couldn't be. But it's he. That's what he looked like. I remember more of a child, but no less him. The realization hit me hard.

That's Gil-ad. That cute, good, courageous, considerate kid. The kid who came and went without my finding out his name. Happy is she who birthed him.

Monday, 25 Sivan, June 23
Kidnapping Day 11

Matriculation Exam Day (History)
For twenty years this has been one of the most significant days to me. All year, every year, I do my best to prepare my students for this day. But no other year has been like this one. This year my head is elsewhere.

This year my son is making history, I think to myself.

As a civics and history teacher I've been part of a civics lesson never seen before and on which I've never before been tested. I console myself with the fact that at least I finished checking all the prep tests. I don't want even a single student to suffer from the fact that I'm not functioning.

In the evening the plaza at the Eretz Yisrael Museum in Tel Aviv hosts a round table discussion organized by Ram Shmueli's *Mit'chabrim* ("Connecting"). It's the first such event of this time, and the phenomenon will grow tenfold in the months ahead.

That evening religious and secular, settler and Tel-Avivite, young and old come together for round-table discussions. It's powerfully impressive. No doubt, people talking to one another is an amazing, constructive thing.

I get pictures of the event on my phone, and my heart expands. The same day students representing the town of Shoham contact us from Geneva, Switzerland. They tell us that on Tuesday there will be deliberations about Israel in the UN Human Rights Council. Anyone who wants to address the panel may do so for two minutes.

"The mothers have to go there to speak," they tell us.

The Fraenkel and Yifrach families come to Talmon. We sit together for a short meeting, strengthening one another and being strengthened. We, the mothers, decide to go. It turned out later that the Ministry of Foreign Affairs had decided not to send any representatives, since the gathering had more than just a whiff of antisemitism. But the UN itself has no moral mandate to refuse the request of three families to speak at its meeting, and thus we found ourselves trying to organize a trip to Geneva in less than a day, still doing everything possible to free the boys.

The Ministry of Foreign Affairs announces our trip to the public, even though we would prefer to keep it low-key to prevent antisemitic demonstrations outside the UN building.

Afternoon

It's a nighttime flight, and I even managed beforehand to attend my daughter Hallel's flute recital. The school year is almost over and the girl wants to display her talents in performance. I try to clear space in my thoughts for it, and go with her to the show. I'm with her and not with her, but completely proud of her and happy to see how much she's progressed in a year.

That evening my daughter Meitar has a joint Bat Mitzvah celebration for all the girls in her class. At that hour I have to be on my way to the airport. As a mother I have to decide, and with a heavy heart I know I won't be at the Bat Mitzvah. I'm aware of my daughter's understandable anger and frustration, but the thought that my trip can help Gil-ad's return even a little is decisive.

I get ready for the flight.

I've never packed like this.

A neighbor advises me on what to wear; another packs a respectable carry-on; a third suggests that a hat will look more dignified and official than a headscarf. Armed with sundry bits of advice, a big bag, and a heavy heart, I rush to the airport.

My thoughts won't leave me alone. Is this what will help us bring the boys back?

Rabbi Yonatan Hayut, the Rabbi of El Al, meets us before we board the plane. He showers us with blessings and supportive, loving words. Do you have everything you need?" he asks. "Maybe something to eat or drink?" Our refusal is rendered pointless when he empties two shelves of drinks and sweets from the bar and shoves them in a bag. Provisions.

What a nation we have, I think. G-d, are You watching? You see?

I meet Iris Yifrach at the airport. Racheli Fraenkel flew earlier and will meet us in Geneva. Discover an amazing friend. A strong woman of faith. The connection between us, which began under horrific circumstances a few days ago, grows stronger as a result of this trip.

It's clear to us we'll have to speak in English. I'm very stressed by that. It's not my mother tongue. It's been a long time since I learned the language or used it. Who would have thought I might need it under such conditions? I'm tense and try, unsuccessfully, to rehearse some relevant English sentences. I suddenly understand my students' difficulties repeating historical dates.

I'm sitting on the plane, waiting for takeoff. I'm armed with drops to help me sleep to conserve my strength. I swallow a few drops but the pressure won't let me fall asleep. The anxiety, the responsibility, the foreign language, the emotion – they all accumulate to form immense pressure inside me, and render useless even the mightiest attempt to shut my eyes and catch some momentary rest.

I've always loved flying, enjoying nature's beauty from up in the sky.

This time I can barely look left or right. I'm so focused on my goal I barely notice anything. I'm so worried, so anxious. But then, right in those few minutes, a white strip of the sunrise shines through the window in front of me. Glowingly beautiful, smiling Good Morning at me. How grand are Your works, Hashem.

Maybe, I wonder, it's for the purposes of this UN trip that Hashem has pulled the rope tight for so long. Maybe, I say to myself, trying to spin threads of hope within, after this mission, today, the waiting will come to an end and the boys will come home safe.

Tuesday, 26 Sivan, June 24
Kidnapping Day 12

It's early morning and we land in Geneva. There isn't much time until our session with the UN. Little chance to get organized. Rabbanit Yaffa Dayan, the wife of Chief Rabbi of Geneva Yitzchak Dayan, greets us with a big hug.

The first meeting with the Deputy Chairwoman of the UN Human Rights Committee gives a clear example of the nature of the distorted arena where we now find ourselves. As a mother herself she shows empathy for our situation, but nothing more. She forgot she has a job and is unwilling to do more than that. "What about condemning the kidnapping? What about demanding the captives' immediate release?" We ask. "Listen, it's not so simple..." she stammers, and refuses to issue an official condemnation.

I try to express our position to the UN representative, but the translator refuses to translate my words. It seems too much to her to ask for the prisoners' immediate release. I explode, intensely frustrated. I promise myself once this terrible journey is over I'll learn English properly. It's unreasonable for my heart to be overflowing – with criticism, insights, and reactions – and is blocked from expressing its treasure by a language barrier.

Afternoon

We enter the room where the UN Human Rights Committee sits. I feel culture shock: protocol dictates that each speaker gets two minutes, and then they move right to the next one. No listening, no discussion, no responses. Discourse at its finest, I think to myself, and notice that those who look up at the camera and speak up induce some delegates to listen. I point that out to Racheli.

Racheli speaks well for her allotted two minutes, representing us quite honorably. She tells a little about each boy and says we're in the midst of a mother's worst nightmare – our sons didn't come home from school. Isn't it every boy's basic right to return home from school without risk of being kidnapped? Her voice breaks when she begs the committee to do everything in its power to bring the boys back.

It looks like most of the people in the hall are listening. We don't stay to listen to the rest of the speeches – it turns out almost all of them denounced Israel that day. Our feeling of frustration grows stronger.

Everyone knows kidnapping is beyond the pale. Everyone knows the boys' lives are in danger – but politics is politics, and no shout or cry will breach its walls.

Over the next couple of hours we give interviews to the foreign and Israeli press. Draining but important. There's no door on which we're not ready to knock for our boys.

A few days later it will become clear that the UN's ignoring the boys' kidnapping and its hostility to the subject will actually increase support for our cause throughout Israeli society. The realization that *Am Yisrael* must take care of itself – If I am not for myself, who will be for me? – along with an understanding that we're surrounded by hostile audience, will strengthen the Israeli public and awaken brotherhood and a sense of shared fate.

Late that night we fly back to Israel, exhausted and anxious. Was it right or wise to go to that place?

One clear, unequivocal feeling does accompany me, with no ambiguity: a mother will go anywhere in the world to bring her son back.

That day our eldest daughter, Shirel, writes to the soldiers on behalf of the sisters:

> To the IDF soldiers – our brothers,
> A week and a half have passed since our beloved brother Gil-ad was kidnapped.
> We want you to know that Gil-ad is an amazing brother, spoiling us and taking care of us.
> A brother full of joie de vivre (we're sure when he hears about some of the things happening now at home he won't stop laughing at us), sociable, smart, and righteous, who bakes incredible cakes for us.
> Since the kidnapping we can't sleep at night.
> We know you're not sleeping at night, either, and are doing everything to bring him back with Eyal and Naftali, safe and sound.
> We feel each soldier going out to search for Gil-ad is like a brother to us, a real part of the family.
> We can't go out and look for him ourselves, so you're doing it for us, in our stead.
> We don't have the words to thank you for the tremendous dedication and concern.
> We believe you'll succeed in bringing our brother home, back to his mother's arms. With Hashem's help Gil-ad will become a soldier himself and be proud to wear the IDF uniform.
> We hope that Hashem grants you the strength and ability to

continue, not to let up, not to give up; to search everywhere, in every corner, every hiding place.

Here at home we're trembling and longing for our Gil-ad. Thank you for everything!

With love and appreciation,

>Shirel, Tahel, Hallel, and Maor (Gil-ad Shaer's sisters)

Wednesday, 27 Sivan, June 25
Kidnapping Day 13

Morning

Again we're riding in a convoy to the Knesset, this time for an encouragement meeting with female MKs, organized by MK Shuli Moalem-Refaeli, called "Waiting for the Boys," using a Hebrew abbreviation for MK that creates the pun, "From Female MKs to the Boys."

Behind our car is another carrying a delegation from the town that coordinated the event. The clock is ticking and they're feeling pressure not to be late. Suddenly they ask us to wait at the Ofer roadblock. Ofir and I have to get out of the car and go over to a vehicle waiting at the side of the road. Inside it sits Yinon, of the liaison staff, holding a page listing prizes for members of a Bnei Akiva youth movement chapter. "Do you know whose this is?" he asks. At first glance it doesn't look familiar. We call a friend of Gil-ad's from the staff of our chapter, who doesn't recognize it either. We let out an extended groan. It turns out it was a random piece of paper found in the search zone, but not connected to any of the boys.

During that time the searchers collected many items, and when the possibility arose that one belonged to the boys, they would immediately contact the families to check it out. Any such object could be a lead. Every object causes butterflies in our stomach, in the commanders' stomachs, in the searchers' stomachs. The emotion from this item is in vain. There's no connection to any of the boys.

The women in the car with us are stressed, and don't understand why we stopped. If they only knew...

We continue on our way to the Knesset and arrive late. Before the planned meeting with the female MKs, Speaker of the Knesset Yuli Edelstein invites us into his office for a personal meeting. Warm, friendly Edelstein gives us encouragement and remarks on the excitement, the spiritual awakening among Jews worldwide, and gives special mention to the displays of solidarity and partnership with Israel following the boys' kidnapping. He suggests holding a video conference with the heads of Jewish communities abroad, and we consider together how to move such a project forward.

In the end it didn't happen for technical reasons. Nevertheless, we get messages nonstop from the leaders of Jewish communities all over the world about the impact this episode is having on so many Jews wherever they are.

We get to the conference hall. Dozens of MKs and ministers are sitting there, from almost every faction. All the female MKs come as one to support the families together. It's a powerful encounter, an embrace.

At this event I meet Minister Uri Orbach, of blessed memory, for the last time. I won't forget his words.

While everyone else was speaking in praise of the families and holding their endurance up as an example, Uri, typically, speaks the plain truth: "These aren't extraordinary families. This is how our community acts. Many families would conduct themselves in this manner, with restraint and responsibility. That's how we were raised." I thank him for his humanity and for his open, unvarnished truth.

I never thought within a few months he would "move in as a new neighbor" at the Modiin cemetery.

That morning I spoke from the depths of my heart:

> Dear women,
> I come to you as woman to woman, mother to mother. I'm speaking to you from the blood of my heart.

A day, another day gone, and my heat burns – I want Gil-ad alive, with me at home. I'm heartbroken, but not broken.

I want to share with you that during this difficult time I draw strength mainly from the support and love flowing to us all the time – from all parts of the Israeli spectrum. Our souls are also filled by the prayers and songs we sing. One of the songs that touch the most sensitive, pained parts of my heart is that of our mother Rachel from the book of Jeremiah:

> A voice is heard in the high
> place Wailing, bitter weeping
> Rachel is crying over her sons
> Refusing to be consoled over her sons, for they are gone.

The prophet continues:

> Thus says Hashem
> Refrain your voice from weeping
> And your eyes from tears
> For there is payment for your works, says Hashem
> They shall return from the land of the enemy
> And there is hope for your future, says Hashem, and the sons shall return to their border.

Our Sages tell that when the Temple was being destroyed the forefathers of the people prayed for the restoration of *Am Yisrael* to its land from exile.

The great figures of the Jewish people, including Avraham, Yitzchak, and Yaakov, prayed extensively, but Hashem only listened to our mother Rachel, because she had special merit.

In her youth she gave her sister Leah the special signals Yaakov had given her so her father, the evil Lavan, would not replace her with her sister. When their father indeed made the switch, on the wedding night, she gave Leah the signs so as not to embarrass her sister. Rachel did an inconceivable act, rising above herself for something exceedingly important. The power of that act made G-d guarantee that her sons would return to their border.

It turns out life also creates crossroads at which we are required to rise above ourselves.

Beyond our private pain – searing and unrelenting – we must rise above ourselves and place the concerns of *Am Yisrael* before us, of the IDF soldiers, of the security forces, of the Government of Israel standing against the enemy, and of this mysterious mission Hashem has placed at our doorstep.

I have complete confidence in the system.

I know it is doing everything for my son, and for Naftali and Eyal.

This morning I got up and couldn't believe my ears. The news reported that the prime minister is prepared to reach an agreement with hunger-striking prisoners, who are demanding improved conditions for security prisoners. Could it be? Is it possible?

Gil-ad, Naftali, and Eyal are held in some unknown place by vile captors, Hamas members, and the prime minister wants to appease them? If the prime minister knows who the kidnappers are, then he must act in every possible way to press them to return our sons alive: stop transferring funds, worsen prisoners' conditions, apply pressure on the Palestinian Authority. Make

Hamas understand that kidnapping, especially of children, does not pay.

Ramadan is coming. Does it make sense that while our people is living in uncertainty and deep worry, the Palestinians will open their Ramadan festivities?

Yitzchak Aharonovitch, sir, Minister of Internal Security, you're all confused!

An agreement with the hunger strikers would be a severe mistake. We're doing everything to keep the people united, and we grasp the immense responsibility at this moment.

We feel that beyond our private pain there are tremendous processes taking place, the power of which we do not yet understand. All of *Am Yisrael* is united in pain and prayer for the return of our kidnapped sons, but we will not accept irresponsible behavior by our decision-makers. Reaching an agreement with the hunger strikers at this time would be an irresponsible act toward *Am Yisrael*.

Dear MKs, you have power. You're here too – all of you together, rising above political disagreement, for one important shared goal. The more we act together, the greater our power as mothers. I believe in the power of femininity and motherhood, and am sure each of us sees each of the three boys as her own son. What would you do for your son in such a situation? From here I send great thanks and appreciation from the depths of my heart to the mothers of the soldiers in the field, and to the wives of the commanders in the forward posts. We hear you're overturning every stone to find the boys and bring them back alive, but maybe the time has come to think differently; maybe we need not only to turn over every stone, but to lift it up? Are we thinking outside the box? Has the decisionmaking echelon opened new search avenues and new operational possibilities to bring the boys home safe?

Dear MK, you have one important task at this time – rise above political disagreements and act for the return of the boys – Gil-ad, Eyal, and Naftali – home safe and soon.

Mr. Prime Minister, members of the cabinet: your deeds will be examined by the result. *Am Yisrael* will test your actions by the outcome.

Would that the merit of our mother Rachel and of her children's unity serve us. I believe our mother Rachel continues to supplicate before the Master of the World for her sons, who are gone. Would that we see the swift fulfillment of the hope "and the sons will return to their border."

At the end of the conference we get a tremendous embrace from MKs on the Right and Left. The event is unifying, moving. On our way out the journalists await, and some of them interpret my words as criticism, for which they've waited more than a week.

I know and feel my faith in the system remains steadfast; but I can't ignore the push for an agreement with the security prisoners when the fate of our sons is unknown. A few hours later I received a call from the prime minister's office clarifying that there is no, and there is not supposed to be any, agreement with the prisoners, and we can relax.

One of the reporters wants to interview me on live broadcast. I put on the headset and go on the air. After a few on-topic questions I realize he's trying to steer the exchange in a political, critical direction; he's trying to elicit anger and frustration at the system from me, but that's not what I feel. It's not like me. Without a second thought I thank him for the interview and tell him we're done. I remove the headset and walk away from the camera.

Emily Amrusi, accompanying me that day as a friend observing from the side, can't believe her eyes. "No one dares stop that reporter in the middle of an interview, and you just took off the headset and walked away!" I don't understand what the big deal is. Apparently there are behavioral mores in the media of which I'm fortunately unaware, so I follow my inner sense.

That day at the Knesset we also find time to meet with a large delegation of community leaders from the Jewish Federations of North America. The JFNA group was being hosted by the Knesset, and that gave us a chance to have a heart-to-heart talk. Organization Chairman Jerry Silverman and Director of the Israeli office Rivka (Becky) Caspi move us with their warm words. We didn't know this chance meeting would lead to an enduring connection that remains today with Diaspora Jewry in general, and with that organization and its leaders in particular.

On the way back home at Shilat Junction we see dozens of people standing and waving flags and signs, calling for the boys to be returned home. We stop and get out to hug and encourage them. People are investing their time and energy to do good things for others. It can't be taken for granted at all.

Thursday, 28 Sivan, June 26
Kidnapping Day 14

Another morning, another day.

My head is occupied with the thought: what haven't we done that is possible to do?

A prayer rally is planned for the evening, this time in Nof Ayalon. I hope I have the strength.

We get to the house in Nof Ayalon. The rabbis of the towns speak. The head of the Rome Jewish community, now visiting the country, also talks, trying to encourage us. Later he tells us he is trying to arrange a meeting with the Pope in the Vatican. We're prepared to do anything to keep the issue on the public agenda.

At the end of the gathering, on the way out of the synagogue, a neighbor shows me on her cellphone an announcement by the army: "The names and photos of the kidnappers have been released." The liaison staff had already updated us with the names, but we've been trying not to occupy ourselves with evil and thoughts that weaken us. We rely on the Government of Israel and its decision-makers to act accordingly.

That doesn't prevent one of our daughters from crying all the way home. For her, the worst wickedness and evil on earth just got a face and a name.

Late at night; we're told there's an all-night event in Tel Aviv. Tonight, all the cultural and leisure institutions in the city are open and teeming with people. Dozens of teens have gone to the Tel Aviv City Hall Plaza and collected hundreds of signatures in a call to bring the boys home safe.

Tomorrow, before Shabbat, a neighbor from Dolev brings us a huge sign with signatures and good wishes from those Tel Aviv youngsters. We hung the sign in our living room, on the windowsill, and it stayed there for many weeks.

There was something about it that gave us a real sense the whole nation was with us.

Friday, 29 Sivan, June 27
Kidnapping Day 15

Where are all the fortune-tellers, the mind-readers, the mystics and Kabbalists who work miracles? Why can't any of them find the boys? That's what I think in moments of weakness.

Many good people give it a try. Too many.

From the first moment Ofir and I agreed not to allow space for "mediums" of any sort; the delusion, to which many good people resort in times of distress, isn't like us, and we won't have anything to do with it. Still, in moments of weakness, I so yearn to hear some true, rooted statement that everything will be restored to its place and the boys will come home.

Lots of folks try their hand at such things in these moments, and the army even checks some of them out, because no one wants to take the chance of failure to follow up. At the same time, no one knows exactly what to do with the information.

Fortunately, most of the attempts are blocked by Ofir, Shirel, or neighbors who field the call. It's so helpful that someone spares the family from the dreams and delusions people invent in such moments, as if they lack for things to cope with. At times such as this you need someone realistic and strong who can filter out the mediums, who have no mercy on the family.

It seems there were many: people sent pictures or imagined descriptions, claiming they knew where the boys are being held. A controversial Kabbalist tried to make an appointment with me for days and I refused. He called my sister and insisted he had information about the boys' whereabouts and that they were alive, but he could only give the details to the mother. I consistently refused to listen to such people. In this case I was subject to intense pressure. The day before the bodies were found I relented, and agreed to a meeting, which ended up not happening; G-d decided to spare me the unpleasantness.

Third Shabbat, Parashat Chukat, 30 Sivan, June 28
Kidnapping Day 16

A quiet family Shabbat. We turn inward, seeking quality time with the girls, after another intensive week of searches. It's hard for us to believe we're entering the third week. The fear that the security forces will slow down or despair gains momentum. The worry that the prime minister will decide to release some of the soldiers really weakens us.

How long can a whole country withstand this tension? I ask myself. How long can we remain steadfast?

Ta-te, have mercy on us, my strength is failing...

Saturday Night

We find ourselves escorting the departure of the Shabbat Queen with the singer and composer Udi Davidi.

How? Udi called a few days ago and told us he'd written and composed a new song dedicated to the boys' return.

A song? I'm astounded and moved inside; a song about my son?

I hear myself saying to him, "Come, we'll listen gladly."

And he came. He came with his song "Soon You'll Be Coming."

Reports of his expected arrival spread quickly. Dozens of the town residents join us, sitting on mats and chairs in the yard and listening. And the song is so on, so palpable, so touching. I listen with growing emotion and the tears gush.

The olive tree in the garden
Reminds Imma you'll be coming soon
And she holds back her tears
Just hug her when you come.

Only her lips are moving; her voice can be heard at night
Opening the door, she waits
And you'll be coming soon.

Angels plead
Prayers bang on the Gate of Mercy
And Abba knows you're strong
Without fanfare, know they're waiting.

Only her lips are moving; her voice can be heard at night
Opening the door, she waits
And you'll be coming soon.
"May the angel who delivers me from all evil bless the boys."

In the midst of listening to the song a Shabak man beckons us to enter the house. We're called into the room.

They found glasses in the search zone and want to know whose they are. They sent pictures. We call the optometrist and try to ascertain the exact model of Gil-ad's glasses. He had a unique greenish pair I loved.

It turns out the glasses belonged to Eyal Yifrach. The discovery still doesn't offer any insight into the boys' whereabouts.

We would get Gil-ad's glasses later, broken, burnt, and mute, unable to recount what he went through in the last moments of his life.

At the time we still didn't know the implications of the find. Just saying to ourselves: finally, something relevant has been found that definitely belongs to one of the boys. We're clutching hope, and to us, all the possibilities remain open.

Sunday, Rosh Chodesh, 1 Tammuz, June 29
Kidnapping Day 17

The third week begins. Seventeen days have passed since the kidnapping, and I refuse to believe we're entering the third week of this horror story.

The media have started to pack up their photography equipment and leave the crowded street. I worry they're starting to lose interest in the episode. It's one thing for the media to do so, I think to myself, but what about the whole country? The leadership, the soldiers searching – what will become of them? How much more strength will they all have? Will we all have?

Already at the start of the searches we really wanted to meet with the fighters doing the search, with those whose dedication means no shut-eye, day and night, to bring the boys back home. After almost two weeks the army responds to our request and organizes a meeting with the soldiers looking for our children.

In the early morning we travel to the Tarqumiyyeh roadblock to meet the soldiers. A year later I would find out that the army tried to put off the meeting with the parents out of concern we would express anger, criticism, or frustration that our sons hadn't been found yet.

We get to Telem Camp, located in the search zone. I grasp the immensity of the occasion only when I stand before the soldiers face to face. It's an emotional encounter. They stand in front of us with eyes bloodshot from sleeplessness and emotion. We thank them for throwing themselves into the efforts and for their extraordinary contribution to the mission of returning the boys.

"You're the soldiers who will find Gil-ad and bring him home," I say to them. "You're the ones who are giving of your time, of your sleep, of your family lives for the sake of my son, for the sake of Eyal and Naftali, and for our sake, the parents. I've always been moved by people who give; giving, unfortunately, can't be taken for granted in the modern world. This giving warms our heart especially. It's impossible not to be awed and moved by it."

These soldiers haven't been home for more than two weeks. Most of them haven't slept much since the kidnapping. The commanders told me with excitement that after a day searching, the soldiers would ask to join the nighttime operations, again and again giving up hours of sleep. They understand time is of the essence, and every bit of reinforcement could be valuable.

I stand in front of the soldiers, in tears. We've been through quite a bit in the last two weeks, and still, something in this face-to-face encounter with the searchers makes me very emotional. A big lump appears in my throat and doesn't let the words come out.

"I wish I could hug each of you," I say.

How do you express immense gratitude and appreciation in words?

Every word seems small, insufficient. Tears roll down my cheeks. Not only mine. The soldiers sitting before me, soldiers from the most elite combat units, called in specifically for the search effort, wipe tears from the corners of their eyes.

The atmosphere in the room is charged as if by electricity. It's impossible not to be moved. They also want to thank and encourage us. "We're looking for your sons as if they're our brothers," they say, and I feel it thoroughly, believing every word.

One of the soldiers gets to his feet and vows: "We will bring your sons back home."

"Thanks to you we're strong," I whisper.

A year later an amazing woman, married to a career soldier, shared with me that on the same Friday the kidnapping was reported, her husband and his buddies in the unit were scheduled to come home after two weeks of operations. But in the WhatsApp group of the soldiers' wives, they all asked their husbands to stay in the army and take an active part in this search of utmost importance.

One of the senior unit commanders, who would end up not returning home for eight consecutive weeks – from the beginning of Operation Brother's Keeper through the end of Operation Protective Edge – shows me a text message he got from his ten-year-old son: "Abba, find Eyal, Gil-ad, and Naftali. Don't come home until you find them." In the following days I'd realize that boy wasn't the only one; many children told their soldier or officer fathers, "Don't come home without the boys."

By the way, that commander's wife gave birth to a daughter about a week into the operation. He saw her for the first time a month and a half after she was born.

I'm moved by the dedication at every level, from the most senior officers to the soldiers in the field.

I see a wedding ring on a commander's finger. "You're married?" I ask. "Do you have kids?"

"You confuse me," he says. "This isn't what was supposed to be in the protocol... we were expecting parents angry and frustrated at the system..."

"How long have you been away from home?" I ask with concern. He doesn't understand the extent to which his and his soldiers' dedication to the search for my son leaves me awed and moved. An entire nation that enlists to look for three boys who didn't come home. It simply can't be taken for granted.

Happy is the nation with these as its children; happy is the nation with these as its soldiers.

From there we proceed to an observation post overlooking the area where the search is concentrated. It will emerge later just how close they were, but no one had a clue.

The tour concludes with a drive to the Alon Shvut Junction and a retracing of the estimated kidnap route. Chills run through my body. I try to visualize what happened there and it makes me weak. I try to focus on what's happening in front of me. It's not easy.

In the afternoon we come back home, exhausted from the trip but energized by the intensity of the encounter with the soldiers. It's a preparation in miniature for the exalted encounter awaiting us this evening with the people at Rabin Square in Tel Aviv.

Afternoon

We go with the girls in anticipation, hoping the rally will draw many people and unify hearts. The motto of the rally, "Singing Together for Their Return," catches my eye as we arrive. We sit in the first row, excited and worried at the same time.

On stage, Avri Gilad emcees. The finest artists sing their songs and touch all of us. The Chief Rabbi of Tel Aviv, Rabbi Yisrael Meir Lau, and President of Israel Reuven Rivlin address the crowd. We three mothers also do our part, sharing words of blessing and prayer.

I get on stage with Ofir and my breath catches; there are tens of thousands of people before me filling the square, the edge of which I can't see. Emotional, I address those in attendance:

> Good evening.
> Our Gil-ad, my sweet child,
> We're going through a difficult time – you, we, and all of
> *Am Yisrael.*

103

I'm here with you, with Abba and the girls. I want to tell you you're not alone.

There's an entire nation with us, waiting for you.

An entire nation embracing, praying, and wishing for your safe return home.

In Israel and around the world the whole House of Israel has come together in welcome, unifying action in anticipation of your return, of Naftali and Eyal's return.

When you come back, you'll discover our family has greatly expanded; that you have additional brothers and sisters, grandmothers and grandfathers all over the country and the world.

The special feeling present during this period in Israel reminds me of other special moments of unity and exaltation when a people was put under pressure; first among them the heroic Yoni Netanyahu, may Hashem avenge his blood – the brother of the prime minister, whom we wish long life – who rushed to the aid of brothers and sisters he didn't know and covered a distance of 3,800 kilometers to rescue them from the enemy. The sense of shared fate has created a reality. That sense continues to today.

We are brothers, and brothers do not remain still until their little brother comes back to them. They do not stop and do not remain silent. Yesterday it was at Entebbe; today in Gush Etzion; tomorrow it will be in Sderot or the Golan. The places change; the togetherness remains. Always.

We are brothers, and thin threads of pain hold us together, hold us up so we won't fall. Beloved Gil-ad, your name contains within it immense power: eternal joy. Joy is positive thinking, good vibes, intensity.

> We're here singing together – song is prayer.
> Song can strengthen, unify, embrace, free.
> Prayer is a longing for partnership, for connecting in the face of difficulty.
> Any feeling of sharing or partnership is prayer. It's song. Whether from a printed *siddur* or from the *siddur* of the heart.
> We support and embrace all those working day and night for the boys, from the prime minister and his cabinet down to the last soldier.
> We pray for the welfare of the IDF soldiers and commanders; may G-d protect you and make your mission successful; may all of you return safely from the mission to bring back our dear sons safe and sound.
> We want to thank everyone who came to this square tonight; everyone watching us; and anyone who devotes a good thought or a good deed in anticipation of bringing our sons home soon.
> "Our Father, our King, have mercy on us and answer us, for we have no accomplishments.
> Perform *tzedakah* and kindness toward us, and deliver us."
> Look, our Father, how many of Your children came today for the sake of their brothers' welfare.
> Thank you very much.

Much later the rally in Rabin Square would be remembered as one of the defining events of the *chai* days – a deep encounter with all parts of Israeli society, an encounter embodying connection between diverse people, of extraordinary unity. An evening with spiritual exaltation felt at every moment, with the sense that any moment now, the boys are coming home... In fact the next day they would find the boys.

Lifeless.

A week later, during the Shiva, a tour guide who was present at the rally with a group of Christian tourists would describe their experience at the event. "That was so powerful," the group told him. They also felt the spiritual force that was present, even as they merely looked on from the side at our people.

"Now we understand why you're the chosen people."

Monday, 2 Tammuz, June 30
Kidnapping Day 18

So far we've been acting mainly based on our understanding, our sense, and good advice we get from various people, most of whom aren't experts in such crisis situations. Nevertheless, our heart has led us faithfully. One of our friends in the town described it well: our senior adviser is the Master of the World.

As a couple who usually make decisions in a reasoned, rational manner, we felt it necessary during this episode to make space, perhaps even more space, alongside the intellectual considerations for our feelings to guide us. We go to the media with our gut feelings and make decisions based on our heart's leanings. We're surrounded by a large group of friends who provide answers to our questions and requests.

The great responsibility for the boys' welfare causes us not to close our eyes for a moment, so constant is the worry. Our heads keep trying to think of whom else we have to meet; what else we need to do; whom else can we pressure to make the searches more effective and speed up finding the boys. We know the entire system – governmental and security – is involved, and we really appreciate that. Still, the bottom line is the boys haven't been found yet. We try to urge everyone to think outside the box. The entire period we've been having meaningful meetings with the most senior diplomatic and security personnel.

G-d has sent the right people to be with us and escort us. We appreciated that greatly during that time. We appreciate it even more today. A sober look reveals to us just how such responsiveness can't be taken for granted; other scenarios definitely come to mind.

Nevertheless, we sense the people around us are getting fatigued. It looks like we have to engage some professionals to navigate the ship.

We decide it's time to explore the involvement and assistance of professionals, and make a six p.m. appointment in Tel Aviv for a meeting of the three families with a big PR firm to construct a plan in case the searches continue for a long time.

Ofir and I decide to take advantage of the trip out of Talmon to stop in Raanana, to console one of the liaison staff members sitting Shiva in his house. We look at the clock – it's already five. We part from our friend with a hug, not knowing that the next time we see each other he'll be coming to console us; we order a taxi to Tel Aviv. The driver recognizes us and we exchange warm words; we get encouragement and a blessing from him.

The very fact that we need to have this PR meeting is hard for me. It's tough to admit we must put anything long-term in to action. They're hinting that the searches may take a lot longer, and I have a hard time reconciling myself to that possibility. We get there and meet the Fraenkels. We're told the Yifrachs will be late. We go up to the office and wait for them.

It's six o'clock. Ofir's cellphone rings; it's a member of the liaison staff. Ofir goes outside to talk. "Drop everything and come home. There's an update," he's told.

To this day Ofir remembers the pavement where he was standing when he got those instructions. "What happened? What's so urgent?" Most of the time, these updates are reports that there's nothing to report...

"We ask that you drive carefully and get home as fast as you can," the liaison staff member repeats laconically.

Ofir comes back to update me. Shock. We exchange looks full of concern. Minutes later we're in a car with our friend Yaakov Netanyahu, who's driving us back to Talmon.

Forty minutes of driving that seemed an eternity. It's the longest trip of my life.

Yaakov drives in silence you could cut with a knife. He doesn't open his mouth, glancing at us all the time in the rear-view mirror.

Conflicting emotions wash over me. On one hand I want to get there as quickly as possible to remove the tremendous doubt and the worry eating away at us inside as a result of that phone call. On the other hand I don't want the trip ever to end so I don't have to face what's waiting for me. Not to confront the bitter truth, to still have a few more moments of hope...

The trembling that overtook my body during that trip will never be erased from my memory.

We get near our house and the worry intensifies. The media are back in force. The town rabbi has come, and the police have returned to block the street.

Town representatives are trying unsuccessfully to keep people from gathering in front of our house. At that moment, Emily is inside with our daughters. She's been updated; she's at wit's end and beside herself. She decides to prepare dinner and tells the girls their parents have decided to come home early to eat together with them.

Shirel gives her a suspicious look: "But we just finished eating dinner..."

"OK," answers a restless Emily. "So you'll eat again." "What happened?" Shirel persists.

"Military activity in the Hevron area," answers Emily.

Shirel begins to realize something's amiss, as she would later tell me.

We arrive and Emily leaves. She can no longer separate her professional duties from her friendship. The burden on her shoulders was heavier than I'd imagined at the time, and I wasn't privy to most of her deliberations. One thing isn't in doubt – friendship has won out this time.

The looks we get on our way into the house tell us everything. The army doesn't depart from official procedure.

They bring us into a room and give us the official notice that they found the bodies of the three boys.

I immediately want to gather the girls and tell each of them individually and directly.

A failed attempt a few days ago with a professional psychologist who tried to help me explain to little Maor what was going on, but who I feel only complicated matters, makes me insist we parents need to speak to our kids alone, and that's what happened.

They came in one by on and we gave them the worst possible news.

Those moments, during which you know you're going to change your child's world, seem as tormenting and soul crushing, no less than the conveying of the news itself.

We protected them so much during those *chai* days; we tried so hard to shield them from trauma. And here G-d reminds us again that not everything is in my control.

That evening the Talmon youth gather into discussion groups, by age. Everyone's falling apart. The optimism that had infected everyone has now burst, and the fact that the boys were found dead leaves a most difficult emotional mark. Social workers from the Regional Council, who rushed to help our amazing youth, are nevertheless surprised by their openness and maturity, and amazed by the endurance against the intensity of the pain and loss and of its willingness to touch them.

Someone made sure to bring in professional psychologists to help the dear people of Talmon, who surrounded and supported us through it all. Gil-ad's group from Bnei Akiva is taken care of by an adoptive local family: an amazing young couple who are there for them, providing hugs and encouragement.

Everyone needs something to lean on.

Including us.

All over the country, people gather in their grief. Hundreds of people stream spontaneously to Rabin Square. They light candles, sing soulful music, and cry. A friend who lives near the square told us emotionally what he saw with his own eyes. People came together to hug and shake off the sadness together.

The shock, the disappointment. The worst possible ending.

Nighttime

The need to be practical and decide immediately where to bury Gil-ad, plus other technical things, gives me the capacity to face things without falling apart. Falling apart will wait until later: now we need to make decisions.

The decision to bury the boys in one plot seems obvious to us. The kidnapping became a national event, and we understand the three boys were connected by a single fate. First we try to get approval to bury the boys on Mt. Herzl. Later the three boys would be called "the first casualties of Protective Edge." The government refuses adamantly for fear of creating a precedent for burying civilians in military cemeteries.

The three families − from Nof Ayalon, Elad, and Talmon − reach out to the city of Modiin for a place to bury our sons. We decide to make it their final resting place. Mayor Hayim Bivas goes out of his way to help us in these difficult moments, and he's not the only one. As just an example, an announcement went out to the entire town that evening: "A group of women from Beit Shemesh is willing to send babysitters from Chashmonaim or Beit Shemesh to enable people from Talmon to go to the funeral. If that would help you, send an email or text and let us know how many families are interested."

We can tell the entire nation feels part of our tragedy, feels our shared fate and is willing to help one another.

Tuesday, 3 Tammuz, July 2
Day of the Funeral

Today I understand the extent to which we understood nothing. How hard the news is to absorb. How incomprehensible it all is.

What it means to lose a son, to be a bereaved mother; the change of one's status to a bereaved family.

Writing a eulogy for my departed son is the most terrible thing. How? What?

How do I make words from the tears of a broken, bleeding soul? Where will I get the strength to charge words with a task beyond their capacity? No word in human language exists to suitably convey such pain.

It was decided to begin the funeral procession at the home of each boy, following eulogies by family and friends, and proceeding to the joint burial in Modiin.

Our decision to invite Yair Lapid to deliver a eulogy seems natural to us, a direct continuation of those *chai* days, during which we felt connected to every part of the nation. Some people raised an eyebrow; I, on the other hand, think unity is something you create, not just talk about.

I'm amazed by the fact that both Yair Lapid and Rabbi Dov Singer chose the same instruction of the Holy Ari to mention in their eulogies. It prefaces the daily morning prayer liturgy with the declaration, "I hereby accept upon myself the positive commandment to 'love your fellow as yourself.'" Another unexpected connection. Another connection that proves no matter your appearance, we are one people.

After several meaningful speakers we got up to speak our hearts. Ofir began his eulogy:

> My Gil-adush,
> "Toward this boy I prayed," my only son.
> I'm sitting in your room to write this; I take the photo album from Tahel's Bat Mitzvah that you designed, as a surface to write on; I refuse to absorb; I can't believe this. How can I condense your life into a few words? How can I distill your accomplishments into a few short sentences?
> A gargantuan challenge was placed at our doorstep eighteen days ago – just a regular settled family, in both senses.
> We've had to exercise incredible strength, which we drew from *Am Yisrael*, to escort you on your final journey. Incredible strength we draw from your character.
> Since the moment we heard your courageous whisper into the telephone, my posture went erect and I heard in you a mighty, hidden voice, a voice that has stayed with me through this whole difficult time. That voice is getting stronger, reaching from one end of the world to the other – what resourcefulness, what heroism, what power in someone yet to reach seventeen years of age!
> My precious Gil-ad, a week ago I told *Am Yisrael* how much I miss wrapping you in my *tallit* for the Priestly Blessing. I didn't tell them how insistent I was to do so even when there was tension or disagreement between us. How when I wrapped you up you gave yourself over to my embrace, even though

we disagreed. How I was so proud when you got taller than me and I had to raise my hands to wrap you up.

And now, that *tallit* is orphaned; it envelops your pure body before that body is buried in the ground of our land that you so loved.

I want to tell you, Gil-ad, as your mother said at the rally, that you're already part of a huge family – the family of *Am Yisrael*. An IDF officer who took part in the search for you said it plainly – you have your private pain, but there's also something much bigger here.

I feel that.

I believe many future generations will be raised in your light; they'll tell your life story and be awed at the way you departed this world – you, Naftali, and Eyal. Your final journey and your ascent to the heavens have broken down barriers, brought hearts together, and unified an entire people.

Many of those who came to visit recently heard about the odyssey we took together before your Bar Mitzvah, on the theme of "In all your ways know Him." At the time we studied a book written about Roi Klein, may Hashem avenge his blood, and we were present at his memorial ceremony at Mt. Herzl. I saw how you kept his example and devotion in your heart.

Who could have believed you would also become a hero of Israel, while still a boy. In this week's *parasha* we read about Moshe and Aharon, and of the miraculous blooming of Aharon's staff as it produced almonds before *Am Yisrael*. We're used to gradual processes – first the blossoming, then the withering, then the fruit emerges. But in people of greatness there's no contradiction. All at once, the flowering occurs in all its glory even as the fruit emerges in all its splendor.

That's the meaning of "in all your ways, know Him." The ability to connect, to integrate, to do things at the same time without them conflicting.

You loved to bake cakes, yet you immersed yourself in the spiritual; you loved to sit back and enjoy life, yet you were goal-focused and achievement-oriented.

I managed to speak with you shortly before you left on your way home. I heard your calm, loving voice. I waited for you to come back, and now, here you've come back to us.

We always knew how to grow and overcome life's challenges together.

But now I'm facing the challenge of my life – and I know you're with me from your place, sending out a supportive hand.

And here, standing before you in final moments of parting, I ask you for forgiveness.

Please forgive me, my beloved son, if I made a mistake, if G-d forbid I hurt you. My dear daughters – Shirel, Tahel, Meitar, Hallel, and Maor, my heart breaks with yours, yet beats strongly in all of us.

Girls, you've always been proud of your one, special brother. You certainly are now, and after you, all the generations you bring into the world will grow up with his legacy and be proud of him – of how he lived and how he died.

Our hero.

People of Israel: we're all hurting together, but in the end we'll all grow stronger. The murderous kidnappers tried to weaken us, but we won't weaken. We'll connect, unite, and together intensify our hold on our homeland.

Rabbi Harlap wrote the following in a letter on Sunday, Rosh Chodesh Tammuz 5688, to the family of Shlomo ben

Yosef, who was the first to be hanged by the British Mandate authorities:

"My dear son, his dear wife, and your dear child, may Hashem be with you.

"Indeed our thoughts are stormy at the hanging of a Jew, in vain. All the pleading did not work; all the begging failed; and all the windows of Heaven were closed. All the prayers, the crying out, the imploring, and the supplications – failed to breach the clouds.

"Fortunate is this man who was the cause for so many stirrings of repentance. Fortunate is he for being the catalyst for all of Yisrael uniting around one point. But alas, what has become of us; why has He closed off our prayer?

"Nevertheless, we trust in Him, may His name be blessed, the He will avenge the blood of His people before our eyes, and may we soon see the rebuilding of Zion and Jerusalem, the construction of our Holy Temple..."

Those are the words of Rabbi Harlap in 1928.

But now, "how can I go to my father with the boy not with me..."

My Gil-adush,

Your developing character, your personality growing more powerful before our eyes, sparked immense pride in me.

We will keep you *gil*, you joy, *la'ad*, forever.

I salute you, my beloved son. May your memory be blessed.

Abba

I stand at Ofir's side, sensing that he had a hard time delivering his eulogy, and wait for Shirel to speak also:

Hashem, who dwells in the heavens, You're the one who arranges our lives down here. Today I'm giving You my best friend, my only brother. I don't even know what he felt, thought, as he fought for his life.

The last time I was with Jilder it was at our grandparents'; he was studying for his matriculation exam in history. When I got ready to leave, I went to say goodbye to him as always.

Suddenly, without thinking about it, I gave him a hug.

Hashem, You know how close Jilder and I are; he's my best friend. I was always the annoying sister who called to find out what's going on, to try to plan a Shabbat together at home, but Jilder's always busy... the Ofarim youth movement, yeshiva, the guys... but our rapport is strong.

Am Yisrael has just been through tremendous upheaval. Three Thursdays ago we were thrust into a movie whose ending could be the worst possible. That's true. I don't have a brother anymore. But we've undergone something huge in the last couple of weeks, and we have to nurture it. Jilder and I are good siblings, very close.

We all have brothers and sisters. Take one of Jilder's good traits by being loving brothers and sisters. Fighting can be a part of it...

Ever since we were small we loved to imagine what it would be like when we grow up, and I always thought about you being a soldier. A soldier in *Am Yisrael*'s army. I imagined worrying about you. Well, Hashem, that's one thing You've made sure I don't need to worry about anymore. From now on I know he's protected and treasured next to Your throne. I love Jilder and really appreciate him, but I never realized I was growing up together with such a soul.

Jilder, you ended your life with a sanctification of Hashem's name. When you departed, all of *Am Yisrael* began a process. You raised *Am Yisrael* a level on the path to redemption. That's just like you. A *mensch*, a child with desires and struggles.

I also remember the arguments when I tried to wake you up in the morning, and you got annoyed at me. But even then you did it with respect. Sometimes I felt like you were my older brother, worrying about me and protecting me, taller than me. You're joining a long, sad list of heroes of Israel, and not by choice, but, it appears, destiny.

A month ago, during your last Shabbat, at the youth movement clubhouse of course, you needed to come up with an activity. I gave you some sources on "covenant of fate" and "destiny" by Rabbi Soloveitchik. I believe in it, and you believed along with me. So now, you've fulfilled your purpose. And now I'm going to have to deal with that, as destiny. Not fate. Would that you three be the last entries on that list.

Shirel

I take a deep breath. I can't believe we're here doing this now, at such a bitter end. I have to give a eulogy for my only son:

Our Gil-ad, my sweet Gil-ad.
Who would have dreamed two days ago, as we stood in the square together with tens of thousands of precious, loving Jewish hearts, that the next words I would deliver would be a eulogy. I, who usually knows what to say and how to say it, can't find the words.
I, who so loves to write, am out of words...
I'm sitting in your room; I can't absorb the news. The whole

nightmare that began *chai* days ago is inconceivable, and here we are at the worst possible outcome; I simply can't digest it. I'm not the only one silent. The fish you kept in your room, which you loved so much and became a trademark of yours at the yeshiva, are silent.

Beloved Gil-ad,

We were so careful to write your name with a hyphen so it wouldn't be mistakenly read as Gal-ed, a monument. Who would have dreamed that at age sixteen and a half we'd be putting up a Gal-ed for you.

Gil-ad, my heroic child, a proud Jew, full of resourcefulness. A child in years, an adult in your path and conduct.

Mature in the responsibility you took for your studies, for your friends, and your charges in the youth movement.

At thirteen the celebration of your Bar Mitzvah carried the theme of "In all your ways know Him." You connected to that with such power.

You studied Torah, you engaged in kindness, your good heart overflowed with generosity, but not out of a sense of concession or sacrifice, but of joy, integrity, internal wholeness you felt with life, born of a love of life and the joy of living.

We believe that when the soul ascends, it's serene and happy in closeness to Hashem. My Gil-ad, your soul was serene and satisfied down here, as well. You were whole with yourself; you set goals for yourself and always met them with ease.

A child with such high and great aspirations. It was obvious you'd succeed in life. Still, we never imagined how high a level you'd reach, to what heights you raised the whole nation with you. You certainly know, from that place where you are now, about all the wonderful daily learning that took place in our yard and didn't stop for even a moment – all credit to you and your soul.

You started out on your way home *chai* days ago, but only arrived now. You gave us, your family, another *chai* days in which to live. You gave *Am Yisrael chai* days of spiritual exaltation, of unity, of prayer and kindness. *Chai* days of unconditional love.

In death you've left us with a legacy of unity – us, our people. Gil-ad, a hero *la'ad*, forever. I'm so proud of you. For the call you made, for your last words, for your whisper that will echo for all time, for the resourcefulness, heroism, and dedication you showed.

My Gil-ad, you will forever be a Gal-ed to generations of boys and girls.

You were kidnapped and murdered for being a Jew. They tried to hurt your pure body, but couldn't overcome your pristine soul. Your body is pure and your soul is pristine and clean as the day you were born.

You were and are a proud Jew, a lover of your land and people. Despite your young age you'd already begun to debate how to serve your nation best with the incredible abilities Hashem had given you.

Oh, G-d, we so expected different news. Everyone wanted a different result – You promised us "The sons will return to their border."

We've been whisked into a role about which we weren't asked and for which we weren't trained. Please, G-d, take the reins into Your hand. Please.

The faith that You've given us the strength to cope until now is what will give us the strength to keep going. But please – do not hide Your face from us; shine Your face and let us be delivered.

G-d, You've given us six precious gifts, six treasures entrusted to our care. Gil-ad is the only son among five beloved daughters. All these years I've felt it a tremendous privilege to be mother to these children.

My amazing girls, you can be proud of your brother.

Now we're being called upon to return the deposited treasure, our Gil-ad. It was called due before its time; it didn't last long enough... we never got the chance...

My Gil-ad, raising a strong-willed child who knows what he wants and does what he wants – that's no simple challenge for parents. I ask forgiveness from the depths of my heart for the moments I didn't function as a worthy mother. Please forgive me.

My Gil-ad, as I've already told you, you're no longer only mine. The extended family, which now includes all of *Am Yisrael*, is with us today, holding you in your last moments before we part from you, but we're not really parting from you.

"We are all one living human fabric, and if one of us departs, something inside us dies." You won't be alone, Gil-ad. As long as we breathe we will visit you, and when the day comes we will be reunited.

Be at peace, my beloved son; Imma says goodbye.

After the eulogies we stepped quickly from the Talmon synagogue plaza into the cars that left in a procession to the Modiin cemetery.

Later our friend Yuval Ben-Yehuda sent us what he saw in the synagogue plaza during those moments:

> The eulogy ceremony for Gil-ad is over, and the large crowd surges into the area where the eulogies were spoken in order to greet and embrace Gil-ad's family.
> Ministers, MKs, and other dignitaries are pushed toward the family; the crowd is pressing in and the tumult is great.
>
> The family won't wait; they try to get out of the plaza quickly to get to the cemetery. To my left I see in the throng Rabbi Aharon Lichtenstein (Rosh Yeshiva of Har Etzion, where Ofir studied) stepping slowly, supported by his wife Tova and daughter Esti. Suddenly, Gil-ad's father, Ofir, looks back, sees the rabbi, and as if it were the Splitting of the Red Sea, retraces his steps, crosses among the MKs and ministers as if they weren't there, and falls upon Rabbi Lichtenstein's neck. They're hugging each other and the floodgates of tears open; the two of them crying and crying copious tears, each on the other's shoulders for many long seconds.
> Ofir takes his leave of Rabbi Lichtenstein and again crosses the plaza fast, toward the exit. Even after Ofir's departure Rabbi Lichtenstein continued to stand there, exerting great effort, and weep bitterly as if he were seeing his own son lying in front of him.

Yours is a king's funeral, my son.

Many cars escort us on our trip. A convoy of motorcycles surrounds our vehicle front and back. The people of Nili and Naaleh crowd the junctions and greet the procession with signs, flags, and a loving embrace. We're awash in tears, pained and moved.

The trip takes longer than expected. The organizers expected large attendance, but hadn't counted on more than a hundred fifty thousand participants, as the police would later assert.

The car we're in gets stuck at the entrance to the cemetery, and, absurdly, I'm afraid we'll be late. I feel uncomfortable inconveniencing the waiting public, and can't imagine what the masses of people are experiencing at the moment – masses who in their dedication covered great distances on foot, parking their cars at the roadside and walking to the cemetery under a blazing sun. No one complained, we'd be told later. It was clear to everyone they were taking part in something bigger than themselves.

All this wasn't lost on the journalists, one of whom would describe the tens of thousands who came patiently, quietly, calmly. So painful and so sad, he would say. And yet so restrained and impressive. In the presence of tens of thousands, the President of Israel Shimon Peres delivered a eulogy for our son, as did Prime Minister Binyamin Netanyahu, Chief Rabbi David Lau, and Rosh Yeshiva of Mekor Hayim Rabbi Dov Singer.

In the painful sea of those moments we don't really absorb the number of people who came to pay their last respects. We're immersed in our own grief, but at every moment sense the power surrounding us – a sea of power.

The Shiva

Wednesday, 4 Tammuz, July 2

The first morning of Shiva.

We wake up to the bedside phone ringing. A Jew from far-off Peru calls to console us.

Ofir gets ready for morning services in our front yard.

Each day begins early in the morning and ends in the wee hours. The neighbors help us function properly throughout the whole period. They make sure we have time to rest every afternoon and eat lunch with our daughters.

In contrast to the *chai* days of the kidnapping, which I remember with relative clarity, the Shiva days are a blur to me. But even within the fog one fact stands out prominently and never ceases to amaze me: the unending stream of visitors, those who promised to return for our celebration of gratitude over the boys. The people and the stories are foggy in my memory, and in fact, as a good friend would say, in retrospect, we were different during the Shiva.

During the *chai* days, hope injected us with strength. We hung our hopes on the fact that the search was temporary; we were wrapped in optimism that everything would end well. We clutched faith, from which we drew the endurance to get through each day.

Rabbanit Yaffa Magnes, who with her husband Rabbi Yehoshua Magnes, ran the girls' high school in Tel Aviv where I studied, told me a year later that when she and her husband came to visit during the *chai* days, she asked how I was and how I was coping. I told her that in each moment I was living the minutes when Gil-ad would open the door and come home. Hope enabled me to breathe. During the Shiva there was nothing to breathe for.

I compare my body to a deflated, wrinkled balloon, as if someone took all the air out of my body, and I'm not sure it can ever be reinflated to its natural size.

Thursday, 5 Tammuz, July 3

We are told that in New York, a Chabad family from Brooklyn held a *Brit* for triplet boys, whom they named Eyal, Gil-ad, and Naftali.

In the evening a group of men come in holding a Torah scroll. The scroll was donated for the merit of the three boys by a benefactor from England who wished to remain anonymous. They want to finish the writing at the homes of the three families. They have already visited the Fraenkels and the Yifrachs, and finally came to us. The emotion is intense. Who thought of such an initiative so quickly – not just thought, but accomplished it? Writing a Torah scroll for the departed is an important mitzvah and a tremendous privilege. The other visitors who came to console us are similarly moved, and break out into song: "May this moment be a moment of compassion and a time of desire before You..." Ofir completes the letters *gimmel* and *ayin*.

The anonymous benefactor lets the families decide where the scroll will reside. In a joint decision we all agree on an IDF base. Several months later it will be inaugurated in a moving ceremony at the training base of the paratrooper brigade in Lachish.

We are privileged to hear stories nonstop and meet special people. Amir Sandler, Deputy Secretary General of Bnei Akiva at the time, tells us that when he came back from the funeral a discussion ensued among all the leadership training department heads of all the youth movements in the country – a group saturated with competing ideologies, desires, and disagreements – about the role and mission of youth movements in Israeli society.

They decided unanimously to visit us in Talmon – Gil-ad himself was an "exchange" counselor (serving in another nearby branch of the movement) in Ofarim. For many members of the group, crossing the Green Line was no simple thing. Amir suggested the idea carefully, and was stunned to discover the proposal was accepted without objection.

It was not an easy decision: summer is the busiest season for youth movements, but still, people left home at five in the morning from the forests up north and seminars in the south to meet at 10 a.m. at the Shilat Junction and proceed from there together to Talmon. Just picture the image in your head: one vehicle crowded with the coordinators from the Scouts, Bnei Akiva, HaNoar HaOved VehaLomed, and Ezra. And each is receiving a practical lesson on the importance of dialogue with the other.

The visit fills everyone present with inspiration. They come in when the house is already crowded with visitors: Minister of Defense Moshe (Bogie) Yaalon and a delegation of rabbis from the Golan. The youth movement representatives approach Ofir, concerned they will be swallowed up by the crowd, but they manage to find seats facing us. We really want to talk to them.

Opposite us sit coordinators from the Scouts, HaNoar HaOved VehaLomed, Beitar, HaShomer HaTzair, Mahanot HaOlim (immigrants), Ezra, Bnei Akiva, the Agricultural Union, and the Council of Youth Movements. I tell them about Gil-ad, a dedicated counselor who invested in his charges. I add: "I don't know most of the people sitting here, but to me you represent the power of *Am Yisrael*." We talk about spirit and the strength that *Am Yisrael* provides right now, which enabled us to make the trip to the UN Human Rights Committee.

During the conversation Sarah, the widow of Roi Klein, enters (may Hashem avenge his blood). I don't recognize her immediately, but a moment later we're hugging. I tell the coordinators about her and about her husband, and Ofir passes around the book about character improvement that Rabbi Kastiel wrote in Roi's memory, and which Gil-ad had studied with Ofir. We're all so moved, but the youth movement coordinators even more so when Ofir tells them we want to stay in touch.

Later we would discover the visit served as the beginning of a joint initiative by the movements that would lay the conceptual foundation for a joint seminar of all the groups. Bnei Akiva would be represented by friends of Gil-ad.

After the Shiva we got a letter from Nelly Markman, training coordinator of the Scouts, who had participated in the joint visit:

> I remember the trip to the meeting. I remember my senses on alert, mainly the great fear that enveloped me. Fear of a different place, of different people, of awkwardness, of not knowing what to say – even just fear of hurting someone.
> It's a crazy time; the country is awash in pain, sadness, and war, and in the midst of all that I'm riding in my khaki uniform to some isolated settlement to console mourners.
> Is this right? Will my visit be welcomed? Is there even sense to this trip?
> Tons of things went through my head during that drive, but all of them, including the fears, vanished the moment my foot crossed the threshold and I encountered an inviting, welcoming smile.

Today I no longer have any doubt:

That meeting between a family that had just lost its most precious possession and a group of optimistic people promoting ethical educational activity, was right, important, and precisely what was called for.

A meeting that sought, specifically in the midst of chaos, to convey a message of inclusion, of understanding, and of reconciliation. A meeting that asserts that despite all the conflicts, the mutual fears, the stigmas, and the contrasting perspectives, we know how to feel pain together and know how to dream together of a different reality.

A tremendous thank you for the privilege I had to hold this meeting. Thank you for the smile, the listening, the moving stories, and the meaning you gave to our visit.

It really cannot be taken for granted.

Evening

A bashful young man enters the house and sits on the side. Neighbors who came in with him introduce him to us and tell us he landed just a few hours ago, straight from New York. I look at him, touched. I ask:

"How are you? How was the flight?"

He gives a shy smile: "*B'ezrat Hashem*, just for the flight it was worth coming here." I don't quite understand what he's getting at... I look at him, wondering, did this precious man take such a long trip just to comfort us? He explains: "I came to represent the Knesseth Yisrael community of Far Rockaway, which charged me with consoling the three families." He was almost offended when I expressed surprise at his long trip just to be with us. "Of course I did it," he says, "a Jew is in trouble, so we're with him — the whole community." That night he couldn't sleep and sent a moving letter to his community:

> In all sincerity, I don't know where to begin. The trip to the airport Wednesday afternoon was accompanied by sadness and serious concerns. I've never been so sad going to visit Eretz Yisrael.
>
> Numerous questions gnawed at me: will my presence mean anything to the beloved families? Will they look at me like just another guy from some organization fulfilling a PR obligation? Will I even have a chance to explain where I came from? To tell them we're grieving with them and that I came to bring a message of support from all our brothers and sisters in America?
>
> I started the trip on the wrong foot. A two-hour delay of the flight made me think I was too late, and that I wouldn't arrive in time for the noon meeting of the delegation of OU rabbis for a visit with the three families. It wasn't a good feeling, but it turns out I was wrong, absolutely.
>
> The trip will be forever etched in my heart. It was much more meaningful than I anticipated, and I want to share with you what I felt and experienced.
>
> During the flight the attendant talked to me, asking when I planned to fly back. She was surprised when I said I'm returning right after Shabbat.
>
> "What kind of a trip is so short?" she wondered. I was forced to share that I was sent by my community to console the families of the three boys, to deliver the amazing letters written by community members, and to tell them our love for our brothers and sisters in Israel knows no bounds.

The flight attendant began to cry. "Your community is something special and extraordinary."

Suddenly she goes to the microphone and announces to the entire sold-out plane, with many Birthright groups on the way to Israel: "Ladies and gentlemen, we have a mitzvah emissary on out flight. Come meet the rabbi sent by his community to fulfill the mitzvah of consoling mourners, people who feel like family, like real brothers and sisters. Our plane is safe because we have a mitzvah emissary with us."

That caused a tumult. It took some time for me to get back to my seat, at which point a twenty-six-year-old fellow from Washington came over and introduced himself. It was his first trip to Israel, and he wanted to borrow my *tallit* so he could perform a mitzvah he hadn't done since his Bar Mitzvah – for the boys' souls. He took out a card from his pocket, from which he recited the Traveler's Prayer, in Hebrew. It was the only prayer he knew to recite in Hebrew, and he wanted to say it wearing a *tallit*. But he wasn't done. He also asked for my *tefillin* and started to put them on in front of the other stunned passengers, who couldn't help but photograph and video the extraordinary event.

The story doesn't end there. This fellow, with a piercing in his ear and a tattoo on his arm, won't leave me alone. He asks me excitedly, "Rabbi, I'm so excited. In Washington I don't have *tefillin*, but I want to keep doing something for the souls of the three boys when I get home. What can I do?" I was stunned.

All of a sudden a Satmar Hasid sitting behind me turns to him and says, "My sweet fellow Jew, if you promise me you'll put them on every day, I'll make sure you have a set of *tefillin* sent to your home in Washington." They immediately exchange addresses. I landed in Israel two hours late. I'd missed the visit with two of the three families, so I went straight to the Shaers in Talmon. I got there at about 3:30, and we were told by the police that the family wasn't accepting visitors in the afternoon. The OU rabbi representative decided to go back and not to wait, so I found myself wandering the streets of Talmon tired, hungry, and sweating.

Out of nowhere a young woman from the town asks how I am. When she realized I'd just landed two hours earlier, she opened her home and gave me plenty to eat and drink. We then went out for a walk around Talmon. Everyone who heard I came from the U.S. to bring condolences to the families cried, moved that in America they share the families' pain. I saw an extraordinary sight. Whole families, young and old, were going around giving out bottles of cold water, fruit, cakes, and sandwiches to the hundreds of visitors. It's hard to describe the love and good vibes that prevailed in Talmon.

People came in throngs. The house was stuffed to the gills. Suddenly I heard Ofir and Bat-Galim asking everyone to clear space for the rabbi who came from America. I was greeted by the Shaers with a huge hug, with warmth and great love; they were shocked that our community had sent me to console them.

Despite the signs on the walls asking people not to take photos, Bat-Galim asked a dear neighbor to memorialize the moment in pictures, which I sent to you right away, to thank you and to try to share with you the intensity of what was happening there. That moment I decided to spend Shabbat in Talmon. I went to visit the other two families, the Yifrachs and the Fraenkels. I was also welcomed there with a big hug. Each moment I felt the tremendous privilege of being part of the Jewish people.

I feel that the verse, "Who is like Your people Israel" is manifest on several levels:

Who is like Your people Israel, who feel deep connection with one another;

Who is like Your people Israel, who feel a sense of obligation to one another and discover amazing powers in moments of difficulty and crisis;

Who is like Your people Israel, who are ready to do anything for one another, even people who don't know one another;

Who is like Your people Israel, who together undertake to make the world a better, more meaningful place.

I want to thank you, the community, and our rabbi, Rabbi Eytan Feiner, for allowing me the privilege of this meaningful mission.

Yours truly,

Rabbi Shai Shechter

A deep connection was forged with Rabbi Shechter, and later with his wife Rina. An amazing family that continues to be there for us today. Brothers in heart and soul. They would name their third son Michael Simcha, after our son Gil-ad Simcha. They were born on the same date, seventeen years apart.

Saturday Night, Parashat Balak, Eve of 8 Tammuz, July 5

Masses of Jews crowd into the house. They forms rings around us, holding us, supporting us.

I look up and suddenly see the singer Avraham Fried sitting there quietly, on the side. I rub my eyes in disbelief. I grew up on Fried's songs; they touch every heart. I compose myself, send somebody to get a guitar and ask Fried to "say a song." Noam Yaakovson, sitting next to him, takes the guitar, and the two of them, beside themselves with awkwardness, grant my request.

"What should I sing?" Fried asks gently. "It doesn't matter," I answer. "Something for the soul." The last thing on my mind right now is his repertoire, and for a moment a thought flashes inside me: What are you doing? A mourner during Shiva isn't allowed listen to music! But the knowledge that his songs give me strength and touch my soul remove all doubt, and the only song that comes to mind is a verse from Psalms, "It is good to give thanks to Hashem."

Avraham Fried raises an eyebrow and cooperates.

When the song ends I share with those present a question that bothers many people: "Where did all the prayers go? How could the search for the boys end this way?" I stress that the question isn't directly relevant to our story: unfortunately they were prayers to change something in the past. Still, we're sure prayers aren't wasted. They operate in ways we can't see or understand.

Amid all the terrible pain, we recognize how much kindness is embedded in our story. First, we were able to find the boys and give them a proper burial. Second, the boys didn't suffer from the crime. Third, no soldier came to harm during the search. And fourth, the incredible unity we've been privileged to see. There is what to be thankful for amid all this immense pain.

I want to keep holding on to this magical moment, fearing it will dissipate, and request another song. Fried sings a song with lyrics from the prayer of Rabbi Elimelech of Lizhensk, which best expresses what I'm feeling right now. It moves us all, plucks my heartstrings.

> Master of all, place in our hearts the desire for each of us to see our fellow's strengths, not his flaws; that each of us speak to his fellow in an upright, worthy fashion acceptable to You; may no hate arise for anyone by his fellow; and may You strengthen our connection to You with love, as is revealed and known to You. May everything give You satisfaction.

I'm thirsty for more such exalting songs and prayers. "We have all evening," he smiles.

I think to myself he must have no idea where I'm coming from. He sings as Noam plays, and my heart sings and cries with them.

Sunday, 8 Tammuz, July 6

We have a moving, special meeting with people from the Kfar Etzion Field School who found the boys' bodies. They visit our home and try to recount the magnitude of the miracle that led to the discovery. In the afternoon of Thursday, 28 Sivan – June 26 – a number of people got together, including Avital Sela, Roi Simon, Yaron Rosenthal, Elisha Meidan, Tzahi Cohen, and Ori Shechter, all field experts and alumni of field units. They felt they couldn't sit by idly, and that they had to enlist in the search for the kidnapped boys.

They concluded that disciplined, thorough work based on knowledge of the territory and its topography would make precise identification of the place where the terrorists hid the boys more likely. The group stressed that it trusted the army, which was doing everything to find the captives, but in their opinion, another direction of thinking, another avenue of searching, could bring about a breakthrough. On Friday afternoon they presented their plan to the commander of the Etzion Brigade, Colonel Amit Yamin. They described a humble, attentive, and special man. He listened, accepted the data on field conditions, and agreed to the proposal, gave it precise direction, and began to lead its implementation with gusto. He created a new conception of cooperation between the military and civilians, in terms of analyzing topography, in terms of search methods, and in terms of depending on skilled field personnel.

Immediately after he gave his approval, during Shabbat the group marked possible locations on the map, and an uninterrupted stream of people who heard about the initiative came to participate. Religious and secular, from Tel Aviv and Gush Etzion, paratroopers and Golani infantry. In the work rooms there appeared geologists, archaeologists, aerial photography experts, Geographic Information Systems experts, experienced field school personnel from all over the country, graduates of elite units, and independent guides. All of them left their homes, rushing to join this mission with all their souls. Ready to help with anything necessary. The mitzvah-observant worked even on Shabbat, not sleeping nights. Their top priority was one goal: bring the boys home.

Extraordinary collaboration took place between the army and the civilian field people. The brigade commander pushed for and oversaw optimal analysis of the data, allocated integrated personnel, and attached superior field personnel to each group.

They estimated the search would take weeks.

Baruch Hashem, after three days, fifty meters from the spot marked on the map, one of the volunteer scouts, Aharon (Ahrele) Levi, spotted a bush bent at a strange angle not suited to the terrain. He approached, moved the bush... and the searches came to an end.

Ori Shechter, a civilian "war room" staffer, describes the Kfar Etzion Field School personnel's scouting mission alongside soldiers:

> We didn't know whether they were alive or dead. We went out into the field full of hope. With all the pain, we're happy we found them. We could have not found them for years. We didn't give up; we spared no effort; we worked day and night. The whole people's will was incredible. Reservists who weren't

allowed to enlist brought food and drink just to feel a part of the national effort.

What happened here? It was a civilian initiative and the Establishment's attentive ear. There was unlimited investment by the army. There was cooperation among wonderful people from all levels of society. And there were prayers. Once again we've been exposed to the beautiful, painful face of our country.

I look at the face of Ahrele the scout. His whole body showed emotion. "I came for one say of searching," he recalls. "I left a late-termpregnant wife at home with two small children and took a bag of things I thought would be useful.

"At the time we found the boys I got a call from my wife that she wasn't feeling well. I couldn't share the news with her yet, and called a neighbor to ask that she stay with her.

"At the end of the day I came back home confused and agitated. 'You did a tremendous kindness for the families,' my wife told me when I shared what happened."

We feel deep, burning pain accompanied by relief and profound gratitude to all our friends, but most of all to the Creator, who helped bring them home.

Ofir wants to speak his heart to the searchers in our home: "The whole period we felt the need to say thank you. Just on Sunday, the day before the boys were found, they gave us short notice we're going to Tarqumiyyeh to meet the divisional and operation commanders. We always had the feeling the army was with us. We saw eyes red from crying and fatigue; we knew they were making an effort to find them alive. From the top of the chain of command down to the last soldier, the assumption was they were alive. The cooperation between soldiers and civilians that led to them finding the boys is a reflection of what's happening in Israel and around the world. Unity. Military and civilians acting with humility."

At the same time important rabbis from the Religious Zionist movement came to visit.

The arrival of the rabbis and the soldiers at the same time wasn't planned; I feel the encounter that was created here between the rabbis and the search personnel symbolizes something deep and important that characterizes this episode, and I address those present: "During the searches we had a tent in our yard for Torah study. Twenty-four hours a day there was constant learning that didn't stop for a minute. A spiritual principle guided us, leading us to maintain a strong connection between physical and spiritual striving, to hold both 'the scroll and the sword,' a manifestation of 'Do Moshe's hands decide the war?' (Mishna Rosh Hashanah 3:8)."

Prime Minister Binyamin Netanyahu wishes to pay a visit with his wife Sarah and their son Yair.

Security procedures dictate that before the visit the house undergo a comprehensive security check. We're told we have to clear out all the visitors so a proper check can be conducted.

What will we do with the continuous flow of visitors that's only increasing?

Someone comes up with an especially creative idea and while the check is underway, seats us in a nearby public park. Two chairs are placed under a tree, and the surreal scene has us accepting many condolence-callers for an hour.

The meeting itself is intimate and moving. The Netanyahu family takes interest in how the girls are doing and shows empathy and solidarity. The prime minister shares his private pain and tells of his coping as a brother with his grief over his brother Yoni. "It's like losing a hand," he says. "A kind of disability. You learn slowly, through great pain, to live with it, but it's a daily struggle." He does not hide his pain.

Tuesday, 10 Tammuz, July 8

We get up from the Shiva on the day Operation Protective Edge begins. Our personal story developed into something much bigger and more complex.

We go to the grave.

There's still no stone.

The name Gil-ad Michael is scribbled next to Eyal and Naftali Yaakov. It's a difficult sight.

The fact that Gil-ad came home, but not as we intended or anticipated, is too hard to bear. Hard to digest. Hard to understand.

We come back home while it's still early morning and fall into bed for a few more hours' sleep.

We go back home to our lives, which we must now rearrange and reorganize.

Piles

Suddenly everything is tangled and complicated.

Everything has accumulated into piles –

Piles of laundry.

Piles of clothes.

Piles of papers.

Piles of letters.

Piles of bags.

Piles of food and drink.

I don't know where to begin.

Two sweet girls come to help us sort through all the letters we got from *Am Yisrael*, from Israel and the world. Two dear neighbors, Uli and Hodaya, take it upon themselves to help us compose letters to send back.

They sort, file, and place before me stacks of sorted letters.

Piles. Piles.

I try to make some order out of the mess, but barely find the strength. I feel like the disorder isn't just external, not just in the house, which is normally neat but looks like a storm passed through. The mess is mainly internal – where will I draw the strength?

Where do I start?

There are so many decisions to make.

Suddenly everything that seemed so natural or simple in the everyday now looks like a threatening, never-ending pile.

Between the Shiva and Shloshim

Wednesday, 18 Tammuz, July 16

The days pass like a shadow.

The days keep passing and we're busy with intensive activity that seems to leave no room for processing the pain.

But you can't escape the pain.

The pain is material, physical. It establishes a place in your mind.

In your heart; deeper, even – in your soul.

We feel the absence, the longing, more and more.

We're starting to experience what death means, more and more. But we still don't understand a thing...

A sea of tears, a river of drops that flow without stopping.

I find myself going to deliver speeches of encouragement, to hold meaningful meetings, and crying all the way there and back.

During the speeches I try very hard to be with the audience; years of teaching experience do their part. I'm usually able to grasp pretty quickly who's sitting in front of me and to direct my talk to the heart, and that's a huge help from Heaven.

I share with the listeners the insight that there's no such thing as being strong in the face of death. We've fallen apart, we're hurting, longing. "Strong" isn't applicable.

I try to challenge the audience to find a more suitable word. I haven't found one yet.

We're always engaged in a conscious effort – and we choose to go on living. We choose to go on and to amplify the meaning revealed by Gil-ad's death; we choose to go on through action and commemoration, trying not to get sucked into the gaping abyss of pain.

It's not always possible.

We also give space to the pain. There's something liberating, cleansing, in crying. It's important to me that the girls see it's OK to cry. Because it really does hurt, and it's not easy for them. It's not easy to see Imma and Abba crying.

Ups and downs; we get up and fall down.

We just cope. We just go on. We just live.

My thoughts frequently return to the *chai* days.

How was I so optimistic – where did I get the positive thinking that I clutched to so tightly most of the time? How certain I was everything would end well...

I worked so hard to keep the girls from emotional wounds from the event, and here the Creator reminds me who runs the world; they will always feel wounded by Gil-ad's death.

It's hard for me to absorb that reality has thwarted the affirmation, "Think positive and it will be positive."

I can't come to terms with the fact that the positive thinking I so nurtured doesn't actually work.

We thought positive, and it ended the worst way possible.

I look back and am filled with wonder that I managed to control my thoughts with such consistency and dignity. We're used to exercising self-control in our behavior, in our actions, our speech; but controlling my thoughts?

It seems impossible, but look, I did it.

I remember going to sleep exhausted at the end of the day, not just from worry and powerlessness, but also from the constant work on my thoughts. Don't give the negative thoughts any room... it's draining, fatiguing.

Gradually it's becoming clear to me that "Think positive and it will be good" doesn't necessarily mean reality will bend itself to our will, follow our brushstrokes. There's Someone who runs the world, and He decides; we don't.

It's so hard to accept.

In such a smart, opinionated generation, a generation that ostensibly knows and understands it all – suddenly a hurdle appears. We suddenly realize we don't understand everything, and it's hard.

You need a lot of humility.

Against the backdrop of that initial realization, there's a new meaning forming inside me of that charged affirmation. A person is limited, after all, in how much he can control his life. Think positive so you'll be best able to cope with reality, and that'll be good for you.

Try to create sturdy, fireproof tools that will allow you to handle reality.

A person has finite capabilities when it comes to controlling his life. The big challenge is grappling with the reality that hits you uninvited.

Our choice lies in how to cope with the current reality in the best way, and that's not easy at all. We have to be creators of tools and vessels such that we can choose, in a complex, dynamic reality, which implement is suited to each situation, and through which we can illuminate reality.

We often don't want that reality.

Most of the time we fight reality instead of accepting it and trying to determine how to manage it best with what we have. Sometimes we fight reality with closed eyes or try to force it instead of accepting it and then thinking, with the help of the tools we have, how to manage it best.

The rule is: cope with reality with eyes wide open, and clarify as thoroughly as possible when to fight and when to let go.

In other words, think very well how to make things turn out well for you.

So what was the alternative during those *chai* days, I ask myself.

Fall apart? Break? Be pessimistic and agitated?

With the help of G-d I succeeded in being truly optimistic.

It was hard to accept the ending, a huge shock, but because of our optimism we managed to navigate those days as something possible, without drowning in them. Positive thinking enabled us to cope, to get through the chai days the best way possible for us, a path that gave us lots of strength.

Monday, Rosh Chodesh Av, 1 Av, July 28

Operation Protective Edge is upon us; the spirit of mutual responsibility has spread into the war effort and contributed to support for the soldiers at the front. An entire nation goes out of its way to encourage and support the soldiers protecting the homeland with sacrifice. The experience sharpens the awareness that regardless of where you live, the Jewish People have one fate.

Am Yisrael – its power is in prayer. During all the *chai* days mass prayer rallies took place. We heard about most of them only afterward; we probably still haven't heard about some.

"Pour out like water your heart facing Hashem" (Lamentations 2:19): I'm moved by the public's amazing readiness to pray for the welfare of the fighters. Criticism sometimes comes up that we only know how to unite in times of trouble but not during the day to day, when it seems our disagreements and rivalries cross all red lines. Not only do I not take that lightly, I actually find it quite encouraging that when "it is a time of trouble for Yaakov" we immediately cast off the outer shell of division. We know how to come together and show mutual responsibility and care.

There's no other nation in the world that knows how to close ranks like this in times of trouble and emergency. "One for all; all for one" became a rallying cry at the funeral for Staff Sergeant Sean Carmeli, in which all the diverse elements of Israel's population participated. About twenty thousand people came together on short notice for this lone soldier who immigrated from the U.S. and fell during Protective Edge.

An entire nation encourages and supports its children, its soldiers, at numerous rallies for prayer and encouragement. One such rally is close to my heart, because it took place where I spent many childhood years, and I'd like to elaborate a bit on it. I'm referring to Givat Shmuel, where I was invited to address the rally:

> Beloved friends, good evening.
> We're gathered here tonight with the residents of Givat Shmuel, the setting of my childhood, to pray together.
> What is prayer?
> Prayer is a yearning to share, for connection in the face of difficulty.
> Any feeling of sharing and participation is prayer.
> We support and encourage all those working day and night for the welfare of our country – from the prime minister and cabinet to the very last soldier.
> We want to pray for the welfare of the IDF soldiers and commanders; may G-d protect them and grant success to their mission; may you all return safe from your important mission protecting our homeland.
> *Am Yisrael* has undergone a revolution in the last month and a half.
> Judaism is a way of life. Judaism is a world unto itself.
> We are a people who believes, a people with a great and glorious past and a present full of challenges.
> To meet future threats and dangers we need emotional strength.
> Some of that strength was displayed when the boys were kidnapped, and it hasn't weakened.
> It's still with us because we don't let it diminish, through effort...

Am Yisrael, in its painful moments, reveals unbelievable power...
I want to share a little story with you about Gil-ad:
As a child Gil-ad made sure his teachers always wrote his name with a hyphen. His fourth grade teacher told me he didn't understand why it was so important to Gil-ad to have his name spelled that way; he would correct teachers and tell them to pronounce it and write it correctly. He even went to the secretary to make sure the records all showed his name with the proper spelling, with the hyphen.
A boy full of smiles, full of *joi de vivre,* a boy who loves life. A boy full of joy, *Gil*. That *Gil* unfortunately became a Gal-ed, a monument.

Our job is to be strong despite the pain, the grief, and the gaping absence... People ask us: where do you get the strength? How are you batteries always charged?
And I answer: the source of our power is the unity of *Am Yisrael*. That's our battery. From the day of the kidnapping to today – *Am Yisrael* has been encouraging, wrapping us in an embrace, caring for us as full partners in our brokenness and in strengthening us.
From across the country and around the world – Jews are sending letters, flowers, posting notices, sending emails, and just embracing us hard, saying, "Gil-ad isn't only your child; Gil-ad is all of ours."
That incredible revelation of unity is a source of strength on a national level.
As a nation we've had no small number of challenges since the founding of the state, and many more await us.
Look at the might this nation has when it's united; look at the power it gives the soldiers in their holy work.

I ask myself: why do we have to wait for when it hurts to be together? Why do we wait till it's so difficult until we realize we have to come together?

Here's another little story:

Last week we went to console the family of Dror Hanin, may Hashem avenge his blood, from Beit Aryeh, a civilian killed while engaging in his act of kindness: distributing food to soldiers.

What a great man, all about love for Israel and giving.

The head of the regional council there, Avi Naim, was sitting there, and asked me what he could tell children who ask him, "We prayed so much, but the boys were murdered, and Dror was killed..."

I answered him that we're not the G-d's deputies and we don't really understand where all the prayers went, but in our case the precise nature of things doesn't leave room for doubt. The murder happened long before the prayers for our sons, but perhaps because of those prayers the bodies were found and given a proper burial... and maybe because of them we've been privileged to see miracles when thousands of missiles were fired and we weren't harmed. And maybe, with all the difficult losses, the prayers prevented an even bigger tragedy... who knows?

To me, the deaths of young men in their prime is actually supposed to strengthen our prayer, to strengthen our choice to live, to highlight the deep meaning of doing good, because life is so short.

Since the murder, some have tried to make Gil-ad a symbol.

But I'm telling you as his mother that Gil-ad was a fantastic child, but a normal kid. And there are a lot of Gil-ads walking around among us.

Think about it: many of us are growing such flowers in our homes.

Last week I met his friends from yeshiva and thought, really, each of them is such a flower. In *Am Yisrael* there are tons of children, flowers like that. Those powers are inherent in many families. You don't need to wait for events like these!

We have to look at ourselves hard in the mirror and ask: why did this all happen – *for what*? We can't get caught up in the "why" of things, because we'll never get our questions answered.

We have to broaden and deepen our gaze at ourselves and at our place in the world. If we realize that this revelation of unity in *Am Yisrael* is the source of our strength, if we realize that unity doesn't require uniformity, but provides space and respect for the other, we can properly meet all future challenges.

I am filled with prayer that we maintain this unity and find the strength even in our daily lives, not just in moments of crisis.

With great love,

Bat-Galim

During the Shloshim period we get a phone call from Ronit Dotan, of the Federations of North America, whose representatives happened to meet us at the Knesset during the *chai* days. We're invited to a conference in Jerusalem with delegates from 120 Jewish communities in the U.S. Ofir is asked to address them, and when he's finished we witness an event that astounds us.

Side by side, dozens of representatives of Jewish communities are standing and sharing with us the prayers, classes, and gatherings that took place in their communities during the *chai* days for the sake of the boys. Jews from all streams – Orthodox, Reform, Conservative, and even those not formally identified with any movement – prayed, beseeched, and cried there abroad while their hearts were with us here in Israel.

We stood energized by the warmth and love they showered on us. The embrace grew stronger as the months passed, and revealed insights to us about the essence of the intrinsic connection between Israel and the Jews of the Diaspora – insights that we as native Israelis had not reached before.

The Shloshim

Tuesday, 2 Av, July 29

A month has passed, gone without you, Gil-ad.
Our life has turned upside down at home.
Never a dull moment.
On the Shloshim we go to the burial plot, and I speak to Gil-ad, at his grave.

> My heart burns, my body hurts, and my head can't digest it...
> From the moment we discovered your body was found, your soul, Gil-ad, connected to mine.
> Your body was taken from us but your soul is with us all the time.
> A beloved soul – it turns out we were raising a great soul.
> I wasn't always wise enough or clever enough to cope as a mother.
> Your absence is present in everything.
> During the few days of rest we tried to arrange several days ago, we remembered how much you loved to hike and have your picture taken; how you swam like a fish in water; and how you'd lift your little sisters up high. On Shabbat we waited for your delectable cakes and the mess you'd leave in the kitchen; the plums on the tree waiting for someone your height to come

and pick the ripe ones from the upper branches. I so hoped you'd come back and together we'd arrange Meitar's Bat Mitzvah celebration as only you and I could.
I so hoped you'd come back and we'd dream together about our house under construction...

My beloved Gil-adush, *Am Yisrael* has undergone upheaval since you were taken from us so unexpectedly with Eyal and Naftali.
You always loved productions, going big, thinking of all the little things that make the difference.
So you arranged a heck of a production as you love to do, big-time, with meaning, with intensity...
Gil-ad, our eternal hero. Your mother is so proud of you. Proud of the call you made without the kidnappers noticing, proud of your last words, including the whisper that will echo forever. Proud of your resourcefulness, the heroism, and sacrifice you displayed.
Ribono Shel Olam, Master of the World, how we anticipated different news.
How we yearned for the fulfillment of the promise, "and the sons will return to their border." Now in the blink of an eye we're called to a role for which we were never consulted and for which we were never prepared. Please, G-d, take the reins. Please.
My Gil-ad, you now have a new role.
Please make sure we have the strength to endure the lack, the pain.
Please protect our soldiers doing their faithful work at this crazy time.

Pease watch over *Am Yisrael* that we may know how to continue nurturing this wondrous unity and national resilience; that we continue to be proud of our Judaism and our people. I miss you. I love you. I hurt.

We come home from the memorial ceremony and just fall into bed. Two grown-ups who don't know the meaning of sleeping in,
 conk out into a deep slumber till the afternoon.
 It felt like we could sleep like that another few hours.
 My body wants what my soul can't find – a little respite, a little calm. But the girls need lunch.

Afternoon

The war that grew out of the kidnapping only strengthens within us the sense that we have to put on a major event for the Shloshim.

This time, as well, Yaakov Netanyahu of Dolev agrees to help; he was at our side with devotion during the *chai* days. After many hours of deliberation and organization, and in partnership with the Jerusalem Municipality, we decide to hold a major rally in memory of the three boys at the Jerusalem Great Synagogue. Thousands come, many of whom remain stuck outside, forced to watch the event on huge screens set up on Keren HaYesod Street. At the rally, personalities from across the Israeli social and political spectrum speak.

Before I get up to speak, a clip is shown in memory of the boys, called "I Seek My Brothers," sensitively produced by Yoav Elitzur.

The images hit me hard in the stomach; the voices echo within me and my throat catches.

I choke back the crying, wipe away my dripping tears.

How can I get up to speak in front of all these people now?
I take a deep breath and begin:

> *Am Yisrael* has undergone a revolution in the last month and a half.
> Since the kidnapping, since our insides turned over, something incredible has awoken in *Am Yisrael*.
> *Chai* days of anticipation, of hope, stoked great hopes in *Am Yisrael*, and not only for the return of the boys, Gil-ad, Eyal, and Naftali, home.
> During that time we thought the dead were alive – we can therefore call it "The Days of the Resurrection of the Dead."
> Days during which values, conduct, and patterns of behavior thought dead in Israeli society came back to life.
> Days in which our understanding of reality became clear and simple to so many: accurate truth without cynicism;
> Truth that touches each and every one of us.
> *Am Yisrael* realizes who its real enemy is and whom we have to protect. The soldiers understand their mission and the civilian understands he has to take responsibility for his life, because life is so short and meaningful.
> The leadership understands its mission to make courageous decisions to protect the welfare of its citizens.
> We all understand we cannot accept an existential threat to Israel that passes without response; we all trust the leadership and the system to do everything for the benefit and protection of the citizens; we all love our homeland and are proud to be part of the Jewish people.
> Gil-ad, Eyal, and Naftali – despite your youth you'd already begun to debate where you'd serve your people best.

Who'd have thought you'd become the first soldiers of Protective Edge.

Who'd have thought you'd be the first casualties...

We can only try to imagine the encounter of your souls with those of the holy soldiers killed during this operation; your voices, the mutual admiration and affirmation. How up there in Heaven you're giving satisfaction to the Creator of the World and to the founding fathers of our people, in your contribution for the sake of Am Yisrael together with the heavenly host.

For thousands of years we've invoked and sought the protection of our people's fathers and mothers, and begged for mercy upon the children in the merit of our ancestors. Now we ask for heavenly mercy and are certain Israel will be redeemed because of holy and pure children who sacrificed their lives, their dreams, and their personal desires for the sake of an entire people.

Our hearts are with the wounded, hurting soldiers, soldiers who chose this immense mission of protecting every Jew, no matter where.

My Gil-ad, you will always be a monument, a Gal-Ed, to generations of young men and women.

Traits with which you were graced can serve as examples to so many of us.

You have received charm and a good mind from Hashem; you loved to learn, to know, to understand. Everything piqued your curiosity. You knew how to analyze the situation and cope with difficulties in a manner beyond your years; you showed patience in grappling with so many situations. I remember when you first came to yeshiva you had a hard time adjusting to the new schedule, and you called, crying and homesick.

And within that great difficulty you amazed me with your observation that the difficulty stemmed not from any challenge in connecting to the yeshiva itself, but the fact that you were far from home and having a hard time adjusting to the many hours of study each day. With emotional maturity you noticed that the passage of time would help, and you'd manage, *B'ezrat Hashem*. We watched you as parents and saw how you blazed your own trail in serving Hashem; we sensed how each year the spirit of the yeshiva beat stronger in you. You showed the patience of knowing that nothing is built in a day...

Patience is the attribute we needed during the *chai* days.

Patience is the attribute we all need during this difficult time.

Patience is needed now to help us both weather and value this time.

Patience will help us maintain Jewish unity and our endurance as a people.

May Hashem always help us, Amen.

Gil-ad with his winning smile, age 1, winter 1999

Loved the holidays and was excited for their arrival, age 6

Gil-ad, child of nature, age 4

Gil-ad, age 3, with his sister Shirel, before his ritual first haircut
by Rabbi Mordecai Eliyahu z"l

Gil-ad, age 4, with his sisters Shirel and Tahel

Age 10 – Gil-ad knew how to enjoy the little things in life, a true joy in life

Age 13 – An unfulfilled dream to be able to play guitar

שמי: _____

נולדתי בתאריך: _____

הורי קראו לי בשם זה כי: _____
_____

המקום בו נולדתי: _____

תחביבי: _____

הצבע האהוב עלי: _____

השיר האהוב עלי: _____

מה אני רוצה לעשות כשאגדל: _____
_____

הספר שהכי אהבתי: _____

אילו ניתנו לי 3 משאלות הייתי מבקש:
1. _____
2. _____
3. _____

Childhood dreams – age 8, but with big dreams

Excited with his father to lay tefillin at the Western Wall, one month before Bar mitzvah

Celebrating his Bar mitzvah

With mom and dad at his Bar mitzvah celebration, Talmon (Photo: Ilay Levin)

Bar mitzvah preparation meetings

With Rabbi Haim Sabato, Ma'aleh Adumim

With Rabbi David Grossman, Migdal HaEmek
(Photo: Lior Solomon, Archive Bureau Rabbi Grossman)

With Prof. Yisrael Aumann, Jerusalem

Eighth grade, with friends at the end-of-year party (third from the right)

The star of the show at the bar mitzvah – "The Lost Key" – a performance in the spirit of S. Y. Agnon

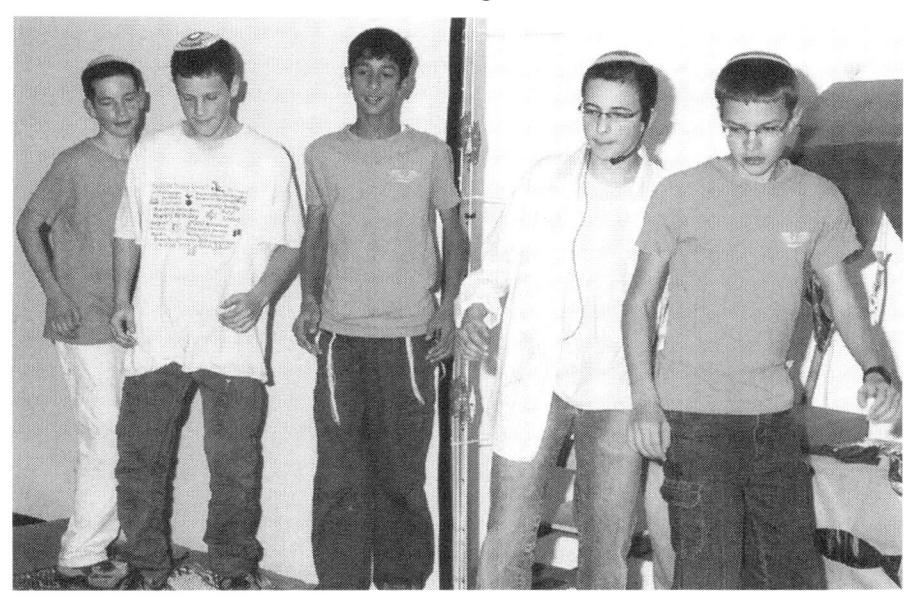

During prayer

Rosh Hashanah eve, 2013, annual holiday photo in grandpa and grandma's garden

Study time at the yeshiva, 9th grade, 2012

Family trip to Nahal HaShofet, age 15 and a half, month of Nissan, 2013

Family trip to Eilat − He loved extreme sports, age 16, Hanukkah 2014

With mom in Eilat

More from the trip to Eilat

He loved making his little sisters fly

With dad in Eilat

With Shirel at the Kinneret (right) and at the Bahai Gardens in Haifa (left), 2013

Human pyramid, with Naftali Frenkel (Photo: Ehud Dahan)

Sports day, with friends from yeshiva, day before the kidnapping (Photo: Ehud Dahan)

Seventh trip with the yeshiva to HaMachtesh HaGadol (the Big Crater) (second from right), Passover 2014 (Photo: Ehud Dahan)

ידיעות אחרונות

שיחת חינם ‎*3778

| תעריך לשטה: ד"ר ה. רוזנבלום ז"ל | דעתוך האחראי הראשי: יהודה מוזס ז"ל | עורך: רון ירון | העורך האחראי: אריאן מוזס | רסים גלוי רח׳ מוזס 3, תל אביב | Yedioth Ahronoth יִדִיעוֹת אַחֲרוֹנוֹת | יום ראשון, י"ז בסיון תשע"ד 15.6.2014 גליון מס׳ 22960 | 5.00 ש"ח 4.20 ש"ח (בלי מע"מ) |

אלפי חיילים ושוטרים עוברים מבית לבית במאמץ למצוא את הנערים

אייל יפרח (19) מאלעד   | גיל־עד שאער (16) מטלמון | נפתלי פרנקל (16) מנוף־איילון

אלכס פישמן
מבחן הממשלה
עמ׳ 2

שמעון שיפר
לשנות כיוון
עמ׳ 8

יועז הנדל
דילמת האסירים
עמ׳ 14

חטופים

מקום החטיפה, אמש: נערות תופסות טרמפים

מבצע חיפושים ענק אחר שלושת הנערים שנחטפו בחמישי בלילה לאחר שלקחו טרמפ מצומת גוש עציון ● ההערכה: החטיפה תועדה במצלמות אבטחה ● באזור נמצאה מכונית שרופה שכנראה שימשה את המחבלים ● נתניהו: אבו־מאזן אחראי ● המחדל: מוקד 100 של המשטרה קיבל בשעה 22:25 הודעה על חטיפה, אבל עידכן את הצבא רק אחרי שעות ● משפחות הנערים: מבקשים מעם ישראל להתפלל שיחזרו בשלום ● יוסי יהושע ועקיבא נוביק, עמ׳ 2־20

"אין לנו דרך אחרת לנסוע", הסבירו עשרות הנערים שנועדו גם אמש בטרמפים בגוש עציון

עדכונים שוטפים ב‎ynet

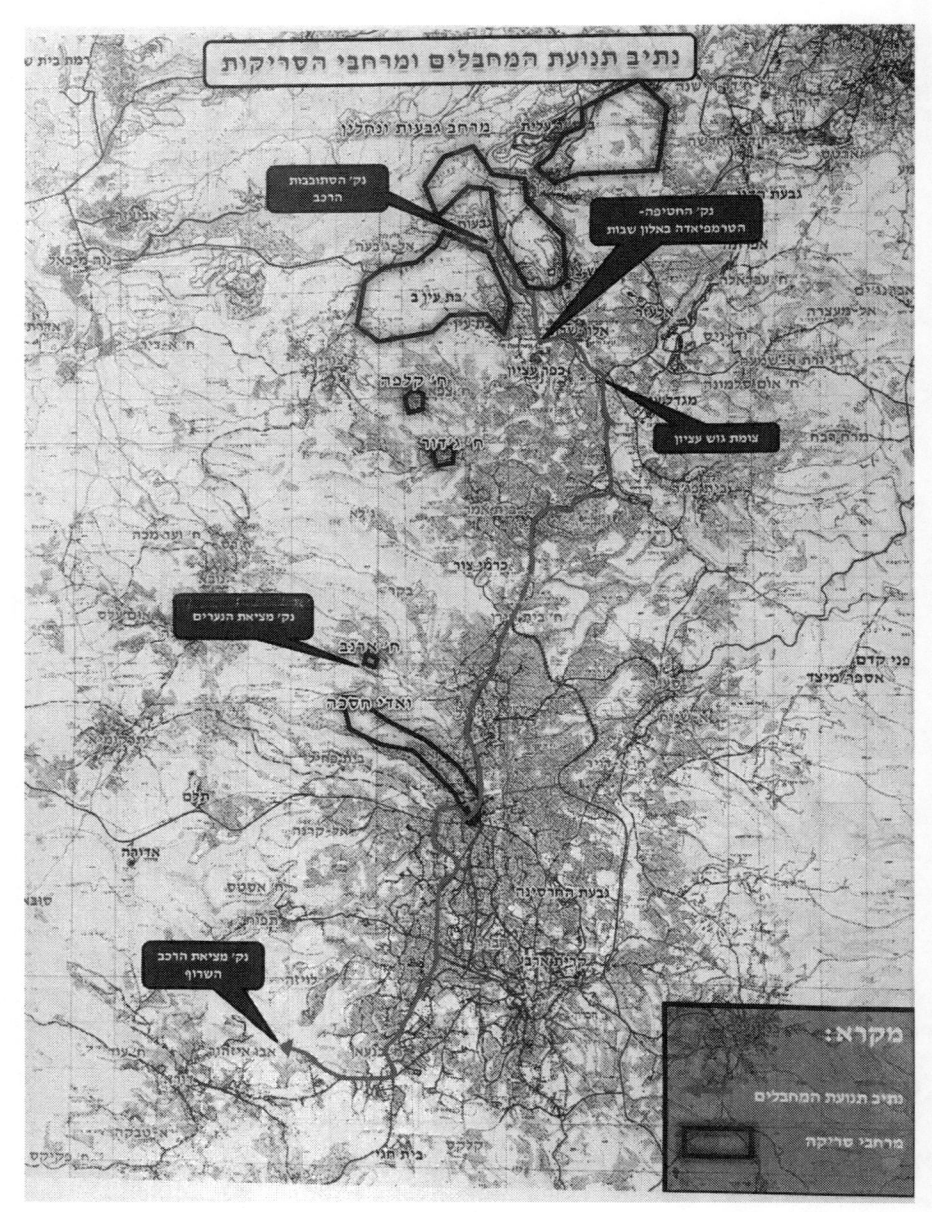

The route of the terrorists' movements and the search areas for the boys

Summer 2014,
chai **(18) days, the**
searches
(Photos: Tal Shachar)

(Photo: Reuven Shimelman)

Ofir and Bat-Galim come out to the media in Talmon; the media offers a warm embrace

(Photo: Miriam Tzachi)

The three mothers – Racheli Frenkel, Bat-Galim Shaer, Iris Yifrach (right to left)
(Photo: Alex Kolomoysky)

The three fathers – Uri Yifrach, Ofir Shaer, Avi Frenkel (right to left)
(Photo: Alex Kolomoysky)

Rafting in the Kinneret – "And return sons to their borders"
(Photo: Afi Sharir)

Solidarity meeting and support for the Knesset, "Waiting for the Sons" (Photo: Alex Kolomoysky)

White night in Tel Aviv – the youth writes to the families and prays with us for the boys to return home in peace

Picture of the three boys in Times Square, New York, during the *chai* (18) days
(Design and photo: Yali Hakalir)

Bring Back Our Boys – a tremendous mobilization around the world for the release of the sons
(Photo: Daniel Astrin)

Prayers for the three boys – Yeshivat Mekor Haim, with head of yeshiva Rabbi Dov Zinger (from right) and head military rabbi Raffi Peretz (from left)

A demonstration in solidarity with 700 primary school students in Givat Shmuel, Israel
(Photo: Avi Revivo)

Mass prayers at the Western Wall (Photo: Ohad Zuigenberg)

The three fathers praying at the Western Wall (Photo: Barel Efraim, ynet)

Talmon during the *chai* (18) days, endless embrace (Photo: Yuval Chen)

Birthday celebration for Brigadier General Eitan Madmoni, a significant figure who accompanied us throughout the period (Photo: Motti Kimchi)

"Singing together for their return" – strengths and connections in Rabin Square Tel Aviv, first in the evening, 6/29/14 – a day before the boys are found
(Photo: Tal Shpizes)

(Photo: Yuval Chen)

Bat-Galim giving a speech in Rabin Square
(Photo: Yuval Chen)

Embraced by President Shimon Peres z"l, with the parents of the three boys
(Photo: Mark Neyman, GPO)

Embrace from members of Harley Riders of Israel in Talmon (Photo: Michal Avior)

The stop where the boys were kidnapped, Tzomet Alon Shvut, Gush Etzion
(Photo: Alex Kolomoysky)

Monument established near the location where the boys' bodies were found
(Photo: Miriam Tzachi)

Eulogies for Gil-ad in Talmon, 7/2/14 (Photos: Motti Kimchi)

State funeral at the cemetery in Modiin. Over 150,000 people came to pay their final respects
(Photo: Miriam Tzachi)

Rabin Square, at the moment when the nation learned of the boys' death
(Photo: Dana Kopel)

The cemetery in Modiin, before the laying of the gravestones (Photo: Yuval Chen)

The gravestones. Architect Moshe Shapira wanted to give each one a personal place, but also a national expression in the form of a Star of David

Every year Unity Day takes place in Israel and around the world, in memory of the boys
(Photo: Eitan Morgenstein)

Oz VeGaon Forest (Gil-ad, Eyal, and Naftali) was established at the Gush junction on the day of the funeral
(Photo: Gershon Elinson)

Ofir and Rabbi Shai Schechter from New York, with his young son Michael Simcha, named after Gil-ad Michael

Top left: Project Connection – Jewish Unity – sending care packages to Jews around the world. **Top right:** "Sing, Brothers" evening in Raanana, one summer later, in a spirit of unity and in memory of the boys. Summer 2015 (Photo: Tzvika Tishler). **Bottom left:** Project "Sweet Heart" occurs every year in Israel and around the world on Gil-ad's birthday – from the Facebook group "Gil-ad's Kitchen" (design: Aharon Benafshial). **Bottom right:** "Song of Gil-ad" – spiritual center and synagogue established in memory of Gil-ad in Talmon (Photo: Michal Avior).

Cornerstone laying ceremony for the branch of Bnei Akiva Ofarim, with the participation of Gil-ad, 5/13/14 (Photo: Mor Sha'ashua)

Dedication of the branch of Bnei Akiva Gil-ad, Ofarim, in his memory, 8/30/2015
(Photo: Mor Sha'ashua)

Page from Gil-ad's diary found near the burned vehicle

Thursday, 4 Av, July 31

In the afternoon powerlessness overtakes me. I feel crushed.

Here it comes... no desire for anything, not even to think. Just nothing.

How do you go on? I ask myself. How do you cope?

And then our friend Rani Sagi comes, as always with perfect timing, and finds just the words to encourage, shake up, clarify, focus, and dream. "How will you look your best in two months?" he asks us. "What do you have to do for that to happen?"

"I don't have the strength to think about how tomorrow looks, and you're talking about two months from now?" I feel profound internal weakness and lack of desire to think, to cope.

But Rani doesn't let up. "Dream: where do you want to be in another year and a half? What would make you feel good?" he continues.

Gradually his words penetrate, the tune can be heard, and positive energy flows in. I begin to collect myself and climb up from the abyss.

We will yet know many other moments like that. Moments of weakness, of powerlessness. Time hasn't yet begun to work its magic.

Evening

A knock on the door.

An old, unfamiliar couple steps in hesitantly. "You don't know us, but we know Gil-ad very well," they say.

"Sima," I say, and she's blown away. "How did you know?"

"Come on in, we're happy you came. We waited for you," I say with a smile, and she's surprised I even know she exists.

Just a few days earlier I said to Ofir in bafflement, "Strange that Sima hasn't come." Not that I remember all the visitors, but I waited for Sima.

For the last Passover of his life Gil-ad wanted to work and save up money for a trip to Poland that summer. A friend from yeshiva arranged cleaning jobs for those interested, and Gil-ad found himself at Sima's house in Modiin, cleaning and scrubbing the kitchen and windows along with the various other implements that need cleaning in a Jewish home before Passover.

The two developed an affectionate connection, and Sima asked Gil-ad to keep cleaning her house another couple of days, but it didn't fit the schedule of the guy who'd set everything up, who had Gil-ad set to clean another house already.

Sima didn't relent and asked Gil-ad to work in her home privately. Gil-ad felt it unethical to do that; he declined, and later that evening consulted me for my opinion. In the end Sima insisted and prevailed. Gil-ad continued to work for her at her request another few days, with the consent of the guy in charge.

I laughed so much with Gil-ad at her stubbornness in engaging him specifically and not to let him be replaced by some other cleaner. It's not every day that such a connection develops between a cleaner, who's just a boy, and a homeowner. I was curious to get to know Sima and expected her to visit.

Sima repeated what we already knew for some time, but this time from her perspective. She told us how special the connection was that arose between them, and how impressed she was by Gil-ad's personality – the reason she insisted he continue cleaning her house.

It's remarkable how an apparently innocent incident, not some big story that attracts extraordinary attention, suddenly becomes – now that you're not here, Gil-adush – such a meaningful and important event.

Friday, 5 Av, August 1

After much deliberation, Gil-ad's friends left for Poland.

Gil-ad wanted to go so much; he was so excited and anxious as the trip approached. He'd worked and saved for it just a few months prior. We supported him and encouraged him, even offering to pay some of the cost.

As an educator who participated twice in such trips, I know just how meaningful and compelling it is, how critical it is in forming a student's character. No history lesson in a classroom can compare, and will never approach the unmediated experience of taking physical steps on the killing fields while hoisting the flag of Israel high.

In our generation there are still some survivors able to tell their personal story firsthand. It's so important for our children, who form the link between the generation of the Holocaust, the survivors, and the next generation, to hear of the horrors from the witnesses themselves, experience the journey with every limb, and pass on this difficult chapter of Jewish history to its children, the children of the next generation, who will only be able to read books about the destruction, about the attempt of an enlightened people to destroy a nation.

I'm fully aware of the controversy surrounding the trip, but still, as a teacher and educator, I'm an enthusiastic supporter. It shapes a youth's maturing character at such a significant age and intensifies his connection to himself, his people, and the Land of Israel, of course only with proper preparation and guidance.

His friends wanted to cancel the trip. They can't go without Gil-ad, they said. It was clear to us that life doesn't stop. We urge them to go, certain the trip will be meaningful for them. In the end they decide to go, and I send a letter with them.

> Dear friends whom we love so much,
> It's Friday, before the holy Shabbat, the spiritual high point of the week, and since the kidnapping, an even more meaningful time.
> I can't help but recall that Friday after the kidnapping, those initial moments of uncertainty and doubt.
> At the time we had no idea what would happen to us and all of *Am Yisrael*...
> As I write these words we're getting news of a soldier taken captive in Gaza.* My heart breaks and my stomach turns.
> Oh G-d, isn't it enough? What haven't we done to appease You? What else can we do?
> So much pain, such a void!
> *Am Yisrael* has a glorious past that carries it through many tribulations; a future full of hope and faith; and a present full of challenges.
> A challenge, unlike a difficulty, leads us to ask *for what* instead of *why*.
> There are some questions that will remain forever unanswered. We have to ask the questions with humility, with the recognition that there is a Creator who runs the world and it's not us – we're not up to it. The questions must be asked with the knowledge that they are likely to remain unanswered,

---
* The soldier was Hadar Goldin, of Blessed memory, who hours later was declared dead and missing in enemy captivity.

because the human mind can't comprehend everything. Perhaps we can learn from the trait of humility at which Gil-ad excelled – during his life we didn't understand just how humble he was.

On the one hand, humility comes from the security in knowing who you are, what you want and your opinions. On the other hand, this is balanced by the recognition that there is truth in the world which is run by G-d, the True Judge. Truth that demands we help others, recognize our abilities so we can share them with others equally and so we can be true friends.

The trip to Poland is an extraordinary one. It's a trip that becomes a trip of life, one that empowers and builds the character of each student participating. During the trip you'll cross valleys of killing that had a single purpose: the extermination of *Am Yisrael*. At the same time you'll visit the graves of *tzaddikim* and yeshivas that formed the basis of the Jewish people, our life's breath.

It's a trip that embodies the story of *Am Yisrael* in condensed form – growth from within immense pain.

Under normal circumstances a mother might write a letter to her son leaving on such a trip.

This time I'm writing to you. You've all become my sons, our sons.

I'm full of hope that you'll come back even more loving and proud – of yourselves, of your families, of the yeshiva where you study, and of our people, the Jewish people. I can't wait to hear your experiences and impressions.

With great love,

Bat-Galim

Sunday, 7 Av, August 3

A mother is always thinking about her children: how are they, are they well? Of course, naturally, our attention is sometimes diverted by myriad issues and impressions that crowd into our brains, so minutes or hours can pass without our wondering about them or making sure they're OK.

There were days when only toward evening I'd find time for a phone call with you, Gil-adush, to check that everything's fine, that your routine is good for you. Usually on my way home at night, on the way back from a teachers' meeting, I'd close out the day with calls to you and Shirel.

But now all of a sudden you're with me more than ever. You accompany me every moment, every hour, everywhere. Everything reminds me of you. That smile that never left your face. A song on the radio. A shirt someone's wearing. Chocolate muffins on their way to the table, or simply when a neighbor asks her son to put something on a high shelf.

I miss you so much it's tearing my heart apart. I don't know what to do with myself.

"Imma, don't worry" – that's what I imagine you saying from up in Heaven, by the Throne of Glory, with your ever-present smile, reassuring me with a sentence you'd say all the time when you were here in the flesh: "Imma, don't worry."

When I'd assume the role of the concerned mother and start to interrogate you and say "mom-things," you'd smile and say, "Imma, don't worry." I'd answer you by saying, "When you tell me not to worry, that's when I start to worry..." and we'd both smile.

The truth is I never worried about you. You were such a responsible kid, always keeping me up to date. I don't remember worrying about you, even when you were little. You had a caution that gave me serenity.

During the *chai* days I was suddenly so worried. I felt so powerless. After all you're so mature and responsible; you can get along fine without me – and now all of a sudden you really do need me, but I'm unavailable and can't help.

The sense of pain, worry, and frustration at that time can't be depicted with any quill or brush.

But now, now I'm no longer worried. Now I just miss you so much...

I hurt and I miss you.

Gil-ad, my son, where are you, my son...

Thursday, 11 Av, August 7

I awake to a tough morning. As soon as I open my eyes the recognition of this unwanted, inconceivable reality lands on me.

The tears flow; I don't have the strength to bear anything anymore. The toughest of mornings.

The sense of brokenness that sounded in me through the searching period comes back to me today, big-time. I can't take anything anymore; I just want Gil-ad home.

I'm tired of the commemoration, of the continuous public action, of the responsibility and thinking about *Am Yisrael*, of dealing with the media. I want to go back to the routine I knew, a routine I didn't always appreciate, to the level of trials I was used to facing. To the life I had before, which was far from perfect – but Gil-ad was there in it. The tears don't let up. The pain in my chest only increases; the burning in my mind spreads to every limb and I feel like I can't take any more of it...

Ofir left this morning for a meeting in Jerusalem with a group of pro-Israel Christians. This whole time we've been having meetings with various communities around the country at our house in Talmon. We feel a tremendous sense of mission in these meetings, so we can say thank you for the support we've received, or to convey messages. We find ourselves dealing quite a bit with communications.

We learned quickly that in the media time is limited and the message has to be quick and to the point. We realized public attention is short, so the formulation of messages has utmost importance. Every conversation or interview demands maximum attention from us in developing the most concise, sharp communiqué; each interview requires preparation. It's not easy for us. In the torturous everyday it's so exhausting and wearing.

At today's meeting Ofir will try to stress in his messaging that the world has to recognize the impossible situation of Jews in Israel. The kidnapping of the boys and Protective Edge have aroused society's awareness that *Am Yisrael* lives under existential threat in Eretz Yisrael, no matter what part: Talmon, Sderot, Jerusalem, or Tel Aviv.

It's one of the things that awaken in us the sense of unity – that strong message, the knowledge that we're all in the same boat. The frustrating thing is that the world doesn't seem to get the message.

Operation Protective Edge continues in all its fury, and Israel is accused of war crimes. The world stands by and accuses us out of ignorance of the complex situation in Israel.

Messaging, messaging – I'm tired of that too. Always thinking about the message you have to deliver, to focus on.

We're planning a weekend with the girls at a hotel in the north so we can give our bodies and souls some rest. The trip was delayed until the afternoon so we'd have time for Ofir's meeting in the morning.

The little ones come into my room and see me crying. It's hard for them to see Imma in tears.

"What happened?" asks Hallel.

"I just miss him," I answer, naturally, but realize it's too much for her. It's not easy to absorb that Imma has no strength left.

I send a message to Rani: "Rani, it's so hard. I don't have any more strength or patience... I need good vibes."

Rani answers: "I get it, I get it; so many of us understand and want to support you. Is it OK for me to come by today?"

He's there within an hour, listening, encouraging, supporting. Just his presence brings positive energy. With a serious look he states, "That's the most meaningful message you've written yet – the ability to admit to the difficulty is new and important." I half-smile to myself. "Admit the difficulty? I've been doing that from the first moment, no?" A short while later Rani says goodbye. I say with an embarrassed smile, "I've got energy now, thank you."

"So many understand and want to support you," Rani writes this morning.

That's all true, but this morning even that desire of so many is part of the distress and frustration.

No compensation, no vacation, and no commemoration project will provide a suitable solution to the pain. The frustrating feeling is that any help is so transitory while the pain is never-ending...

My feeling this morning is awful – such pain and frustration. I can't enjoy anything now. Even the trip to the Kinneret seems impossible to me – but I hope at least the girls have fun.

The Drive Up North

Songs are playing on the car radio; it's the first time in seven weeks that both my heart and Jewish law let us listen to happy songs. The kidnapping episode that lasted *chai* days, the Shiva, the Shloshim, during which we observe mourning for a child or sibling – Jewish law distinguishes between mourning for a parent and for a child. Mourning for a child or sibling lasts a month, whereas mourning observances for a parent last a year.

I heard a true and painful explanation: the pain of losing a child is so great that it obviates the practices to keep the grief present, as it's so out of keeping with the normal course of events for parents to bury their children. The mourning period is therefore shorter for a child than a parent.

The Shloshim ended during the Nine Days, which lead up to the Ninth of Av, when we mourn the destruction of the second Beit HaMikdash; we don't listen to music then.

Our oldest daughter Shirel is about to start National Service in Yeroham right after the Shloshim. A close neighbor raised the idea of taking a quiet family vacation up north, and we now find ourselves driving north right after the Nine Days, just before Shirel starts her year of service.

On the way north the girls seize on music as a source of consolation and joy.

The radio is playing songs and I don't know what to do with myself. I don't want to spoil their happiness, but for me there's nothing more distant.

I used to love listening to music. I remember a discussion we once had – what do you listen to first, the words or the melody; which one is primary? The notes always caught me; they're what I gave priority to, what I gave myself over to. Words were second-place. But now it's all been turned upside down. I find myself putting the words first, and have trouble connecting to the melody. It seems at this stage, when my heart is fluttering about grasping at reality where it can, the word is the nourishment my soul needs. Each word takes on meaning and takes the place that the melody once did in my heart. And the radio, as if to provoke me, broadcasts shooting arrows of song right at my heart: "For there's no love in the world like Imma's love." How spot-on are the words of Smadar Shir, and at the same time how painful.

> I breathe your skin, my life
> I breathe deep into my heart
> I want to keep you close to me, my life
> To keep you and any shade of pain apart...
>
> For there's no love in the world like Imma's love
> And there's no worry in the world like Imma's worry
> And there's no one in the world who'll love you like Imma
> Only your Imma.

I listen to the song and the tears flow by themselves. Beautiful song, beautiful timing... The next song seems not to care how I feel. Eyal Golan singing Avigdor Kahalani's poem:

> I have a land – milk and honey rendezvous
> And the oldest of old – is wrapped up in the new
> It's holy, beautiful – so many want her, need her
> Who knows where it's headed – so many different leaders
> Home after home – from kibbutz to moshav
> And one big city – Yerushalayim shel zahav.
>
> A gorgeous blue sea – but of water nearly dry
> and green desert – from the dew of the sky
> A generation that decided – a flag of blue and white
> Then a generation came – to best time in a fight
> We're here forever – to build and plant
> From dream to hope – our fathers' land.

Zionism at its best, I think to myself. A song that lives and breathes love of the people and land, and we, as parents, were raised and raise our children all our lives with love of the land, including a readiness to sacrifice for it... but we didn't mean for my Gil-ad to be so quick to fulfill that...

I continue my rapport with the radio, and it seems to be addressing me with the song "Everybody's Father" by Elad Shaar:

> If it's hard for you to get up first thing in the morning, bro
> And you ain't got a clue again where'd happiness go
> Smile and be done with it, cuz G-d's with you
> If you can't earn a living and all you feel is lack
> And all around it seems no justice, nothin' on track
> Remember what the tzaddik said: no despair in this world.
>
> So smile at me now
> And you'll see the world is forever perfect
> Because we have a Protector
> Who doesn't sleep – it's Abba, everyone's Abba.

Gil-adush, that smile of yours...

The girls sing along with the song; at least they can maintain their miraculous joy.

Ribono Shel Olam, I always want to be happy...

The next song, "Great Light" by Amir Dadon, might as well not have heard the dialogue playing in my head:

> And I may have been somewhat sad
> Maybe something important came out of that
> Because when it's over, at the ending
> There's a reason for everything

Alone in all the insanity
I think of how the time can fly
But when it's over, at the ending
There's a reason for everything

A great light illuminates what for
And you don't need to ask anything, anymore
I've come to learn from the good, to live
To start all over, begin afresh
Like taking my very first breath
I'm here And not going to waste my time.

The girls sing and I tear up – there's a reason for everything?
   I don't understand anything about Your world, G-d.
   The radio doesn't let up. My hour of self-pity goes way overboard today.

Sunday Night, Eve of 15 Av, August 10

Every year thousands of women gather to dance in the fields around Shiloh, reenacting the ancient custom from the days of the Judges.

Following the horrific episode of "the concubine in Giv'ah" and the end of the three-week mourning period between 17 Tammuz and 9 Av there's a joyful day, a day of reconciliation and love in *Am Yisrael*. It's the anniversary of multiple positive events in Jewish history; most of them are related to love and unity. The custom is for girls to wear borrowed white clothes, to avoid embarrassing the have-nots, and then go dance in the vineyards to find a husband.

With mixed feelings I join this special evening. The wound is still so fresh; my heart is still bleeding. One of the organizers begs me to come, noting that it's a chance to say thank you to the women of the Judah, Binyamin, and Samaria regions, and to the women in general who were such a significant support for us. I can't refuse such a request.

I speak to the women with words from heart.

> "There is a time, a moment for every purpose under the Heavens.
> A time to be born and a time to die... A time to weep and a time to laugh,
> A time to mourn and a time to dance... A time to love and a time to hate,
> A time of war and a time for peace."
> *Am Yisrael* is in a time of uncertainty.

The kidnapping led to Protective Edge, a war that achieved real results and earned the determined backing of *Am Yisrael*, who face uncertainty over whether it will continue.

The uncertainty takes me back deep into my state of mind during the *chai* days.

Chai days of waiting, of uncertainty about Gil-ad's fate, about the fate of Eyal and Naftali.

During that time I insisted on positive thinking.

I didn't make any room for negative thoughts that aimed to undermine or weaken me.

I tried to stay optimistic and focus on the good that was possible.

That positive thinking radiated out to those around me and did good things for me, not only in terms of my thoughts about Gil-ad, but also in my dealings with the government, the security forces, and the media.

Positive thinking is no small thing.

That kind of thinking helped me put the emphasis on the essential thing; to ignore that other women were messing around in my kitchen, doing my laundry, and cleaning my house for me.

This thinking helped us get up in the morning and cope each day with a difficult situation that, looking back now, seems impossible.

It's an approach that preserved our energy for what's really important.

In this time of uncertainty in Israel we need patience.

Instead of always anticipating, always waiting for things that leave us longing for the past or some imaginary future, we need to focus our vision on the here and now, as a way to cope.

On Tu B'Av, this evening, we mark exactly two months since the kidnapping.

At this hour two months ago I couldn't have imagined what I was about to go through only hours later.

Today is Tu B'Av, the day the girls of Israel would go out to dance in the vineyards.

The kind of dancing is called "*machol*" by traditional Jewish sources, a joyful dance of optimism and confidence in finding a mate quickly. They danced in expectation of finding someone right away. Such dancing breeds infectious joy.

But there's also something that can create, *l'cholel*, to give birth to a new reality that didn't before exist.

We all sense that something new, different, formative, is happening now in *Am Yisrael*.

Now is a time of unity in *Am Yisrael*, when we can all feel a concern for others, a time when we're developing a new vocabulary, and we women can birth this new reality. We as women can maintain this special public atmosphere that's been suffusing our people for the past two months.

I pray that just as we danced together in *machol* today, we feel our power to keep creating and improving our reality, to face future challenges.

Monday, 15 Av, August 11

Exactly two months passed; that's how we mark time now. The time before and the time afterward. Life with Gil-ad and life without Gil-ad. The burning in my heart refuses to abate. The physical and emotional pain feels like one pain.

The fact that Operation Brother's Keeper was immediately followed by Protective Edge only intensifies and highlights the pain and loss. Israel's family of the bereaved gained sixty-eight families of fallen fighters almost at once, along with the families of four civilians. *Chai* days, seven days of Shiva, thirty of Shloshim, the Nine Days – the mourning period has been especially long this year.

It's really hard for our daughters. They want to take a break – maybe outside the house they can escape what's inescapable inside. Maybe it'll be easier outside. Coping with the loss is so hard for them, and each one is handling it her own way. I decide to take two of them clothes shopping for a change of atmosphere and to feel the newness of a nice outfit; maybe their mood will improve a bit.

Right away I realize loss is not our only challenge at the moment.

Society's situation provides plenty of others.

We enter the store and immediately notice people's gazes following us. We proceed, as if naturally, to the women's department, looking through some of the dresses off to the side. I can't see a thing. On my back I feel the piercing stares; I spot a mother sharing a look with her daughter; I notice a man's raised eyebrow to his wife. The girls are struggling to come to terms with the public exposure forced on us regardless of its effects, and of how it deprives us of liberty – another unexpected challenge borne of the many recent events.

People are of course tactful and sensitive. Some even approach us to offer encouragement, and that sometimes gives us strength. But the realization that my privacy is gone is tough. All I wanted to do was make my daughters happy with some new clothes – but now they're not just my daughters, they're Gil-ad's sisters.

Thursday, 18 Av, August 14

Vignettes from shopping for Shabbat.

I've been avoiding it for a long time. Simple daily tasks suddenly seem impossible.

For several weeks Ofir was in charge of the shopping, until I decided to jump into the water.

Cereal, Gil-ad...

Chocolate, Gil-ad...

Vegetarian cream, Gil-ad...

Every item I put in my cart wears your smile, your enjoyment, smells of the memory of being with you in the kitchen, baking together. The little things in life.

I pick out tomatoes and put them in a bag.

A woman recognizes me and wants to express support.

I move on to the onions, and another woman does the same.

Turns out supermarket shopping serves as a good barometer for public awareness of the boys.

It'll take much more time till I can get through the shopping without someone coming over and saying she's with us. That everyone's with us. They all approach sensitively, with lots of love. *Am Yisrael* loves and embraces us. Around the anniversary public awareness will increase, then naturally fade.

Tears wash over me in that routine, everyday place, which is all about food. I don't feel like cooking anything; I can't even fill the cart. When I get to checkout I look at and see it's full of memorial candles and tissues. That's more or less what I'd consume for many months yet.

Gradually I'll learn to fill my cart again, but I haven't yet gotten back to the time before, when one cart wasn't enough.

Something in the taste of food has changed. Not sure what, but it's not the same.

Another year and a half would pass before the taste of food would go back to what I knew, and even then not permanently.

I find a pot on the lit stove as if I forgot I'd put it there; chicken and potatoes will sit in the oven way too long – any memory that I'd put it there simply fled my mind; I don't remember whether I've seasoned the food.

That scatteredness and lack of concentration during cooking are not like me.

It's when my thoughts return naturally to you, Gil-ad.

Kitchen time. A time of love.

Monday, 22 Av, August 18

I've read many books about the experience of organizing the room and possessions of departed relatives. I won't connect to the things, I used to think. I won't do that to myself. I'll just give everything away and that'll be it.

But when I went into Gil-ad's room more than two months after his death I didn't act much differently than anyone else. The clothes, the smell, the curiosity of the search, the desire to find meaningful things – it was so tough that morning.

He had a collection of deodorants on the shelf – Shirel asked me not to throw them out. I stuffed them in a bag and set them aside.

Clothes: I try to cram all of them onto just a few shelves. Not many clothes, I think. Gil-ad loved name brands, not choosing to dress like a classic yeshiva boy. In the last couple of months of his life he developed a style of his own. So individual, so Gil-ad.

A few youth movement shirts in his backpack reveal how meaningful the kids were to him, and what a central place the Ofarim chapter was in his life. A Bnei Akiva Sharon-Shomron district pin I suddenly find stands out with the words on it: "Be Big and Heroic." My heart skips – you took every word seriously, I think, and remind myself to investigate where and when that pin was given out.

Binders and notebooks from math and other school subjects are left orphaned on the shelf, waiting for you to come solve another few exercises.

I find an important *dvar Torah* about Hevron and the burial of the patriarchs and matriarchs, getting chills from its relevance. I decide to put it in a plastic sleeve and share its contents at a *Slichot* event to take place at the Machpelah Cave in Hevron a month hence, toward the end of the Ten Days of Penitence.

I'm looking for a sign, a signal, something from you, and I find your book of Psalms marked at Chapter 35. I read the chapter and shiver – did you specifically put the bookmark here?

> To David: Hashem, fight my fight; battle my opponents. Hold the shield and buckler and rise to help me.
> And draw out the spear and close the distance toward my pursuers; say to my soul, "I am your deliverance."
> Shamed and humiliated may those who seek my life become; may those who intend me ill withdraw and be embarrassed.
> May they be as chaff in the wind, as an angel of Hashem pushes them away.
> May their path be dark and slippery, as an angel of Hashem pursues them.
> For unprovoked they have hidden a net for me; without cause they have dug a trap for my life.
> May destruction come to him unawares, and may the net he concealed entrap him; may he be ruined in falling into it.
> *But my soul will rejoice in Hashem, be glad in His deliverance.*
> Let all my bones say, "O Hashem, who is like You, delivering the poor from one mightier than he, and the impoverished and destitute from the robber?" False witnesses rise; they ask me things I know not.
> They pay me evil in exchange for good, bereavement for my soul. But I, when they were sick, wore sackcloth; I afflicted myself in fasting; may my prayer return to my bosom.
> As if for a friend, as a brother, I walked about, as if for a mother I bowed low.

Yet when I stumbled they rejoiced and gathered about me; wretches I know not have torn into me without pause.

In the manner of profane, mocking scorners they grind their teeth at me.

Hashem how long will You watch? Restore my soul from their destruction, from young lions my only one.

I will thank You in great assembly; among throngs of people I will praise You. May my deceitful enemies not have reason to be happy on my account; for no reason they wink.

For not in peace do they speak, and against those who are harmless in the land they speak and think deceit.

They open their mouths wide against me; they proclaim, "Oho! Our eyes have seen!" You see, Hashem, be not silent; be not distant from me.

Arise and awaken to my judgment, my G-d; Hashem, to my fight.

Judge me according to Your righteousness, Hashem my G-d, and let them not be glad because of me.

Let them not say in their heart, "Oho! We have achieved our desire!" Let them not say, "We have devoured him."

May they be ashamed and embarrassed all together, those who take joy in my misfortune; may they be clothed in shame and humiliation, those who make themselves great at my expense.

May those who seek my righteousness sing out and rejoice, and say always, "May Hashem be magnified, He who seeks the peace of His servant!"

And may my tongue express Your righteousness, your praise the entire day!

I examine the chapter and discover the commentators have divided it into three parts: each one ends with a commitment by the poet to praise Hashem once he is saved.

Oy, how relevant this chapter is to the period we went through!

How we asked of Hashem to fight our battle, to oppose our enemies. How we begged for deliverance. How we felt Hashem's kindness and righteousness fill the world at every stage, every moment. And along with the request for protection from evildoers, how we felt such closeness to Hashem!

Now they're looking for the murderers – "Judge me in Your righteousness, Hashem my G-d," and while I don't understand Your ways, I'm sure You're the one running the world, so I will keep pronouncing "Your praise the entire day."

In the afternoon United Hatzolah holds a memorial event for the boys.

Someone donated three motorcycles to serve as emergency vehicles, in memory of the boys – the one for Gil-ad was given to the neighboring town Dolev, and Aviad Hertz, a close friend and volunteer in the organization, drives it. The rest of the year he will report to us amazing life-saving events in which he used the motorcycle, including births, accidents, terrorist attacks, and injuries. He would write to me that each time he went out on a call, beyond the obvious importance of saving lives, he felt added value in the fact that the motorcycle donated in Gil-ad's name meant he, Gil-ad, is memorialized through the preservation and protection of life. We all know of Gil-ad's attempt to save his own life and the lives of his friends in his final moments.

Monday, 29 Av, August 25

The meeting with the One Family organization – which provides assistance to families of terror victims – had already taken place during the *chai* days. The one and only Mindy Levinger, coordinator for the Jerusalem area, came to our home, encouraged and supported us, mainly Shirel (we weren't home at the time). She herself lost a sister in a terrorist attack, and the connection between her and Shirel was immediate and natural; she introduced herself to our daughter and promised to return. "There'll be no need," Shirel answered. "Gil-ad will come home."

During the Shiva, when Mindy came back, Shirel recognized her at once. "You came back," she said, and they cried on each other's shoulders.

It was of course natural for us to join this amazing family once we discovered the bitter truth. On paper we were invited to a family vacation with other terror-victim families to a resort in the north, and then it hit me – that denial, that realization we'd become part of the wide circle of families you usually only read about in the newspaper; a precious family that no one wants to join, but nevertheless it expands unbearably quickly. Who'd have thought we would join, I wonder to myself as I get on the bus that morning.

There's something easier about spending time with families who have known loss and pain. There's an unspoken understanding about unhealable pain and about the endless struggle with it. Still, there's something painful about spending all that time together, as if we're being reminded every moment what we've been through and of the new reality with which we have to live now.

We get warmth, love, and support from wonderful people. The staff does everything to occupy the time and pamper us in the best way possible. I sign up for a massage – my body is so stiff. I try to relax, and remember a shared moment with you, Gil-ad, when you told me about workshops you had during the summer at yeshiva.

You paired off, and at one point you started massaging the feet of your partner on the lawn outside the yeshiva. We laughed so much when you described your friends taking off their shoes and stinky socks, applying cream and massaging one another's feet. A group of soldiers passed by, you told me, and looked at you in astonishment. That delightful situation would seem absurd in any other educational framework, but was so perfectly suited to the sensitivity and attentiveness the yeshiva instilled in you. Listening to one another, listening to body and soul.

Wednesday, Rosh Chodesh Elul, 1 Elul, August 27

Today is the start of the academic year 5775 at Yeshivat Mekor Hayim. At 9:55 I get a message from a friend of Gil-ad's: "Today we're starting our senior year, but it's not the same – Gil-ad is missing.

Today at 'reception' we hope to receive something from Gil-ad. We need him. Let's hear good news."

Boom, right to the gut.

As much as I prepared myself for this moment, it caught me unawares.

My Gil-ad, my yearning for you becomes unbearable at such moments. My heart constricts. Today we were supposed to accompany you to yeshiva, to your first day of twelfth grade. Such a meaningful year for you, one you anticipated so much. You really, really wanted to be a senior.

Ofir would tell me later, "Gil-ad's in a place where he's teaching others; he doesn't need twelfth grade." But that doesn't console me. Reality hits me as hard as it can.

The message reached us upon our return from two days up north with One Family. The whole time I couldn't grasp what I was doing as part of that family, not comprehending we'd joined the family of bereavement.

My tears start flowing; the volume of the pain increases. I can't find comfort.

Gil-ad, I want you here, with me, now. I want you in your natural place in twelfth grade with all your amazing friends that we got to know under bitter circumstances.

The thoughts pursue me; the sadness won't budge. It takes over every

189

fiber. I try to muster my strength, to remind myself we're going back home to our five sweet daughters, five incredible souls who each deserve full attention. Each one a world unto herself, a living, palpable world times five.

Please G-d, give me strenght.

Thursday, 2 Elul, August 28

The stream of events is packed, surreal. We're invited to many places, to address diverse audiences. A radio program for mothers on education wants me to share with the audience my personal insights into the approaching Days of Awe. Three months have passed and they're already sure I have insights.

They introduce the topic of discussion – "From Crisis to Growth" – and, little old me, what am I doing here? All I'm trying to do is cope with the challenges G-d has placed at my doorstep. I don't feel any growth yet; I'm just feeling broken. Nevertheless I share my emotions, my sense, my grappling with things.

The month of Elul this year takes on special meaning. We feel Elul started for us long before its time, and has continued since – days of internal reckoning and introspection, days of prayer in new garb – each word shaking the world.

I suddenly have an interest. I want the Beit HaMikdash – I want the Resurrection. I want the Redemption now! I'm no longer satisfied with what I have; I feel a huge lack.

Several months later I would arrive at a sharpened focus when reciting the words, "He who revives the dead." A new insight would suddenly flash inside me: you can't only focus on those words, but on the words that open that section of the prayer: "He who disburses life with kindness..." In other words, we have to pray for our lives, for this world, to hope for Hashem to support it with kindness, because nothing is automatic. And maybe, maybe even before the Resurrection...

My desire lies in finding the balance between the need to fill the void that's been created – to cope with the unceasing pain in my chest – and the torrent of everyday concerns: the girls, the desire to be a good mother, to realize what amazing souls I have at home. To manage to gain strength from my daughters, who inspire me with their ability to integrate pain with joy, loss with the continuation of life.

To confront reality through looking at the present one day at a time while allowing space for visions of the future and planning the years ahead.

A new kind of training awaits us: training ourselves to accept help; how to live in this new situation in which we've been transformed from givers into receivers. It's really uncomfortable for us to adapt to what we feel is such an unreasonable situation.

Maybe our journey will be softened by a definition of *tzedakah* I heard once. *Tzedakah* is the capacity to give to others while knowing how to receive. *Am Yisrael* wants to envelop us so much; knowing how to accept that giving is a kind of *tzedakah*. In any case, I take encouragement from the expectation that this receiving is only temporary, and I wish to return as quickly as possible to the ranks of the givers.

Tuesday, 7 Elul, September 2

The connection with the media remained throughout this period. Some of them became close friends, interested in our welfare and continuing to encourage us. There was desire on both sides to meet.

During all of the *chai* days I didn't let the media into my home; they covered the episode from outside. We maintained what little privacy we could. Sometimes we went outside to take trips to meetings or to escort some of our visitors. There, outside, we met the press face to face.

This time we decided to meet them in our home. We tried to define for ourselves the goal of the meeting, and focused on four main issues: the human encounter; the desire to process the experience; an attempt to preserve the positive feelings that had been created; and most important of all, expressing our gratitude, just saying thanks. We agreed there would be no filming or photography.

About thirty journalists come to our yard, including cameramen. Plenty of food is served and hearts open. Everyone is moved by the very occurrence of such a meeting, and by the fact that something could motivate thirty reporters to leave Tel Aviv at night. One of the journalists observes with a smile that there's no way he'd find a parking spot in the crowded city upon his return, but he came anyway.

We invite them into a discussion circle.

Two rules were set for the conversation: each person speaks in turn, and each person speaks about himself. There's no cynicism in this circle; no interruptions and no criticism. Each one introduces himself, and is asked to share a significant moment to which he would like to return. They all listen. Many reveal in moving terms how powerful the unexpected, prejudice-breaking encounter with the settler community is. Many point out the human warmth and heartfelt goodwill directed at them. The time spent together and the profound concern creates a connection, a riveting encounter between worlds.

One of the journalists, a confirmed political leftist, brings his brother to the meeting. The powerful impression it created in him by the settler community, the destruction of stigmas within him, surprised even him, and he didn't want that revelation to be limited to him alone. The desire to share that discovery with others inspired a fifteen-minute film looking at the settlers from a different perspective. And the breaking down of stereotypes isn't merely one-sided. It's mutual – we, too, discover the people behind the cameras, the ink, and the keyboard.

In the second round we ask them to share something new they learned, or discovered about themselves.

One of the reporters remembers a moment when he really wanted to meet us in our home. He left the cameras outside, introduced himself, hugged Ofir warmly, and left. Journalists apologize that their profession has been hurt by the incursion of emotional baggage into news coverage. A broadcast journalist recalls with discomfort when she cried upon learning the boys had died, and how she couldn't calm herself even for that evening's broadcast.

I'm surprised. Journalists, like historians, tend not to be objective; the work of keeping emotion out of the picture is contrived, if not impossible. What's so shocking to them about human reporting? Why do they think it's unprofessional to be human, to be real?

An interesting discussion develops about the character of mass media. Many of the journalists contend the people need yellow journalism, that positive coverage doesn't interest the masses. A large portion discover they only get "Likes" for negative stories – they accuse the public of looking for and consuming yellow press. We argue the consumption of yellow journalism can be stopped; the recent episode proves it.

Positive coverage has turned a page; there's demand for a different kind of news media. I have no doubt: *Am Yisrael* has taken it to the next level and rejected negative news. There's demand for positive coverage.

Movement in media: months have passed, and again it seems there's a thick wall between the media and consumers. As if all the positive insights have been erased, the lesson forgotten. A heavy feeling envelops me. Despite the clear sense that people have grown, it looks like the press is still behind.

But then I hear one day about a regular news feature on positive stories, the entire purpose of which is to highlight good behavior. There are viewers and significant responsiveness to the idea. On that program they'll later ask me to talk about Operation Sweet Heart in honor of Gil-ad's birthday, 19 Tevet. The Moreshet radio channel wants to launch a weekly feature with positive takeaways, and every Thursday I've begun to cover current events from a positive angle that is usually not presented to the public.

A good feeling fills me; things appear to be moving despite everything. Slowly, but moving nevertheless.

Wednesday, 8 Elul, September 3

Our first trip to Yeshivat Mekor Hayim since the kidnapping – we're very excited.

We've been asked to attend a ceremony honoring the Keren HaYesod, which donated a minibus to the yeshiva in the boys' names, and we arrive with great anticipation before meeting the students and staff.

It's our first trip to the yeshiva without Gil-ad.

Already in the car I start feeling the tightness in my chest. The intensity of the pain grows the closer we get to the yeshiva. We are shaken by the realization that we're going there, but Gil-ad's not there. My throat is choked by tears.

They start flowing freely while Ofir is in the car with me, as if saying to him I both want and don't want to go.

A few minutes into the drive we discover we forgot an important bag at home. Ofir turns the car around and we go back, ostensibly delayed by only a few minutes.

Later, when we meet with Rosh Yeshiva Rabbi Dov Singer, he'll say, "You didn't simply go home because you forgot a bag." The rabbi again shows his sensitivity and amazing ability to understand how painful and difficult it is for us to come to yeshiva on such a day.

The conversation flows. There's mutual interest in how the family and yeshiva are coping. We exchange impressions, trying to gain strength from each other.

During the meeting a certain booklet keeps falling from the shelf near the rabbi's chair every time he shifts in his seat. We smile and wonder –

maybe the booklet wants something from us; let's browse. Ofir picks it up and is astounded. He recognizes it as a booklet Gil-ad edited last Nisan, a collection of *divrei Torah* written by friends from the yeshiva about the Passover Haggadah. "Gil-ad wants you to open the booklet," says Ofir with a half-smile.

The rabbi opens to the piece Gil-ad wrote with his classmate Nadav Tuchman about rejoicing on the festival. He reads it aloud. It's so natural to me that Gil-ad chose to write about that. He reached the conclusion in his learning that the mitzvah is for a person to make others happy by means of that which makes him, personally, happy, that which adds joy to his life. Each person and his internal joy.

Right after the meeting with the rabbi we go to see the students, classmates, and others at the yeshiva. To this point I've held up well, and the tears have stayed in the corner of my eye, but not for long. When we go out to the students I feel my strength leaving me and the sorrow hits me with great pain.

Where's my son? Why isn't Gil-ad here? It was so clear he'd finish his senior year along with everyone else, that he'd spend another year growing in yeshiva.

I want you here now so much, my Gil-adush, and the tears stream without stopping even before I open my mouth to say anything to the students. I can't control them. I came to support others? I ask myself in despair.

After a few minutes of hopeless crying I try to collect myself, to speak with his friends about the ability to feel pain and excitement at the same time at the start of a new year. When I described to Rabbi Singer how little Maor manages to be happy, dancing alongside her longing and pain, he asserted that the depth of the pain indicates the depth of the joy. Now is the time to give pain its space, to let go.

I hope he's right, I think to myself. I'm good at feeling pain. I hope I can manage to feel joy to the same degree. I'm not there yet right now.

We end the meeting by wishing the friends success in the coming year. That they grow, progress, and utilize their abilities as much as they can. From there we walk with them to the Keren HaYesod ceremony, while in our hearts and lives a gigantic chasm has opened.

Sunday, 12 Elul, September 7

Suspended between heaven and earth, over multiple seas, I try to be reborn in this impossible situation.

The long flight to the U.S. takes my thoughts, as usual recently, to you, Gil-ad. It sits deep in my mind, searing as always. Tears fill my eyes and my frustration explodes. I want you here, with us. How can we take a family trip without you, and a trip to the U.S. at that?

The trip was born of an invitation we received to participate in a big fundraising event for *Am Yisrael* all over the world, run by the Jewish Federation of New York.

I struggle to fall asleep. The thoughts flood over me and don't let me rest. The one who would have enjoyed this trip the most would be you, Gil-ad. Your absence is magnified at these moments; it's so palpable. You're the one who knows how to enjoy every little thing, to maximize what you get out of any trip abroad. You'd be beside yourself on a flight like this. My heart breaks. The frustration increases – I want you here by my side.

A pleasant flight attendant pampers us with a typical breakfast, catching me in a moment of weakness, and asking if I'm OK. There are moments it's not OK to ask, because it makes me burst into a torrent of tears I can't stop.

I made her uncomfortable. I'm sorry, I didn't mean to.

I try to listen to some music to calm down. This trip isn't going to be easy at all.

Your absence, Gil-ad, is felt at every moment, at every family experience. Still, the pampering and the huge embrace by all the Jewish community members we've met manage to break through our barriers, and succeed in improving our moods for a few moments. The atmosphere is familial; the warmth and love radiated by Jerry and Erica Silverman becomes the start of deep friendship.

This kind of family trip will become almost an emotional need each year to rest, to gather our strength, to just spend time together. To breathe. An outsider wouldn't understand.

"Imma, does the plane fly high in the sky?" asks Maor. It's the first flight of her short life, and her intelligent eyes gaze at me fiercely.

"Yes, sweetie, higher than the clouds. Look out the window," I answer, not sure where she's going with this.

"So Imma, will we see Gil-ad?"

Tuesday, 28 Elul, September 23

It's 6:30 in the morning; we awake to a phone call from the Shabak. We get a report that the boys' murderers were killed last night. "We wanted to let you know before it appears in the media," said S. on the other end of the line.

"This morning permission was granted to publicize that following a complex intelligence operation by the Shabak the location in Hevron of Marwan Kawasmeh and Amar Abu Aisheh was identified, the two Hevron residents who perpetrated the kidnapping and murder of Naftali Fraenkel, Gil-ad Shaer, and Eyal Yifrach," the Shabak reported. A firefight erupted and the two were eliminated.

"Chief of the General Staff Lt. General Benny Ganz spoke to head of Central Command Nitzan Alon and praised him for closing the circle. 'On Rosh HaShanah eve the matter was sealed, and we brought to a close Operation Brother's Keeper, which began on Friday, 13 June, and has continued intensely since then. We promised the Shaer, Yifrach, and Fraenkel families we would reach their sons' murderers and this morning we accomplished that. The commanders and soldiers of Central Command have not rested since the day of the kidnapping until the completion of the mission this morning. There is no consolation for the families in their heavy grief and their pain, but I hope their burden has been somewhat lightened upon hearing the report that we got the boys' murderers,'" it said.

We get inquiries from many media outlets wanting our response. In the afternoon we send the following message in the name of the three families:

The security forces updated us that our sons' murderers have been killed during our forces' military operations. We are proud of our government and security forces for their steadfastness in ensuring our sons' murderers face justice. The world has been shown Jewish blood is not free.

We embrace the Special Forces soldiers who risked their lives to restore deterrence to the State of Israel. May every enemy know "that I will pursue my enemies and catch them, and not return until they are destroyed."

The circle of evil has been closed, and this start of a new year we hope that from now on only circles of good will be opened. We send our wishes for a good, sweet year to all of *Am Yisrael*, and wish to thank the entire people in Israel and the Diaspora for holding and supporting us.

The circle closes. The knowledge that the murderers are no longer walking around among us, able to engage in more killing and attacking, and the fact that the citizens know there is a law, there is a judge in Israel, are very important to us.

The whole time I've tried not to bother myself with thoughts of the murderers. Such thoughts weakened me. Maor didn't let it go; every now and then she'd ask if they'd found them. Their demise calmed her very much, and apparently me as well.

Wednesday, 29 Elul, September 24

Rosh HaShanah Eve

The phone rings; it's a good friend on the line. She asks how I am and wants to let us know how she feels:

"Five months ago I got some *etrog* jelly from you. Today it caught my gaze, sitting there on the counter."

I remember – it was jelly that Gil-ad had made.

My heart constricts; another wave from my beloved son.

I've already mentioned the fact that Gil-ad loved the kitchen and was so good at making original baked goods. After Sukkot he'd collect *etrogim* from anyone and everyone and make an especially delicious jam. I gave a jar to a pregnant friend – *etrog* jam is known to be auspicious for an easy birth. Chills overtake me. I ask her to bring the jam to our house; maybe through it I can have a little more of my son to taste.

And so, on Erev Rosh HaShanah, the jam comes back to me. Its taste is the taste of Eden; and the memory embedded in it tastes at once so sweet and so bitter.

Thursday, 1 Tishrei, September 25

Rosh HaShanah 5775
It's the first holiday without you, Gil-ad.

The fear of the festival's approaching footsteps has been greater than the day's own solemn agenda. For many days I tossed and turned in my bed wondering about how to have this holiday without you. Great sadness chokes me. It's a family holiday, and our family isn't whole anymore.

Our extended family invites us to join them for the holiday, to celebrate as in time gone by, but I can't. Your absence, Gil-ad, would be even greater. I can't celebrate the holiday as in past years. I need to do something different.

We decide together to stay home. We invite guests and are invited out to friends, so as not to be alone. Not to be in pain.

The clock doesn't stop, and the holiday begins.

I try to be here, in the present, in the holiday itself.

I'm tired of hurting. I want a happy holiday. For myself, for the girls.

I discover it's possible to have a holiday. I'm slowly learning the complexity of life.

Holiday. Joy. Emptiness. Family.

All mixed together.

Thursday, Eve of 9 Tishrei, October 3

Selichot Event at Machpelah Cave, Hevron, Yom Kippur Eve
Last night the fathers of the three boys went to Hevron for a Selichot evening. They met with the commander of the Yehudah Brigade, Colonel Yariv Ben-Ezra, and heard firsthand about the pursuit of the murderers, which ended in their deaths.

This evening it's our turn, the three mothers. We try to gain strength along with the women of Israel. I address the many women assembled there with the following words:

> Hevron, the city of the Fathers.
> It's impossible to stand here, during the Days of Awe, without feeling G-d's closeness.
> The city of the Fathers – Avraham Avinu, the Hebrew, the first Jew, bought his burial place right here.
> I found a *dvar Torah* that our Gil-ad wrote, apparently for Parashat Chayei Sarah, and the connection between this place and time and his words is amazing.
>
>> The Machpelah Cave, the "Doubled" Cave, bears that name because the people buried there were buried couple by couple.
>> Machpelah Cave was the first property the first Jew bought in the Promised Land. The importance of the graves, their purchase, and the fact that they were relatives, are a

powerful expression of the deep connection family has even in death. It's the reason Hevron has its name, from the root *het, bet, resh*, strong connection.

It's the foundation of *Am Yisrael*: strong connection. The Mishnah in Yoma says that the daily morning offering, the first one of the day, was not offered until the sun shone over Hevron, above the Machpelah Cave. We can learn from this that honoring the family, honoring one's parents, and honoring one another, are the root, the foundation of honoring the divine.

Those are Gil-ad's words as inspired by Rabbi Shimshon Raphael Hirsch.

Rabbi Hirsch sees in Hevron the burial place of our Fathers and Mothers, a symbol of family, of the connection linking all of *Am Yisrael*. He learns from the link between the offering of the *Tamid* each morning and the light shining over Hevron, the deep connections binding family, nation, and G-d Himself. The power of family connection, of marriage and children, both the basis and condition for connection with the Creator. When there is a connected family, a connection among relatives, among the various parts of the people, the basis for connection with G-d is created.

Avraham was not the only one to realize this.

Yosef the Tzaddik was sent from the Valley of Hevron in Parashat Vayeshev to seek "the welfare of his brothers," to find them, in the most positive sense. Here he bequeathed to his children the eternal mission and purpose of "my brothers I seek."

It's the mission we were assigned not long ago in the search for the boys, a mission the army and entire people fulfilled heroically.

During the recent war, as well, when our enemies tried to "lower our heads," we lifted our heads up high.

Here in Hevron, Yosef dreamed his dreams, developing the beginnings of the national idea, realizing the need for leadership and unity among the tribes; that someone needs to shepherd the process.

How much did we hope and dream...

Allow me to seek and dream, here in this holy place.

Please, G-d, give us the strength necessary to cope with the tremendous chasm that's been opened. Grant us the possibility of knowing how to feel joy in life along with pain. Give us family as a place of support, inclusion, growth, and advancement.

Give us this people, embracing, loving, and unified. Give us this people, proud and understanding its power and secret.

Not only our ancestors are connected to this place; Shimshon the Judge and prophet uprooted the city gates of Gaza from the Philistine enemy and carried them to Hevron. It's a contemporary connection to our situation – between the Hevron hills, where the boys were murdered and concealed, and the war in Gaza – Operation Protective Edge.

Here in Hevron the monarchy was established. Only after all the tribes of Israel were united in Hevron with King David at their head could the king ascend to Jerusalem. *Am Yisrael*'s power lies in its unity, in the past, present, and, with Hashem's help, the future as well.

These are "days of remembrance." What do we want to remember in the coming year? Here, we look to remember all the wounded soldiers, to pray for their full and speedy recovery.

G-d, please, heal them. Please.

We want to remember and invoke to the Creator all the prayers, all the desires, all the hopes, and all the good deeds we encountered and experienced over the last few months, that they serve *Am Yisrael* as tremendous merit when we stand before Him this time of year.

We wish to invoke before the Creator that "You have chosen us from all the nations; You have loved us and desired us." We felt Your choosing us, the revealed miracles performed when thousands of rockets were sent at our country; we felt Your love and concern for Your people.

"And You have exalted us above all cultures" – we felt our status as the Chosen People as we stood before our enemies seeking to destroy us.

"And You have sanctified us with Your commandments" – we felt the holiness of the people in accepting personal and communal *mitzvot* this whole time, and then we were privileged to see "And You have brought us close, O King, to Your service." We felt spiritual power and exaltation alongside infinite pain and worry. We felt the Divine Presence among us.

"And Your great and holy Name You have invoked upon us" – our Father, our King, we have no King but You!

We, *Am Yisrael*, seek before the Day of Judgment, to perform a confession – a positive confession – to reflect the good deeds and beautiful actions performed in the last few months.

> We have loved; we have trusted; we have grown; we have spoken of beauty. We have empowered and we

have become empowered; we have remembered; we have smiled; we have taken care of one another. Together we have yearned; we have whispered; we are increasing our mitzvot. We have kissed; we have forgiven; we have done good; we have acted; we have anticipated; we have hoped for good... we have had mercy; we have remained silent; we have remained constant, "Whole you shall be with Hashem your G-d."

May all the actions and prayers act as merit for all of Israel coming before You as this Yom Kippur approaches, with their hands full.
Gmar Hatimah Tovah,

Bat-Galim

Wednesday, 14 Tishrei, October 8

Sukkot Eve
Ofir is coping with the fact that Gil-ad won't help him this year with building the sukkah.

As on many previous occasions, our good neighbors come to his aid, and even expand the sukkah with an additional little section for the girls.

Chol HaMoed
Commemoration of the boys occupies a significant place in our lives. One of the people who came to console us during the Shiva and who went through bereavement himself said that action and commemoration are two things that give him strength. We really connect to that statement. One of the places seeking to commemorate the boys is Yeshivat Mekor Hayim, where Gil-ad and Naftali studied.

After many years of functioning in temporary structures, the yeshiva is expected to build a permanent Beit Midrash in the nearby town of Neve Daniel.

We're invited to the cornerstone-laying ceremony on one of the days of Chol HaMoed. While it's true that in practical terms, because of the holiday and for reasons of conscience, it's merely the removal of a cover from a sign, in an official sense, it's the intent of the organizers that matters. During the moving ceremony I wanted to bless the students and faculty:

The cornerstone ceremony is a meaningful, moving event that symbolizes the start of a building's construction.

The concept of a cornerstone often serves as an expression of establishing buildings and organizations, and sometimes also new, pioneering scientific theories that are not physical structures.

Fortunately, the yeshiva has constituted an innovative, forward-looking institution for years already in its unique educational path.

True to its name, the yeshiva is a Mekor Hayim, a source of life, laying down and drawing an educational approach that gives life to its students during the significant adolescent years and afterward.

Water, too, is known as a Mekor Hayim, and not by coincidence are we laying the cornerstone on the holiday of the water libations.

Tractate Sukkah of the Mishnah describes the joy in the Beit HaMikdash during the libation and the celebration of drawing the water for it:

"Whoever has not seen the joy at the water-drawing has not seen joy in his life. At the conclusion of the first day of the festival they would descend to the Women's Section and make massive installations."

What is this "installation?"

What's more, is it possible to feel true joy only after being present at the *Simchat Beit HaShoevah*?

If that's the case, how does that affect us, we who today can no longer participate or see with our own eyes the *Simchat Beit HaShoevah* in the Beit haMikdash?

In fact, what is joy? What makes a person happy?

A person is happy when he escapes boundaries; its source is in the mind and soul.

The cause of the joy we call *simcha* is an event of breaking through boundaries. The *simcha* itself is the resulting emotional state, manifest in actions that express that breakthrough.

Ostensibly any mitzvah or positive act that a Jew does must be done with *simcha*. It's not always so easy – how do you get to genuine *simcha*?

The paradigm of creation established upper and lower waters, as the Creator commanded.

Parashat Bereshit specifies: "Let there be a firmament amid the waters; let it separate water from water."

The spiritual place of the power waters is below, far from Hashem. When G-d wants us to perform the mitzvah of the water libations, He grants those waters the power to ascend, to break through the boundaries of nature. The water libation deviates from the order of creation and represents leaving one's boundaries, and therefore causes great joy.

That means it's not merely a description of the *Simchat Beit HaShoevah*, but of the profound idea behind it, which has practical implications for our day, as well. To reach genuine *simcha* associated with a mitzvah you have to break through your boundaries and become at one with the unbounded reality of G-d, to cling to Him. In our current complex reality, after the events of this past summer, and feeling Gil-ad, Eyal, and Naftali's absence, we are now bidden to fulfill "You shall be joyful on your festival."

To reach that joy we have to leave our own boundaries. To leave the course of nature and experience joy along with the pain.

The great pain and the gaping lack – how can we be happy?

Maor, Gil-ad's youngest sister, who turned four not long ago, does it very well. I look at her and I see a little girl with no inhibitions, no limitations, no boundaries. She's a happy girl, vivacious and full of energy, but still mature for her age – she understands Gil-ad isn't coming home. She feels his absence all the time.

This is the challenge G-d has given us and this is our Struggle to cope – we have to overcome our limitations in order to experience *simcha*.

I'll conclude with a trait that characterized Gil-ad, his always sticking with joy. When Gil-ad decided he wanted to achieve something, it was clear he'd succeed. He would set a goal and not give up till he attained it.

The yeshiva has long had a goal of a permanent building, and *Baruch Hashem* it's now possible; the vision can be realized.

May it be His will that we set goals and challenges, and that we stick to them until we fulfill them.

May it be His will that we see the dedication of this building soon.

May it be His will that we succeed in experiencing true *simcha* as in the *Simchat Beit HaShoevah*, through the removal of boundaries.

May everyone have a good year.

On Hoshana Rabba eve we host some of Gil-ad's friends from Mekor Hayim in our sukkah. We try to create a pleasant atmosphere, so they feel comfortable coming over. Later on we'd hold such gatherings every few months in our home, on a nature walk, or just a barbecue in the park. Gatherings for discussion and song, of both fun and seriousness. Time for us to be with them, and they with one another. Time to process the absence of the one who should be with us in our place and with them in theirs. We love hearing what they've been doing, what they're thinking. In another year they'll embark on a new journey – some to yeshiva and some to the army.

I smile to myself when I recall how every time Ofir or I would take an interest in Gil-ad's friends, he'd give us an angry smile: "Those are my friends, not yours."

Today, Gil-adush, they're still your friends, but now they're ours, too.

Sunday, 2 Cheshvan, October 26

Five in the morning. We wake up for a morning jog.

Two weeks ago I broke through a significant barrier in my private life in the athletic realm – a group of friends in Talmon decided to put together a running group, and we joined.

Ofir is in good shape despite not having had an exercise routine for a long time – in his youth he loved sports and played basketball. I, on the other hand, never felt much connection to it; I'm not sure why. Maybe my fear of letting my body do things, but maybe the fear of failure. In high school the phys-ed teacher started a special subgroup for me because she didn't believe I could do much. She couldn't grasp why I was avoiding her classes, and finally told me I wouldn't matriculate without a passing grade in gym. Despite my protests and pleas, I found myself a year later coming back to school – during my National Service year – doing forward and reverse somersaults to earn myself a passing grade and matriculation.

The decision to join the running group was, for me, to break through a formidable barrier I'd faced my whole life. In recent years I've suffered severe leg pain, and my head began to realize my body wouldn't last long. I've reached an age when exercise isn't a luxury. To the same degree, and perhaps more, I want Ofir to get into better shape again.

This morning we showed up at 5:30, rubbing our eyes both literally and figuratively – we couldn't believe fourteen people had gotten up this early to run. Hayim the trainer arrived, all smiles and pep. We start walking quickly for three minutes, and then it comes: "Let's go, people, run!"

The point at which my feet leave terra firma surprises me and even proves enjoyable. The knowledge that I can separate myself from the ground gives me a lot of strength.

But soon other thoughts come up. I find myself lagging behind most of the time; the group is in good shape and I don't fit in, I think. A very unpleasant feeling overcomes me – I'm used to being in the lead in almost every arena, and now I'm suddenly trailing most of the time. My will overcame my difficulty – I'm running to prove I can do it!

One of the group members says something wise to me: "in running, each person competes against himself. You're not competing with anyone else; it's completely your game." How true.

My knees don't make the effort any easier. Two weeks later, with the swelling and inflammation only getting worse, I decide to give up. Hayim the trainer won't give in. "That's no reason to stop running," he says. He finds shoes that will give me proper balance, advises me to take an anti-inflammatory, and orders me to show up for the next session.

The power of the group is noticeable in every detail. The support and the affirmation, the encouragement and the pace begin to work. Together we stride and run five kilometers.

Despite being behind most of the time, everyone prods everyone else, mainly me. It's quite an uplifting feeling.

I'm doing this; I'm running.

If I can run, I can fly!

For several months I felt the sky's the limit.

Nothing stands in the way of will, I repeated constantly. Of course that's not the way things are.

The persistent pain in my knees brings me to a dawning realization: not everything is in my control.

Will is important, but not enough to make everything possible.

I've decreased my "dosage" as I try to listen to my body, my capabilities.

To cope with reality as best I can.

Friday, 7 Cheshvan, October 31

A few hours till Shabbat.

The aroma of chicken soup fills the house.

This Shabbat you won't come home.

Next Shabbat you won't come home either.

Not even in a month or two.

Not even in a year or two.

The pain of this shattering, rending finality is inconceivable. Tears of longing and sadness mix with the drops of the first rain hitting the window. Rains of blessing, while my tears are so far away from blessing...

The days pass; the month of festivals is behind us. We're at the beginning of Marcheshvan, which ushers in the month of intensive activity and celebrations in Bnei Akiva.

You loved this month so much, my Gil-adush; you were so happy preparing for it last year.

Even if you were to leave your leadership position in the movement for a bit, as we discussed, you were going to spend this month at Ofarim and give it your all: loving, consulting, treating, encouraging, entertaining, urging everyone to come, to do.

Dani Hershberg, the director of Bnei Akiva, heard about the activity you'd prepared with Shirel and never got a chance to run.

The pages were copied, the pencils were already in a bag, but you didn't come to run it. The activity was supposed to focus on the present, not future plans hanging on nothing.

In the leadership booklet issued at the start of the month the activity was included as an introductory part of a month focused on "Building a More Just Society." A society that knows how to distinguish primary from secondary. A society that knows how to exercise clear judgment and the right priorities, and to conduct itself with a hierarchy of values.

The responsibility you showed in your treatment of the kids is inspiring – you shared with me the importance of the messages, the knowledge, and the experience you gave them. "If I don't take them to Jerusalem they won't get there," you said, and you made good. With a friend, you prepared a binder with a "bank" of activities to record whenever someone had a good activity to share with the other leaders. Each plastic sleeve held instructions with the activity theme, its goal, its character, its process, a list of the necessary supplies, and finally – the result and concluding message.

The awareness that others can learn from your insights; the awareness of the importance of preparation and of the essential need to think about every detail so the activity could be run best – that's what characterized you. I was stunned by the consistency with which you wrote down the details after each activity.

The kids were so important to you; you loved them so much, and they loved you back. What a privilege we had to be introduced to the warmth and charm of the people of Ofarim and be part of something with them. Gil-ad got so much from you...

Thursday, 20 Cheshvan, November 13

Five a.m.
The voice inside me whispering, "Let up, go easy this time, skip this session; you need another hour of sleep (which is true)," while the other voice won't relent, the one that encourages me and contends I've already been working hard for two weeks and can't give up now – that getting out of bed in the morning is always tough.

It's a wonder in itself that I get up so early. I was always a night person; my creativity is at its peak in the late hours, but since last summer something in my internal mechanism has gotten messed up, and I wake up every morning before five, unable to rest.

As with anything, our running has its ups and downs. The trail itself is hardly standard; Talmon isn't flat, and the ascents and descents make the training even harder. My thoughts immediately apply that to life and the twisting, turning confrontation with challenge: ups and downs – that's basically what it is.

Hanan, the father of the late Tamar Ariel – the IAF navigator killed in a Nepal avalanche – would describe the feeling after the loss as "on waves" – ups and downs, the soul stormy and unstable.

The waves don't do good things for me. I want serenity and calm, a little order and a slower pace on our life's running trail. A little stability.

Ofir has abilities of his own. He always says, "Who said life is supposed to be easy?"

A person chooses how to live his life, but not how he dies, I think to myself. Since that's what's been decreed, we can't just ignore the great privilege the boys gave us or the mark they've left.

A deceased person is called a *halal*, a void, because of the lack he leaves when he's gone. The challenge is to fill the space, which often seems impossible.

Don't close your eyes; don't try to imagine. There are things that are impossible to go through and impossible to imagine. There are things you shouldn't imagine.

You can't imagine the absence of someone until it happens, and maybe you shouldn't.

This week I was at a *Brit* (not to compare the living and the dead). The mother of the baby shared her sense that she couldn't imagine before the birth what the addition of the new baby would be like. I remember my pregnancies, the feeling of harmony and family wholeness that prevailed with the existing souls, and my inability to imagine what the family would look like once a new soul joined the existing group.

You can't imagine, but it happens anyway, and a new baby joins the family, not really affecting it in an essential way but slowly and naturally finding its place within. After a few days it seems like everyone there has always been there. Each member moves a bit from the previous niche and simply makes room for the new soul that's just joined, and the family takes on a new and natural wholeness.

On the other hand, I think to myself, what a difference between an addition to the family and the severing of one of its limbs. You can't imagine what goes on inside when a soul disappears from the family. The puzzle changes, but it will never be complete. The abyss that opens is immense, leaving those who remain a space and tasks to perform, new niches to fill, and each one shifts over, but nothing ever gets restored to its place. In contrast to birth, the void is permanent.

A close friend remarks, "I'd sign up for a life like that. Look what he accomplished in his life; look what he accomplished in his death." The friend himself was orphaned of his mother, so he can understand the intensity of my pain. Still, I answer him: "I might choose it for myself, but not for my son."

Friday, 21 Cheshvan, Parashat Chayei Sarah, November 14

I get a letter:

> Hi, Bat-Galim, My name is Ziva Glanz. I immigrated from the U.S. nine years ago (so please excuse any mistakes in my Hebrew here and there!) and I live with my family at a yeshiva in Mevasseret Tzion. I wanted to write to tell you what's happening in Hevron this Shabbat, Shabbat Chayei Sarah, for the souls of Gil-ad, Eyal, and Naftali. But with your permission, I'd like to give some background.
> I had the privilege of working for the Jewish community in Hevron for many years. Through the years I got to know most of the community there, including Ofer Ohana, the Tzaddik in charge of the security staff at Mt. Hevron.
> On Sunday right after the boys were kidnapped, I called Ofer, because I knew how involved he was in local affairs, and asked what we could do to help. He told me three thousand soldiers had come in a single Shabbat, and "they're sleeping out in the open and eating canned tuna..." and how positive it would be for us to support them and give them as much motivation as possible for the search. That was before all the major efforts we were privileged, *Baruch Hashem*, to see for the soldiers' sake.
> So I launched the Help Our Soldiers Help Our Boys campaign,

and I thought we might be able to raise some money from people my husband and I know.

Within a few hours the campaign went viral, and we suddenly started to hear from people from South America to Canada, from Australia to England. People wrote about it and we became the coordinators of all the initial activities. Amazing volunteers joined us (especially welcome, as I was pregnant on bed rest at the time) and we started to organize collection points in all the communities: Kiryat Sefer, Modiin, Yad Binyamin, Yavne, Petah Tikva, Yeroham, and every neighborhood of Jerusalem. People sent so much food that we had too much – so I called Sharon Katz, who runs the Soldier's Corner in Gush Etzion, and sent her some of it (especially the homemade cakes that aren't allowed on IDF bases under military kashrut protocols). She needed help distributing it all, and called some friends – that's how all the amazing volunteer work in Gush Etzion began.

Every Shabbat we held a "Mega-Shabbat" for all the soldiers in the Mt. Hevron area. Each Friday we organized trucks full of food, challot, and grape juice for thousands of soldiers for the entire Shabbat (commercial entities and private citizens participated and contributed). Hundreds of people from Kiryat Arba helped the catering company cook the food and distribute it to soldiers who arrived as late as 3 a.m. and throughout the day to join in Shabbat meals. The next morning the volunteers came at five to prepare and send Shabbat meals to soldiers serving out in the villages who couldn't come to the hall in Kiryat Arba.

It's hard to describe the atmosphere in that hall. I'll just tell a little story: among the group of volunteers were several grandmothers who said that along with the food, they're giving out *brachot*. Believe me – the soldiers stood in line and refused to leave without their blessing from "Grandma!"

During the week we managed to set up a support tent at the old HaMashbir square in central Jerusalem. Entire classes of elementary school students came (especially the Mekor Hayim elementary school) and organized with passersby whole groups for the recitation of Psalms over a loudspeaker in the city square.

Every day I was privileged to see *Am Yisrael* at its best. As was said about Moshe Rabbeinu, we really saw how "his face radiated," how light shone from everyone's face. As individuals and as a people, we became our best selves – truly a nation of angels. It was one of the greatest privileges of my life to see it from the center, and each day I told myself it's too bad I didn't have a video camera with me so the families could see the love from everyone.

It was simply wonderful: one day an immigrant from Ethiopia came. She stopped at the tent with her three-year-old son and really wanted to do something. We divided up sections of Psalms for recitation, and told her we'd recite them and she could answer Amen. But when that was over it wasn't enough for her. She started rummaging in her handbag; Bat-Galim, she stood there no less than five minutes before, with great joy, she found half a shekel. When she gave us the coin she said she has no food and no money, but she wants us to take that money and do something with it for the soldiers and searchers. When she left I said to everyone that half shekel is worth more than gold... I have tons of stories, but I'll conclude just one more. Close to where we set up the support tent, we discovered

225

a panhandler who collects money for himself and his family every day. When that Jew saw what was going on at the tent on behalf of the search effort, he came by hourly to donate the money he'd "earned," half for us and half for himself. Bat-Galim, how we tried to convince him to take the money back! We even tried donating to him at the end of the day from our personal funds, but he wouldn't accept it. He said he's been collecting money for years, but he never has a chance to give to someone else. He asked us to give him the opportunity to give and not receive.

A nation of angels. I remember reading that your husband said at the time he felt *Am Yisrael* was going through some process. I said to everyone then I completely agree with him; it's a messianic process.

That's why we knew this year we couldn't have our Shabbat Chayei Sarah – the Shabbat honoring the Fathers and Mothers in Hevron – without dedicating it to the souls of the boys. So this Shabbat, as thousands come to Hevron, they'll gather to eat in huge tents – and on the wall will be special signs with dedications to Gil-ad, Naftali, and Eyal. And when we recite the blessings together and eat at the Kiddush after services, there will be flyers asking people to pray for the elevation of the boys' souls. This Shabbat we'll again have a "Mega-Shabbat" – this time for the more than five hundred soldiers who came for Shabbat to protect the place. We'll again send food to those in the Mt. Hevron villages, and again we'll try to restore some of the special atmosphere we had this summer in Hevron.

Bat-Galim, I come from a bereaved family, and I know how much this doesn't help and how much you'd rather not have all these benefits. I also know that Naftali, Eyal, and Gil-ad are among the holiest – who says they even need all this merit? But we want to raise them to even higher sacred heights, to Hashem's infinite holiness, for the merit of *Am Yisrael*; to remind ourselves, specifically when we're right here in Hevron again, when we're again in such a difficult time, how great our potential is, and how we can be a nation of angels. I hope you feel, with the families of Eyal and Naftali, a little more consolation and holiness this special Shabbat, and that in the coming Shabbatot we be privileged to end this process and reach the Shabbat of all Shabbatot, the Redemption we need with our righteous Mashiach. Amen!

Shabbat Shalom,

Ziva

P.S. The daughter I had after being on bed rest over the summer I named Rachel Nitzchiyah, after our desire to restore some of the *nitzchiyut*, the eternity we lost when the boys were murdered, and after the revelation of eternity that we saw in *Am Yisrael* that was such a dominant part of my pregnancy at the time. She was born the Shabbat after Tisha B'Av, Shabbat Nachamu, and I hope she indeed becomes a consolation, a *nechamah* for *Am Yisrael* and for G-d.

Friday, 6 Kislev, November 28

Aromatic kitchen moments:
    There's nothing like the smell of chicken soup for Shabbat on Friday.
    There's nothing like the smell of frying onions.
    There's nothing like the smell of a warm cake filling the kitchen.

I never thought smell could hurt.

Being in the kitchen, which once was a time of creativity and welcome activity, cuts my flesh.

Gil-ad would come home and take over the pots and pans. Filling his belly, feasting his eyes on all the dishes, and throw himself on Imma's homemade food. When the fridge was full he'd gush, "That's the way I like it – plenty."

Every Shabbat I'd make three or four cakes. One would be half-finished by the time Shabbat started, as we tried to gather everyone for coffee and cake to smooth the process of getting them all ready in time and calmly. At some point Gil-ad was making some of the cakes – he loved being in the kitchen and trying new recipes. Yeshiva students customarily make a *siyum* upon finishing a tractate. Gil-ad really liked Karin Goren's cookbook, and would say he'd make a *siyum* when he got through all her recipes.

After Shabbat, when he would come back from yeshiva or Ofarim, he'd talk of all the good food they served: Yemini Kubana, Moroccan couscous, everything. Still, he wouldn't skip the post-Shabbat *Melaveh Malkah*, which of course included "testing" all the food we'd had at home that Shabbat.

Often he'd sit with Shirel, also just back from a Shabbat away from home, and talk about the Shabbat each one had had. He'd eat, enjoy, and compliment Imma's yummy food, as if making up for what he'd missed with the family over Shabbat.

It's hard to go back to cooking. Hard to go back to the kitchen.

Most of my time with Gil-ad was spent in the kitchen, the center of the home, among the pots and dishes, and almost never in his room. There. In the kitchen, surrounded by the smells of frying and baking. In the kitchen Gil-ad would update me on the goings-on at yeshiva, on trips he took, on some special activity he prepared for the youth group kids, or just anything that made him happy.

In the kitchen Gil-ad would also ask about how the building of our new house was progressing. Amid the smells of the food we'd dream together about the white kitchen in our new dwelling. And when I was on the edge of despair over how many years it was taking, he'd say, "Mommy, don't worry. You'll have the most beautiful kitchen in the world."

Tuesday, 24 Kislev, December 16

Hanukkah Eve

We're getting ready for Meitar's Bat Mitzvah, to take place on the fifth day of Hanukkah. It all seems impossible. *Ribono Shel Olam*, how will we manage to organize a joyous celebration for Meitar when sorrow envelops us all the time?

At Tahel's Bat Mitzvah two years ago, we decided to put Rabbi Nachman of Breslov's story *The Tale of the Lost Daughter of the King* to rhyme. You, my precious son, asked us to take the story and adapt it to the twenty-first century, and that's what we did. The search for the princess was shown on video and as part of a presentation using Google Maps, Facebook, and other technological means you were so good at using. At the end of the year, as if closing the circle, your grade at yeshiva would choose the same story around which to create the theme for the end-of-year party – a moving production bursting with originality and talent.

You were so prominent in the preparations for Tahel's Bat Mitzvah: the slideshows you made, the album you put together, the script for the play we put on and took in such creative, unique directions – it was all spot-on, perfect, but now – what's going to happen with Meitar? How can we have a party only five months after you've gone?

I can't write anything; I can't tell any tales. I can't connect to any theme. Everything is so sensitive all of a sudden. The preparations seem almost impossible.

I try to relax, to let go, asking the *Ribono Shel Olam*, who already "organized" such an unexpected event for us, to organize Meitar's Bat Mitzvah as well.

In fact, things all but happen by themselves.

Casual mention to a taxi driver that I'm looking for a venue brings me to a beautiful hall, the only one I feel I need to check out. With uncharacteristic decisiveness we close on a date and get on our way. Musician, clothes – it all seems to happen by itself.

As with anything, the preparation for the event was harder than the event itself. It's easy to muster the strength for three or four hours; it's a lot harder to muster it for all the weeks beforehand. Nevertheless, we put Meitar first – she deserves an event like everyone else. There was a band; there was celebration. There were videos, and even a play in which Meitar starred, with the help of our friends Noam Yaakovson and Gadi Weissbart.

Beloved Meitar, we'll overcome everything together. *Baruch Hashem* you had a Bat Mitzvah like you wanted, like you dreamed. Still, Giladush, your absence stood out in the most palpable way.

Sunday, 29 Kislev, December 21

Hanukkah

We decide to go to Eilat. My soul needs to relax and the family wants to be together. The public activity, which infuses us with strength, also takes away from family time.

Our last family trip to Eilat, the previous Hanukkah, still included Gil-ad. It was a fun vacation to remember. It had everything: hiking, attractions, family bonding, just fun.

So much togetherness. So many pictures.

I was never good at photography. I prefer to enjoy the moment, rather than fiddle with a camera. Even during the *chai* days I asked people to keep their cameras out of the house. We wanted to memorialize things in our hearts, to experience the moment. We feared the presence of a camera would distort things.

Photography has now become more complicated. After we looked for good photos of Gil-ad for publicity, after what's left of this boy is just pictures, every photo arouses thoughts; every photo seemingly begs us not to use it for events we don't want, to memorialize the moment but only for positive purposes.

The girls find consolation in the camera. They capture every moment, every flower, every stone. They look with a new eye at Creation, as if they hadn't noticed it until now, as if they forgot that when they were small they'd stop me on the way to preschool to marvel at each flower or bird that crossed our path. The years passed, and the older they got they paid less attention to their surroundings and began to take the flora and fauna for granted, as "mature" people do. Now the shell is getting peeled away and Creation is reawakening their hearts, channeling strength to their bodies.

They choose to photograph what catches their eye from different angles, capturing as if nothing were there until the moment they noticed it.

Vacation. We try to rest, to breathe some fresh air, to escape the public eye. People recognize us, exchange glances. Some come up gently to encourage us. It's not easy to free yourself of public status; it's another challenge our bereavement has foisted on us.

It's hard for me. I want to go back to anonymity. To walk around the mall, to go into stores, to haggle, to exchange an item three times if I feel like it. But it feels unpleasant now – choose, pay, and leave before yet another person recognizes me.

Snorkeling in the Red Sea

You can't be in Eilat and not see the Red Sea, or go diving or snorkeling there. In the water the beauty of Creation seems to intensify. An amazing variety of color; stunning plant life; a whole beautiful, complex world that makes the heart race. No creature is without a role. Each fish has its unique, precise structure, the specific characteristics necessary to find food; each fish is granted a means of protection and of hiding itself from bigger ones. The wonders of Creation.

Last Hanukkah four of us went scuba diving, trying something different. We dove into the depths of the Red Sea for the first time, taken aback by the scale of the experience and the world revealing itself in front of us.

Gil-ad enjoyed it most. Shirel and I were put off by the depth and were scared to take deep breaths. It took us a long time to get used to all that. But Gil-ad took to it like, well, a fish to water: he cooperated and kept close to our personal instructor and emerged from the water with his huge smile, happy and excited by the experience. Meitar also took to the diving smoothly.

It's cold today. We wanted to go in the water with snorkels and remember the familiar, beloved sights.

The joy of diving is now tinged with sadness, and those memories accompany each breath.

The fish are the same colors as before; the variety radiates vitality. The plants move slowly and assuredly, reminding us what we saw last Hanukkah. As if nothing happened in the meantime, they waited for us here all that time, as if we haven't undergone upheaval, as if no one is missing.

It's even colder now. In the body. In the soul.

The girls are happy with what we have, excited by what they see, choosing not to share what their hearts must be feeling.

The chill in their bodies they can't hide.

Friday, 18 Tevet, January 9, 2015

My Gil-adush,

Tomorrow, Shabbat, will be your seventeenth birthday. It's your birthday tomorrow and you're not here...

How can I absorb that?

Maor wants to blow up some balloons before Shabbat.

I explain to her that on this kind of birthday we don't blow up balloons. "Gil-ad won't be coming for his birthday," I say to her, teary-eyed.

You won't come, but you're present, so, so, present.

How am I going to get through this day? What do you do? What do you say? What do you think? Shirel recommends inviting friends and starting a tradition – every year on your birthday we'll have a Shabbat with friends. We connect to the idea right away.

Twenty friends accept the invitation and come on Shabbat to be with us in moments that are difficult for them, too.

The cold weather threatens to disrupt the attendance of some, but in the end almost everyone who planned to come got here, *Baruch Hashem*.

What friends you were privileged to have – we'll come to realize this gradually over Shabbat, as we have over this past year.

Everything is ready; food is crammed in the fridge; but the main part of the story is missing...

My heart breaks.

Already at the beginning of Tevet my anxieties about this day started to grow.

How do you mark the birthday of someone who's not alive anymore? On Gil-ad's calendar all of his friends' birthdays from yeshiva were marked, and most of the time Gil-adush was the one who made sure to organize some sort of celebration. Occasionally he would take a cake from home; sometimes they went out to some nice location; the main thing was to give attention and joy to the one celebrating.

How do you celebrate the birthday of someone who loved birthdays so much and made sure to make his friends feel special on that day?

What do you do?

Dark thoughts surround my head; I don't know how to cope with the approaching date. I whisper to myself again and again, "I hope it doesn't come."

Still, under the assumption it will come, how do you acknowledge the day in a meaningful way? How do you connect Gil-ad with what happened here the summer he was kidnapped?

A good friend, Roni Arazi, director of the company Digital Mashrokit, thought of an original idea. He suggests launching a Facebook page called "Gil-ad's Kitchen," and through it to ask people to bake or cook something tasty and give it to someone they don't know, and to photograph it and share it on the page, all in order to increase unconditional love. On Wednesday evening, three days before his birthday, we put up the first post:

> Gil-ad's Kitchen is a living memorial to Gil-ad Shaer, may Hashem avenge his blood. We've called it "Gil-ad's Kitchen" because he loved the kitchen and spent his leisure time baking cakes, shakes, and other yummy delicacies. We'll be glad if this month you bake cakes, cook your favorite luscious dishes, and upload photos, with links to recipes you love, to this Facebook group. Afterward, distribute the baked goodies or dishes to

your neighbors, your friends, and mainly to people you don't know so well, and ask them to do the same thing – to bake, take a picture, and distribute, and so on, until all of us have warmth and sweetness in our hearts.
We wish all of us togetherness and love in Israel!

Operation Sweet Heart in honor of Gil-ad, Eyal, and Naftali begins. Within a day we're getting amazing reactions and thousands of people joining the group. People bake, cook, and go to give out the food wholeheartedly in hospitals, nursing homes, IDF bases, and elsewhere. The operation is gaining momentum, and I, who was out of sorts leading up to today, say to Ofir before Shabbat starts that I can't wait to see what happens. Here we see *Am Yisrael* again revealed in all its power and beauty, again revealed in its uniqueness, in its generosity, devotion, and desire for great acts. You just need a drop of urging, challenging, and all the good inside that already exists just bursts forth.

Shirel shares some of her words before the birthday:

"Today's your birthday
Look, here's a new-old secret
Slice the bread
Touch something a little perfect
It's already midnight
Thought it might be good to sleep
But something's stuck
Stuck deep in my throat"
(Beri Sacharoff)

A seventeenth birthday
You'll never have.

And I'm left alone to celebrate for you.
What's important on a birthday when you're not here anymore?
Most people define human life
By the number of years from birth to death.
The soul has always existed, and will remain even after we die.
Just as you, Jilder, are with us.

On the day we're born we get talents, strengths, abilities, to meet challenges and move forward,
To be real, good human beings, to make an impact.
We have the power and ability to affect things that happen here in the world, through our choices, through the love we give.
Usually the strength to influence others and make the world better ends when a person dies.
But there are people such as you, Jilder, who are privileged, whose powers of love, of joy, of creativity, and of caring, continue to affect the world and to create goodness and light for anyone who asks.
Your birthday is a date of remembrance, of remembering love for people, love of a life cut short...
On your birthday we tried to draw from the happiness of your life...
I miss you, little brother.
You played a part in so many people's lives, and you continue to add to them...
I hope I find the strength to go on.
In the meantime I'm here, lighting memorial candles on your birthday.

Your sister, Shirel

Shabbat preparations take place in front of a running computer. The Facebook page we started in your memory has prompted extraordinary responses and is spreading quickly all over the internet. Through your love of baking, cooking, and *Am Yisrael*, we're trying to connect hearts again, to bring the distant closer, to bring the different together.

The speed with which the Page takes off surprises us. The number of messages makes my heart tremble. There, between setting the table, doing the last bits of cooking, and setting up the candles, every few minutes we check the phone or computer to encourage, respond, and express appreciation to the many who gave us strength as this Shabbat approached. Many people want to participate; everyone wants to do kindness to you, Gil-ad, to mark your memory, to exalt your soul. Not everyone realizes what kindness they do for me with that act of giving. With that sharing.

From within the worry and lack of desire for this day to arrive, there is born inside me a new reality of curiosity and anticipation to see where this goes. A few minutes before Shabbat I again remember all the messages and texts we got during that long, meaningful period, and am again awash in messages of love and support that give us the strength to go on, to cope, to live through your Shabbat, your birthday, your absence...

A year later we'll run the operation again: girls from the Bayit Vagan College in Jerusalem will discover it and expand it dramatically. They'll announce that on the birthday itself, Thursday night that year, people should bake chocolate cookies – which you liked especially – and give them out at intersections. In more than sixty towns and cities representatives will register their desire to participate. About nine hundred shirts will be printed, and on Thursday, 19 Tevet, despite the winter weather, thousands of cookies will be distributed across the country. A National Service member from London will join and spread the operation among other National Service alumna around the world, and it will take flight in every direction, attracting participants in London, the U.S., and even Singapore and Chile.

In the third year the operation will seem to grow on its own. Your friend from Dolev, Noam Kadmon, will coordinate among dozens of volunteers. In a hundred twenty different cities people will bake cookies, give out goodies, spark smiles, do something good. In ten countries people will participate in this wonderful activity.

The news continues to report attacks, and the media brings into relief the gaps separating different parts of Israeli society. And yet, so many good people are trying to increase love, to bring smiles, to make one another happy. Anyone who wants to feel a little encouragement should go to Gil-ad's Kitchen and see how much good there is among our people.

Saturday Night, Eve of 26 Tevet, January 17

Dedication of a Bnei Akiva branch in Lod named after the three boys.

Your face peers out at me from the wall; your smile is as winning as always.

My heart contracts, and that burning in my soul again washes over me.

My perspective intersects with that of the artist who memorialized your face, Moshe Klehrer. He put his soul into painting the likeness of the boys looking out from the wall.

Ribono Shel Olam, did I ask so much? All I asked for was my son, for my son to be with me. I just wanted to raise children to do good. Inside I'm sure you're proud and happy with the branch in Lod, with the welcome activities that will take place inside walls built in your memory, in memory of Eyal and Naftali.

It's so complicated.

Another branch is under construction right now in your memory, the Ofarim branch. The branch where you led, where you gave and received so much, where you developed so much. You were privileged to attend the cornerstone-laying ceremony for it, a few months before you left us. About a year later the branch will be dedicated in your name.

Your sister Tahel will begin her work as a counselor there about a year and a half after you left us, never to return.

Wednesday, 8 Shevat, January 28

Kitchen moments.

Sunset. The sun takes its leave of the sky, wanting to end its day impressively. It leaves a mark, painting the heavens in red and blue.

There's nothing like Talmon sunsets.

Meitar wants to make the chocolate chip cookies you both liked, Gil-ad.

Music plays on the radio and the girls turn up the volume. A song you loved is playing in the background. The girls start jumping, moving their heads, their hair, themselves in every direction, laughing. Simple, true joy radiates from their faces. They take pictures of one another, trying to capture pleasant moments.

I watch them from the side, with them and not with them. The pain won't leave me alone. I can't connect to that joy, but I do feel gratified by each passing moment.

I have so much to learn from you, my daughters. You enable so much to happen, flowing with and enjoying every moment. Simply living. Simply girls.

Sometimes I think maybe the youngest one doesn't understand, but a dinnertime conversation with them teaches me they all get it quite well, as much as one can – if one can at all...

Maor: "Imma, does G-d have a cellphone?" Hmm, a surprising question, I think to myself.

"G-d hears, sees, gets, and knows everything. He doesn't need a phone," I answer, and add, "it's pretty convenient to be able to talk to Him and tell

Him whatever you want, whenever you want, and He always listens and hears."

Maor looks at me with her big eyes and listens quietly, and then I ask, "Why do you need G-d to have a phone?"

"I want to talk to Gil-ad," she answers.

Friday, 24 Shevat, February 13

It's been eight months.

So much time, a seeming eternity. So little; it seems only minutes. Gil-adush, there's not a minute I don't think of you.

With a smile, in sadness, with immense longing.

The songs you loved play in the background; the girls bought Idan Reichel and Illi Botner disks. I got a new stereo system.

Two weeks ago I started listening to the words – they pierced my soul. Illi stunningly describes coping with loss, a real artistic creation. What did you hear in those songs, my beloved son? What did you hear in those songs that express coping with loss and pain, that bring out longing?

It's great music, touching me deep in my soul. But the words, what words...

"And the distance from longing is the distance from insanity..."

We all live in anticipation – waiting for special events, waiting for holidays, waiting for our birthday, or that of a close family member. Those occasions usually recharge us for the rest of the year and its demanding routine, and become a source of vitality and joy. But now I find myself afraid of them, afraid of festivals.

Every ceremony at Maor's preschool becomes a challenge; every party at Hallel's school seems like climbing Everest...

To myself I even hope my own birthday this year can wait. This week it's Shirel's, and next week, mine. I'll be forty-three.

I need to muster unusual strength to be able to think about what I have, to find what strengthens me.

It's so easy to get drawn into the pain, the void, your absence, Gil-ad.

You loved birthdays so much, loved celebrating for others.

You loved the holidays so much; you loved life so much.

Thursday, Rosh Chodesh, Eve of 1 Adar, February 19

The girls of Shalhevet High School invite me to be coronated as Purim Queen. They're students I taught in ninth and eleventh grades, and gave them guidance through such formative years in so many ways. Girls with whom I treaded a difficult path, but now it's time for the *nachas*.

Such talent, such humor, such an ability to grapple with the complexities of the first high school class of a new school, a class that knew upheaval, crisis, ups and downs. And now they're on stage. Beautiful, talented, self-aware. I am so proud of them.

Again I feel connected to my choice twenty years ago to dedicate myself to teaching. Education is of course a long-term investment, a process, not something you can look at narrowly in the confines of here and now (which is also true of parenting). How much trouble we put ourselves through; how many trials we undergo; how much patience and forbearance we have to muster; and how much crow you end up having to eat, especially when teaching students in the sensitive, tumultuous stages of adolescence.

Often we teachers become targets of frustration when problems seem intractable. It's exhausting work, but when you get to see the light at the end of the pedagogical tunnel, to see the fruits of your toil – there's no limit to the satisfaction and gratification.

And I've been extremely fortunate. I drew so much strength from my students during the *chai* days. Dozens of students I've had the privilege of teaching came to our home, to embrace, to encourage, to support, to show concern, and I felt how lucky I was.

This evening a painful insight hits me – I used to have a normal life.

This year I was supposed to celebrate twenty years as a teacher.

As a result of the summer's events I took an unpaid leave of absence. I'm trying to collect myself and the girls, to focus on the inner work of the family. And yes, to monitor the physical construction of our new house.

But life is much more complex. Reality, which made our private lives public, has become more and more demanding of my attention, and won't allow me the ingathering of myself that I need so much.

Monday, 11 Adar, March 2

Under normal circumstances, the AIPAC Conference in the U.S. wouldn't affect my routine in the least. A tired look at the news at the end of the day would be all the attention I'd give such an event in the routine of normal life.

This year the event took on different dimensions.

A few weeks before the event the three families got messages that they wanted to invite us. A short check led to the conclusion that our presence would strengthen Israel and the bond between American and Israeli Jewry, and we decided to accept the invitation.

Over the long months we went through we gradually learned about the Jewish communities in the U.S. and elsewhere in the world. Entire communities prayed, committed themselves to positive behavior, emphasized and demonstrated unity among different denominations, unity not before seen, as they described it to us.

We felt how the barriers between different groups of Jews were breaking: caring Jews simply want to be part of what's happening in Israel, to embrace and gain encouragement from their brethren settled in the homeland, protecting them from here.

It's an old joke that every town with two Jews will have three synagogues. It turns out that's not far from reality: differences in ideology and approaches to Jewish-halachic life have over the years put great distance between people. But the *chai* days brought hearts together. The sense of special unity that prevailed in *Am Yisrael* in Israel and throughout the world led to a different kind of discourse. Many synagogues held joint prayer services with the other denominations, and conducted discussions aimed at reminding everyone that they had more in common than not. Participation in the AIPAC Conference was a chance for us to meet the American Jewish community and thank them. We were very happy it was made possible.

Preparation for the trip is short and focused. We obviously needed a strong speech, so I asked the assistance of two good, inspiring friends who had helped under other, similar circumstances many times. Two days before the flight I'm holding two good, to-the-point speeches. One of them is sent to AIPAC, which wants a copy in advance so they can prepare everything down to the last detail.

In fact, the organizers prepared their own speech for us, which amounted to nothing more than saying thank you. Frustration mounted before Shabbat began – will our whole trip to AIPAC consist of standing there and saying thanks? We try to add meaningful messages, sensing it's a chance to accomplish an important mission. And so, a few minutes before Shabbat, we send our second speech to them, hoping the organizers can handle these last-minute changes.

It's an extremely difficult flight for us. We're stuffed into a plane for twelve hours and I can't sleep. We land at five a.m. local time, three days before Purim, and I'm all nerves and exhaustion. Uncertainty over the final draft of the speech doesn't help my mood, and everything looks gray and overcast. It's a huge airport, and getting from place to place takes more time than we expected. I take delight in the thought that I'm anonymous again for a few moments, walking around in my ugly elastic socks I wore during the flight, and enjoying the fact that no one recognizes me.

Outside, bitter cold greets us, and a generous driver takes us to our hotel. I'm tense over what awaits us, and a sleepless night on the plane doesn't improve the situation. A thought crosses my heart: So many Israelis go starry-eyed when they hear about a business trip abroad. Few will admit it's no great pleasure. It's not my job to dispel that myth, but still.

Washington is covered in white. New flakes are joining the ones already lying on the ground, and the sides of the road are white. How wondrous are Your works, Hashem; so much beauty and purity. The road is clear and open for travel.

I learn it's possible to drive on a snowy road; smiling at the thought that it's not like that in Israel. Here we have to stay home and shut the education system down, as happened in recent years, when snow took us by surprise. Driving in Israel when snow accumulates on the roads is dangerous and near impossible, but here it's an everyday thing. Routine doesn't stop; students don't get a day off; and people don't cancel their work meetings. Snow melds naturally into the packed day-to-day.

New flakes fall and find their place as if they know where to land, what their place is in the world. Amid them I hope we too find our place in this short trip over the next three days, as if it's the most natural thing in the world.

We have a rehearsal for the speech scheduled at eleven-thirty in the morning. We get organized at the hotel and meet with Uri Yifrach, Avi Fraenkel, and Rachel, the coordinator sent by AIPAC. It turns out there was some confusion, and each family prepared its own speech. The messages are shared, but of course each one put the emphasis on different things. Rachel sits with us, helping us all construct a speech in common, in a way that builds excitement.

In contrast to the American attitude of wanting to know and plan everything down to the last detail, ahead of time, with no changes (something Israelis could certainly learn from), we go through a beautiful process of building a shared speech that satisfies everyone as much as possible. For me, the big challenge will be delivering it in English. It's hard to put in words our excitement before the event.

That morning we were in the convention hall during Prime Minister Binyamin Netanyahu's address. It's a huge hall, full of sixteen thousand Jews with the single goal of telling the Jews of Israel: we love you; we're with you. Gigantic screens show the speakers on stage, for the benefit of those in faraway seats. It's all really impressive. The Jewish pride, the exalted feeling that so many Jews seek the best for Israel, is wonderful. Among the attendees are a large number of non-Jews who also come to show solidarity and support.

I promise myself that next year I'll do everything, with Hashem's help, to convince Israeli media people to cover this event and bring some of that goodness to Israel. If the Israeli public knew what broad backing they had, what support we enjoy in the U.S., they'd stand up straight and feel elevated.

The prime minister says in his speech: "For two thousand years the Jewish People lacked a state, lacked protection, lacked everything. We were completely powerless in the face of our enemies who swore to exterminate us. We suffered horrific persecution and we could not speak for ourselves or protect ourselves. Never again!" His words excite the crowd and he gets a round of applause, with a standing ovation at the end.

Again I feel the strengthened sense inside that regardless of one's political opinion, it's clear that here, in the U.S., the prime minister is on an important mission on behalf of the country, and we have to support him. This is not the time for disagreements; we have to be united in the unequivocal assertion of the need to preserve the existence of Israel.

On the day before Purim I get the powerful sense that history is repeating itself. Just as it happened 2,300 years ago, when Esther sought to unify the people in the face of the evil Haman's decree, we are now called on to "go gather all the Jews." The Jewish people, who at the start of the *megilah* are described as "There is one scattered, divided people among all the nations..." by Haman, later on unites in prayer and battle against the Persian enemy seeking their destruction.

We get back to the hotel late at night.

In Israel it's already Tuesday morning. It's a morning of costumes; this year the girls will dress up without Imma's help or support.

I hope you're all OK, I pray in my heart; I hope you're not left with any scars from this morning, without Imma to dress you up or make you up. I hope when they grow up they'll understand that this trip, for the sake of the bond between the Jews in Israel and Jews abroad, is really important to me.

Tuesday, 12 Adar, March 3

It's our turn to speak.

Yesterday at the dress rehearsal we stood in an empty hall and my stomach turned over with excitement. What'll happen soon before a full hall of sixteen thousand people?

As happened many times before in the past year, we find the serenity and inner power, and on stage in front of the throngs of people, we try to speak from the heart about the support, the warmth, and the importance of the bond between American and Israeli Jews. Our address concludes with words that before our eyes have transformed from cliché into palpable reality: even if two Jews have three opinions, they have one heart.

I think the biggest surprise of the trip, though, was that our speech, which *Baruch Hashem* elicited support and applause, and the huge embrace we got on stage from sixteen thousand precious Jews, weren't the main achievements of our mission.

Over the several days of the conference many members of Congress wanted to meet with us and express their support and solidarity with the Jews in Israel. The opportunity to describe to them the complicated situation Jews face, the sense that no matter where Jews live, there's an existential threat to Israel, is immensely significant to me. The chance to encourage them and say how important their support for Israel is really moves me.

We hold other important meetings, including with Ted Deutch, a Jewish congressman who enthusiastically supports Israel, and Senator

Ted Cruz, who was the first to bring the story of the boys to America's attention – in a moving televised address he told the American people about the kidnapping and gave faces to the boys.

If the citizens of Israel knew how much they love us, how much support and concern we enjoy among Jews in the U.S., maybe we'd have more confidence in the rightness of our path. If we could receive just some of that warmth and love, maybe we'd be stronger and less threatened by all the things that divide us – the things that the media focus on. The feeling that disagreements weaken us resonates in me again and again.

We get back to the hotel late at night. The feeling of absence pinches my heart.

Gil-adush, you'd have loved all these meetings. You'd have known how to leverage them for *Am Yisrael*. With understanding beyond your years, you'd grasp their importance; you'd enhance their impact with your personal charm. The longing and pain don't let go of me even for a moment.

We're on the plane back to Israel.

Baruch Hashem they arranged a more comfortable flight back than the one there. I try to rest; I have to muster my strength for landing so close to Purim. Inside I feel great satisfaction; my heart is bursting with it. The tremendous embrace we got from the Jewish community in the U.S. is empowering. I'm full of emotion at our people, at the great love they show, and the deep connection despite being on different continents.

I stretch out in my seat, open an Israeli newspaper, and a stab of pain pierces my chest. News coverage completely ignores the support and embrace directed toward Israel and its people during the conference; the reporting does not reflect the reality as I experienced it. Oy, what's become of us... the thoughts trouble me and don't let my body rest. I feel the need to write something and send it to the paper.

> Purim Eve 5755.
> We landed a few hours ago and went directly to the reading of Megilat Esther.
> We were in the U.S. for three days, and AIPAC's annual conference.
> My heart bursts... my adrenalin was flowing... so much love for Israel...
> If I could carry it in bags and distribute some to each of you, all of our batteries would be recharged.
>
> Sixteen thousand people, old and young, students and businesspeople, mostly Jews of all denominations, fill the hall and for three days try to tell us how much they are with us, how much they love Israel, how much they support the Jews who live in Israel.
> Sixteen thousand people cheering and clapping, standing up, sitting and then standing again every few minutes as another statement of admiration is made about Jews, about Israel.
> Public figures, influential leaders, come to the conference to say they love us here in Israel, that they support the Jewish people living in Zion.
> Sixteen thousand people cheered Prime Minister Binyamin Netanyahu as a representative of the Jewish People, as the leader of the State of Israel, regardless of their political stance, simply because he represents all of us, the Jewish nation.
> Sixteen thousand people cheered, applauded, and sent waves of warmth and love to all of us, to each of us.

So let's set our egos aside for a moment; let's let those waves of warmth reach us. Let's know that they exist and open our hearts so it can fill up with them. Let's remind ourselves we're brothers. Let's be filled with Jewish pride at the love flowing through those huge halls. Let's recharge our batteries with that love.
It's Purim today, and now as then, our enemies seek to destroy us.
Let's remind ourselves that our power lies in our unity, and let's be filled with pride over the country we have,

Bat-Galim

We land in Israel and rush straight to the synagogue for the *megilah* reading.

Purim goes well, *Baruch Hashem*, as the tremendous embrace by U.S. Jewry fills us and enables us to continue living despite everything.

Friday, 22 Adar, March 13

I'm exhausted after a busy week and decide to go out for a light afternoon run to release energy and unrelenting frustration. A friend joins me. We run, and soon a gap appears between us – she goes ahead.

I'm fine by myself, with my thoughts.

A young man approaches in the other direction and immediately reminds me of you, my Gil-adush. Of course you'd have joined me if you were here... during the last few months of your life you decided to start jogging, after years of avoiding it because of knee pain. Growing pains.

Again that pain; tears flood my eyes.

What's gonna be, *Ribono Shel Olam*? We've received a lifetime "gift" from You? How do I survive this struggle?

So many families in Israel confront bereavement and loss. I'd never realized how torturous it is.

This morning there was a circumcision for a boy born with a twin sister. The mother conceived last summer. The day of the kidnapping she was told she was carrying three fetuses. The day of the burial she found out only two remained. This week they emerged into the world, a boy and a girl. Mazal tov.

I don't understand how You run the world, *Ribono Shel Olam*, but it's nevertheless so clear someone runs the world, that nothing is by chance.

That even when it hurts, it's Your embrace. Let go a little, please; don't hug me so hard; it squeezes so much...

Everyone wishes us joyous occasions.

Joyous occasions, it turns out, are complex, perhaps the most complex thing, but still – only happy occasions.

Friday, 7 Nisan, March 27

Shabbat HaGadol Eve

Pesach is in a week. We shift the clocks tonight, skipping ahead an hour.

Too bad when we can't stop time the way we change the time.

Holiday prep is really tough for me. The struggle sometimes looks doomed to failure from the start, no chance. Who wants Pesach now? Sometimes I envy you, Gil-ad. You've moved on to a world of only good, the world of truth. You've left us so many tasks and chal-lenges, so much pain.

In our world, good and evil are all intertwined. There's uncertainty and confusion. In the world you now inhabit, truth and falsehood are clearly defined. There's no blending.

And the wonderful souls who are with you – what a fantastic group you have around you! Wonderful people have joined the heavenly entourage in the last year. How many luminous *tzaddikim* and humble scholars from the distant past have you met? I sometimes wonder who your study partner is – is it Rav Kook or Rabbi Soloveitchik? The Lubavitcher Rebbe or Rabbi Nachman of Breslov? Does everyone have his own approach to learning there also, or does everything harmonize? Have you found calm and serenity there?

Here everything is so stormy; the country is in turmoil. It's election season.

At home we're unable to make any progress on building the house; the girls cope with your absence every day, every hour. I took a year off and still can't find a moment's rest. Everything is so complicated and tumultuous.

I wonder whether your soul even knows anymore what emotion is, whether it remembers what longing is – if that's just the lot of those who inhabit the land of good and evil.

Saturday Night, Eve of 9 Nisan, March 28

So that's it; you're not coming back.

The inconceivable finality, the pain that won't end.

Finality is something you have to confront little by little when coping with death. We've been trying to explain the finality of it to ourselves from the first moment.

During one of our conversations a student asked me with a satisfied grin, as if asking something no one had ever thought of before, "If Gil-ad came back, what would you say to him?" How innocent she is, I thought. Bereavement is just that: loss and coping with the realization (if one can even understand) that Gil-ad isn't coming back.

The complexity of life alongside faith in resurrection, together with internalized realization of the finality of death is a heavy task indeed. In conversations with my daughters I've chosen, so far, to emphasize the "no return" finality. Avoiding or evading that is no recipe for a healthy life. But awareness of finality doesn't contradict belief in resurrection, and it's a big mistake to bypass it.

One Shabbat Maor fixes her huge eyes on me and says with her winning smile, "Imma, I want to die." I get it at once. "What happened? You miss Gil-ad?" "Yes," she answers. "I want to be with him." My heart contracts. Why does she have to deal with this at her age? I hug her and whisper, "We don't have to die for Gil-ad to be with us."

"Really?" she looks at me with hopeful eyes.

"You know," I continue, "when Mashiach comes, *B'ezrat Hashem*, there will be a resurrection of the dead and they'll all come back. Gil-ad will be with us again."

"What, really? Gil-ad will come back to us? He'll come home?" She asks again and again.

"Yes, *B'ezrat Hashem*. But it'll be a long time from now, and before that *Am Yisrael* has to really work and pray for it. We have to pray all the time."

I look at her small gaze, watching her try to absorb all these earth-shaking ideas. It seems she's satisfied and we leave the topic with a gigantic hug.

A few days later, when I think she's already forgotten, she looks at me in a moment of weakness, as tears of pain well up in my eyes, and says, "Mommy, didn't you say if we pray really hard Gil-ad will come back?"

Great, I think, I've gotten myself in trouble... "It's not so simple," I answer. "We have to pray and be better people – all of *Am Yisrael* has to pray and become better. It will take a long time."

"So, Mommy," says Maor, "Maybe instead of crying you should just start praying?"

Tuesday, 11 Nisan, March 31

The telephone won't rest. Text messages, WhatsApp – *Am Yisrael* gives us another hug. All week long people have been showing sensitivity to the approaching footsteps of the holiday, and sending encouraging messages. I realize the holiday isn't just the Seder night, Chol HaMoed, and seven significant days on their own, but all the preparation that generates powerlessness and emotional blocks inside me. Preparing for any holiday is now not easy at all.

Immediately after Purim all the neighbors start scrubbing and polishing, and the question on everyone's lips is, "Where are you for the holiday?" The pain is accented and increased – your absence has found a new place, as if it had ever left us alone.

The house being slowly built allows us to rationalize doing only a very partial cleaning job this year. House-cleaning time is also a time for cleaning out oneself. A kind of isolated introspection, alone with my thoughts, with the caustic cleansers. My thoughts float among the troubled layers of my soul, finding tremendous, tear-drenched pain. I wish I could wash away the pain the way we wash the walls before Pesach, I think to myself. I wish I could restore things to the way they were.

I feel your absence in the little things, the routine preparations: the lawn is already overgrown, waiting for someone to take the initiative and fill your role. The windows will stay covered in dirt this year, and the excuse that we're moving soon anyway will distract from the thought that you were the last to clean them, with your characteristic thoroughness. When you took something on you were so thorough. Maybe that's what charmed Sima in Modiin when you cleaned her place for Pesach last year so you could earn money for the trip to Poland. Our window tracks will remain orphaned and dirty.

When you join the family of the bereaved you discover things of which the general public is unaware. Preparations for Pesach blend with preparations for Memorial Day soon afterward.

I get a blow to the stomach a few days before the holiday – a telephone call from the Binyamin Council. On the line there's a nice girl who wants to know if we're interested in having the main ceremony on Memorial Day be dedicated to Gil-ad. I think she senses the shock in my voice – she caught me so unprepared. Tears flood my eyes. It takes me a few minutes to recover and answer, "Of course. What a great honor for us..."

Honor and tremendous pain – I can't internalize neither my part in this large family, the family of the bereaved, nor that fact that this year Memorial Day will look completely different.

Friday, 14 Nisan, Eve of Pesach, April 3

Maor is listening to the song "Open Your Heart" written by David d'Or, that he arranged with amazing sensitivity with Keinan Shlomo Ilan – along with other artists representing different sectors of society. She sings along with the chorus:

> How did the three become one
> And command us that we live;
> They ascended in wholeness as a bound deer (Eyal)
> Upon the altar of the boys.
> The Heavens wept over Gilad
> And the Earth shook
> From the winding paths (Naftulim) of the trembling heart
> The three smiled from of the picture.

"Over Gilad," she says. "Why doesn't he say, 'Jilder'?" she asks herself out loud, referring to his nickname among close friends, and causing us to laugh amidst the tense preparations for the holiday.

As I'm preparing things the day before Pesach I get a message from a good friend: "Hugs. I'm sure at a time like this everything comes flooding back again..." Something must have happened, I think to myself, and turn on the news to check. In any case, no, it's not flooding back right now. It's always flooding, all the time. I hear everyone's tense – there are reports of a boy kidnapped near Hevron. The army responds with all possible means; no one is taking risks. Within a few hours it turns out the story was made up and the forces were called out in vain.

My heart contracts: who's going to explain to those pranksters that because of such horrible acts Gil-ad's phone call wasn't treated with due seriousness? Who's going to pass a law to punish youths who think calling the police with false reports and causing the whole system to launch operations is trivial?

Who will teach them you never do that under any circumstances? Anger and pain float up inside, mixed together.

I'm drained when the holiday begins. The fear of the holiday itself, the preparation, the routine hassles that don't let up, the pain, the longing...

As the holiday begins I decide that's enough. I have to let the pain go a little and set it aside.

There are five girls here who want to experience a holiday, as well as Ofir, and I, too, want it. We do manage to feel festive.

A friend tells me, "It's an amazing thing, the ability to control pain. You can't take for granted that you were able let it go for the holiday." Whereas I'm debating whether it's OK to do so: what do you mean, possible to let it go? Can I do that? The friend, a bereaved mother herself, answers me with a sad smile: "Not to worry, the pain will come back."

And here it comes, big-time. It always comes, waiting around the corner for that moment of inattention, to control, to increase, to remind me it exists deep within me.

Monday, 24 Nisan, April 13

Preparations for Memorial Day include another look through photo albums. The screen at home shows a series of family pictures, and you're there in almost all of them. Your friends at yeshiva confirm that you were one of those who loved to be photographed. In every picture you're with friends or family. When I looked for photos of you for publicity during the *chai* days I almost couldn't find any of you by yourself: always surrounded by friends, always surrounded by your beloved sisters.

We try to find photos or video clips that haven't been published yet. Someone asks me if I know of a photo of you in which you aren't smiling. No, I hadn't noticed – your smile gazes out from every possible picture. You changed so much from one picture to the next. At the time I thought I noticed you growing up day by day, hour by hour. Each time you came home from yeshiva you were a few centimeters taller and you had a more mature gaze.

I didn't look at you enough, I feel it now, and my heart aches.

I examine with special longing the man looking out at me from the day before the kidnapping, the famous picture of the human pyramid you made, along with many other good ones just the day before at a "sports day" event at yeshiva. It was a day in which dozens of smiling, happy Gil-ad and Nafatli photos were taken. A day with nothing special about it had you not been taken from us the next with such suddenness and cruelty.

I'm so sorry I didn't hug you enough, you adolescent boy. As a child you loved to share, to talk, to describe every experience you had at length. In the last year I sensed you'd grown, and not just in height. As part of your growth process the depth and frequency of those deep conversations lessened. I noticed you'd found an attentive ear and heartfelt responsiveness with Shirel, and I was happy about that bond between you. I respected your wishes to mature, to distance yourself from Imma's apron.

And now all that's left in my heart is the huge pain of terrible longing for another of your hugs, for some contact... the intolerable finality of grief floods over me again.

Thursday, 27 Nisan, April 16

Conclusion of Yom HaShoah

A week after Pesach, a week before Memorial Day. Thursday night became an evening I won't forget.

Two days ago, on Tuesday, Ofir came back from work and told me about a conversation he'd had with Deputy Police Commissioner Eitan Madmoni. Representatives of the police – some of whom we knew very well – want to come to our home to show us a bag of Gil-ad's clothes and possessions.

Chills.

The expression "blood flows out of my body" exactly fits what I felt.

Will I have the endurance?

Where did the bag come from?

The whole time we've wondered where his stuff was, and they told us it was burned in the car.

You left so few material possessions, and perhaps your death teaches us how insignificant our material existence is. Your spirit stands before us, living, affecting our world. Your soul is with us.

At the funeral, a few moments before the actual burial, someone put a black bag in the grave. When I asked, I was told it was your bloody clothes – my son's blood! – and they have to be buried.

Ribono Shel Olam, it's terrible.

A sense of unease rises in me toward the system in which I had placed complete trust. Where did these things come from? How didn't I hear of them till now?

Here comes the pain again. The choking tears, flowing freely in the space they have known as their own for many months now.

In one of the conversations with Eitan Madmoni Ofir asked him why the security apparatus didn't deem it proper to praise Gil-ad in public for the phone call he made, only remarking on it in private conversations.

A few months after the murder Eitan came to our house excited, and wanted to give us something personal. We were both in shock – he took out a police Medal of Honor, a pin he was awarded personally many years before. Now he wanted to give it to Gil-ad. "I know what those moments are like, facing down a terrorist," he said. "Gil-ad's reaction deserves praise." We had a hard time accepting the pin from Eitan – it's his personal pin! But Eitan, with characteristic humility and modesty, insisted, and asked that we keep it a secret. That's the kind of people who were with us during and long after the *chai* days.

Now Eitan reveals to Ofir that a replica of the pin has been produced, and that he started wearing it all the time since our tragedy. As far as Eitan is concerned, Gil-ad's call is worthy not of appreciation, but admiration. The ability to make a phone call without his captors knowing, the ability to take responsibility under such pressure, to exploit a few seconds of the kidnappers' inattention to make a call that would give such significant information to the police. Information that would lead to the names of the kidnappers by Shabbat eve. Information that gave the security forces much more than a mere lead.

Gil-adush, to me you're a true hero. I'm so proud of you and I love you so, so much.

I'm restless the whole day. From the moment Ofir told me about the impending meeting with the police my soul can't find respite. What more could they have to tell us? I wonder to myself, unable to imagine what news they'll bring.

The day itself passes as if routine. Morning meetings in Jerusalem and a dental appointment in the evening for the little one, who's been complaining of a toothache – you have to take care of it. Even though it's most inconvenient and my thoughts are elsewhere, the appointment is at six, while the police are supposed to come at seven. Of course when we get to the clinic we're told there's an hour delay. What do you do?

My daughter has been complaining of a toothache for three days. Even I, with my non-professional eye, can see the hole developing in her tooth. But there's no way we can be late for our meeting with the police this evening. With pleading and trembling I speak to the wonderful assistant, and explain to her there are important people waiting for me at home and I can't be late. She stuns me with her immediate responsiveness. She approaches the dentist and a waiting client, says what she says, and opens the door for us.

The treatment begins at once, and at six-forty we're already on our way home.

Who knows what the delayed client is thinking; she mustn't have the foggiest idea where I'm trying to get and why. I hope she thinks well of me. How much goodwill we need; how easily she could get angry at being forced to wait another twenty minutes in line because of me! I appreciate her very much and thank her explicitly when we leave the clinic.

On the way back I contact the police reps. "Take your time," they request.

I try to calm down. The last time anyone asked me to drive calmly was that Monday when they told me the worst thing possible. We had to drive from Tel Aviv to Talmon to hear it. I remember the trembling that overtook my body during that trip.

I'm not sure why I'm so anxious about this meeting with the police. It seems my body understands what my head doesn't... I get home and rush to send the girls off to neighbors and tidy the house ahead of the police arrival. Shaking and anxiousness seize my whole body. Here they come. Four police cars come onto our little street. Four officials, each in a separate car.

This is how it will feel at the Resurrection of the Dead, I think to myself, unable to remain calm for two days in anticipation of this police meeting. After accepting the fact that your personal effects disappeared along with you, and the few remaining ones are packed away on a few shelves in the closet of your bedroom – all of a sudden here they are. Suddenly something's been found.

The whole time I hoped, I wanted intensely to find some journal of yours, and as time passed I resigned myself to that not happening. But suddenly, miraculously, they found a diary.

Suddenly, according to the police, a bag came to the forensic laboratory with a notebook and diary. A police warehouse in Hevron held many items collected during the *chai* days; someone was reorganizing the place and discovered it – it was almost thrown away. Found miraculously, saved miraculously. Miraculously sent to the forensic lab. The initial examination revealed that in addition to a biology notebook, there was a personal diary in which you plucked your soul's strings and recorded their tones in writing.

They tell me in tears the words that jumped out at them from the text – "I really love my mother!" and felt it was too personal to touch, so they brought these pages to us, here, home, just now.

Wow. Unbelievable – what a treasure! What a treasure was my son, what a treasure's been found! What a treasure, G-d. Thank You, Father, just thank You...

With trembling hands they take out a clear plastic bag, then another. With even more trembling hands we open it.

I'd regret two things at the end of that evening – what we opened and what we didn't.

My head said don't touch. The diary is falling apart and could get damaged. It's best to leave its deciphering to the experts. Everything is crumbling, charred, and has clearly been soaked. My heart is bursting – I want to know what's written there, what the message is. Now, this moment! To find words that might give me some consolation, that might tell us things about you we didn't know.

I'm afraid to touch. Ofir, as if drunk, leafs through the diary with intense focus, as if trying to find his lost son.

Enough, I can't take it anymore. The destruction is immense, the information is important... we have to overcome our curiosity. "Take the diary," I request. "We'll look at it after it's deciphered." It'll be hard to wait, but the diary is too precious.

A few other items were retrieved from Gil-ad's bag. Items that were collected near the car, some by our police, some by the Palestinian police. Items that flew from the car as it burned, which is why most of them are charred. Some are wet from the water used to put out the fire. A few items of clothing. A *tallit*. Glasses.

"They said, 'This we found – can you recognize it – is it your son's garment or not?'" Yaakov's sons ask their father after they've thrown Yosef in a pit in Parashat Vayeshev (Genesis 37). "He recognized it" and mourns for his son "many days".

I feel we're seeing the beginning of the repair of Yosef's brothers' sin.

273

In Operation Brother's Keeper, how fittingly symbolic, an entire people searched for three lost boys, looking for them like they were their own sons, their own brothers.

The police show us photo after photo and ask us to identify our son Gil-ad's garment. It's not an easy sight. My thoughts return to, focus on, loss and death.

The military rabbi recommends burying the items without seeing them. In a stroke of heavenly assistance we tell them the gravestones have yet to be erected, so the items can be buried immediately. We ask for a night to absorb the information and be able to reach a decision with greater serenity, and we escort them to the door.

An ambulance can be seen at the end of the street. "We called it," they explain with some embarrassment. "You never know how a Jewish mother will react."

"I know the moment we leave your pillow will be soaked with tears." Eitan takes his leave of us with a sense of complete partnership.

The pain is enormous; the lack deepens; nevertheless my pillow is happy tonight.

I got the most meaningful greeting I could from you, Gil-ad.

Miracles happen, I smile to myself.

Still, Mashiach could come quickly. Maybe Gil-ad will come back sooner than we can imagine.

As soon as they leave I'm sorry – about what we opened, the diary, and about what we didn't, the items themselves.

Photos? I want to touch, to feel, to smell the clothes, the *tallit*.

The green-framed glasses that so symbolized you.

Tomorrow I'll call and make an appointment with them, and then they can bury what they see fit.

I can't shut my eyes the whole night. The anxiety is immense. I can't believe they found Gil-ad's diary.

I wanted so much to find things he'd written, and my heart ached because I didn't find much in his room. True, the diary was written by a child. Maybe it doesn't contain profound statements about life. The quick leafing we did indicates it's a very personal journal – revealing some things and concealing more. The fragments we saw speak to the inner workings of the soul, Gil-ad's soul.

Hesitation, deliberation, love, and frustration. Lots of soul.

Who knows what we'll discover in the diary? Another long journey awaits us.

What's certain is that it will contain some great truth.

Tuesday, 2 Iyyar, April 21

Memorial Day Eve

We got the blow to the gut in the evening, when the siren sounded. I prepared myself and the girls this year for the national day of remembrance, a day when we wouldn't have so much time to be with our own private Gil-ad, because of the national character of the kidnapping episode. We were invited to ceremonies and important events; many requested materials, stories, and pictures, and it looks like the boys are present at almost every possible ceremony throughout the country.

We began the evening with a "singing and remembering" event at Sultan's Pool in Jerusalem. The preparations at home looked like those before any conventional family event. Showers, nice clothes, cutting veggies and packing sandwiches for the girls. It's surreal, I thought. Unfortunately, I've felt that many times this year.

We rushed to the ceremony to be in time for the siren, and then, when it began, I felt the blow right to my gut. Gil-adush, who'd have thought I'd be thinking of you in the minute of silence during the Memorial Day siren?

I remember the feeling of wanting to feel the day, to connect to the fallen. I remember the attempt to concentrate during the siren and think about those soldiers and heroes who gave their lives for *Eretz Yisrael*, for *Am Yisrael*. I recall the effort to think, to find something to think about in order to feel, to identify with, to be part of it. And now all of a sudden it's you. What are you doing in all this? You hadn't even been drafted as a soldier.

"We so wanted to see you in uniform," Tahel would say the next day, reading words she wrote to share with the audience at the Wadi Hermia ceremony. Here's yet more evidence that it's impossible to separate the pain over your death from the national pain that forges *Am Yisrael* into a single unit. As if we need proof.

The need to get to another Memorial Day Eve ceremony at the Knesset doesn't leave us a chance to really connect with the event at Sultan's Pool; we're forced to leave the program in the middle. The moving from ceremony to ceremony is hard on the girls. They want to be in one place, to sit with the pain, with Gil-ad. What's with all the running from place to place? I feel tortured by their difficulty, by the public price they have to pay. I tried to prepare everyone for this not being our day of the year. We won't even have time to visit the grave.

I'm well aware that it won't be like this in the coming years, and we have to be grateful for this enveloping public remembrance. There's something in the embrace by *Am Yisrael* that strengthens, that provides death with some meaning. You can't know who's going to remember in future years, and you have to give thanks for the public awareness the episode generated, even at such a horrible price. There will be enough time for our private pain. I'm prepared to pay the personal price, but the family price pains me; I feel it's too much for the girls. I hope when they grow up they understand.

Wednesday, 3 Iyyar, April 22

Yom HaZikaron morning

The magical vistas of the Binyamin region conceal immense pain. An idyllic vista that promises infinite good, adorned on occasion by a swift passing deer or beautiful hyrax. The natural beauty is sometimes disrupted by a powerful red bloodstain that seems to discolor all of nature, leaving a mark on the vista, but even more so leaving a mark on so many people and their relatives. It's a manmade bloodstain, made by men who reveal their inhumanity in their choice to commit evil, to take life. A despicable choice made by people seeking to cause pain to others. People who were raised and raise their children to hate. Neighbors, physically close but ideologically and morally far, far away.

Not all of them.

Life in its complexity has taught us there are more than one kind. There are those who want to live together, who understand the good on both sides that emerges from this extraordinary connection. There are those who appreciate what the State of Israel gives them every day. In this area there are people who live as models of our ability to coexist.

But there are those who don't.

The trip to the ceremony in Wadi Hermia on Yom HaZikaron is long and uneventful. Deputy Commissioner Eitan Madmoni came to our house to accompany us today, in both senses – both with his calming presence, his becoming a true friend under painful circumstances, from the moment he appeared in our home at the beginning of the episode through all the days it continued, when he did everything he could to give help and support; and by literally escorting us to perform the technical work of clearing traffic ahead of us. Eitan is not just a policeman, but a mensch.

Approaching Hermia Junction there's traffic. Cars are slowing down, almost coming to a full stop. I can't help but think of the terrorist attack that took place here on March 3, 2002. A sniper took position on the adjacent hill and murdered seven soldiers and three civilians. Every year since, a memorial service for them has taken place at the Binyamin Regional Council. Here. Right here.

This year they wanted to remember Gil-ad. To talk about him.

I remember a sudden phone call I got before Pesach. A young woman from the Council called and asked permission to center this year's ceremony on Gil-ad. Shock. A stabbing feeling. The pain. My son... what's he doing as part of Yom HaZikaron ceremonies? What could he ever have to do with them?

Of course it's fitting to talk about Gil-ad on this day, but still, it's so hard to accept the fact that he's the subject of such an observance. I prepared myself for this public, national occasion, but the moment we got there and I saw all those familiar people, the teachers supervising the readings and recitations as I had done for my students, it hit me again, hard. I couldn't believe we'd become the objects of the day. That Gil-ad is at the center of Yom HaZikaron.

I look at the faces of the people who want a story, a poem, or skit so they can sense, feel, connect to the pain for a few hours – I was once like that. I would check over a ceremony I'd organized or in which I'd participated, and try to calibrate it to the sensibilities of the audience. I'd always focus on which poem to select, how the texts would be read, the background against which they would be recited; maybe I could find a selection that made things concrete, so the audience could connect, be moved, internalize and absorb the power of the words better.

And there I stood, tears flowing, as pain washed over me, absent any of those dramatic elements. The pain has resided deep inside me for months already. It's a pain that will not end when the ceremony concludes or when the day is over; a pain that doesn't require a poem or skit to be aroused; a pain that doesn't care whether a text is read one way or another. Just pain.

I don't know jealousy very well. *Baruch Hashem* I'm usually happy with my lot, but in this moment – what I would give to be like everyone else.

Tahel, our third daughter, spoke at the ceremony and moved everyone to tears:

> Jilder,
> That Friday morning when I got up and heard Imma worried on the telephone, I got ready for school as usual, and a few minutes before I left she said to me, "Gil-ad is missing but don't worry, they're looking for him."
> I thought to myself it had to be just some mix-up, but in my heart I sensed it wasn't like you not to answer your phone for no reason. That day I came home early from school because I didn't understand what was going on. I felt disconnected.
> I got home and there were tons of people and security forces. I noticed that Shabbat was getting closer but you weren't home. At Shabbat dinner we even set a place for you. Next to me.
> I waited for you.
> I hoped in my heart that tomorrow, at the next meal, you'd be sitting beside me already. That night I couldn't stop thinking about you, about where you were and how you were doing.

Shabbat afternoon I was told you were alive. It filled me with hope. Saturday night the house was pandemonium. News reports about you, all three of you! During those whole eighteen days, every time I got home and saw all the people and security personnel I thought the moment was at hand. You're coming back. But no. That's not what it was. I waited for you and kept imagining what I would say to you.

On Monday I was with friends at a barbecue and I got a bad feeling. At about nine o'clock a friend came over to me and said, "Tahel, you're being called home." I asked her, "What happened?" "I don't know," she answered.

I assumed the family was sitting down to dinner or something like that. On the way home I got a text: "Is it true they were murdered?" I turned off my phone.

I got home. There were so many people in the street, police and neighbors. I understood.

I said *Baruch Dayan HaEmet*. Blessed is the True Judge. I was told they found you.

Life has changed, Jilder. Nothing will ever be the same. So many people came to accompany you on your final journey. Your final words keep echoing in my head along with the cries of pain in that recording, "I've been kidnapped."

Now, Jilder, there are only girls in the house. I don't have a big brother. I don't have a brother anymore. I envy my friends who talk about their big brothers at home, in the army. I always dreamed you'd be a soldier but I never got to see that come true. You're missing in everything. Sukkot came and you weren't there to build the sukkah. Hanukkah, and you weren't there to light candles. On Purim you weren't there to bring joy.

> I missed you even more on Pesach. And now here we are at Yom HaZikaron, your day.
>
> You're missing, Jilder.
>
> I miss you so much, but I know you're protecting and watching us from above.
>
> I love you so much.
>
> Tahel

The ceremony ends and we rush to another one, at Mt. Herzl, for victims of terrorist attacks. The trip is relatively quick. Even where there's congestion Eitan impresses us with his modesty, without his siren, by clearing a path, and we arrive at the mountain about half an hour before the ceremony.

About ten months ago we joined a one-of-a-kind family, a family of wonderful human fabric, but one that nobody wants to join. A family whose fate is constant, unending sorrow.

A family for whom "longing" isn't merely a sensation, but a deep physical pain.

A specially selected family that has sacrificed its most select.

On this special day, Yom HaZikaron, a whole people tries to unite, hold, simply be and remember, to honor the fallen. On this special day past meets present, present meets future, a people grows from within the pain, paying a price for what it believes. The eternal people doesn't fear a long road. I was asked to speak on behalf of the bereaved families:

> Honored guests, beloved families,
>
> "Oh, G-d, do not keep silent."*
>
> At times silence is the most powerful sound in existence;

---

* Tehillim 83:2.

at times silence carries more than words can. The subtle, silent voice has accompanied the People of Israel from time immemorial, when Aharon the High Priest accepts the decree of his two beloved sons' deaths with, "*Vayiddom Aharon*," "And Aharon kept silent."*

Language and speech mean the ability to comprehend. The ability to communicate with one another. Music rises beyond language in its capacity to convey the emotional in ways that words cannot, but silence – silence rises even higher.

The unique nature of this day, Yom HaZikaron, is expressed in its characteristic silence. Everyone is silent (*dom'mim*) because everyone is bleeding (*m'dam'mim*). Silence is not ordinary muteness, but a cry so powerful it goes beyond words.

"I carry with me the sorrow of silence," Shlomo Artzi sang, the words of the poet Yaakov Orland:

> I carry with me the sorrow of silence
> The mute vista we once burned at fear's swell,
> For you said to me, "The city's so vacant"
> For you said to me, "Be silent together a spell."

Words cannot describe the depth of feeling, the depth of the pain. The sanctity of the day lies in its silence, unspeaking, wordless, hesitant, embracing glances. Let us be silent together for a while today. A still, silent voice, a whispered voice. A whispered prayer. Gil-ad's whisper in his final moments. Moments of prayer. A voice that stayed with us during that whole difficult period, the very voice that keeps strengthening,

---

* Vayikra 10:3.

growing to reach the whole world – what initiative, what courage, what strength for someone who had yet to reach the age of seventeen!

This mountain has known numerous sacrifices, the mountain of youth and of youths, as the poet Natan Alterman wrote in his poem "The Silver Platter":[*]

> And the land will lie still; the sky turns red
> Slowly fading
> Smoke at its rim.
> Then a nation will stand – heartbroken yet breathing...
> To receive the banner
> Alone...
>
> She prepares for the rite. She rises to the crescent moon
> tands before daybreak, garbed in festive fear.
> There emerge facing her
> A boy and girl, youngsters
> Before the People, together marching here.
>
> Wearing dust and belt, heavy shoes,
> They stride up the path
> Mute as they march.
> Their clothes they've not changed, let alone washed away
> The marks of hard labor, of night's line of fire.

---

[*] Natan Alterman, *Maggash HaKesef* ("The Silver Platter"), from *The Complete Works of Natan Alterman* (Hebrew), Vol. VII. HaKibbutz HaMeuchad, Tel Aviv, 1972, pp. 154-155.

> Endlessly tired, forsworn of rest,
> Bullets of Hebrew youths' dewdrops –
> Silent, they approach,
> And stand, unmoving.
> With no sign whether living or killed.
> Then the Nation asks, awash in charmed tears.
> She says: Who are you? And the pair, in their silence,
> Answer: We are the silver platter
> Upon which the State of Israel was given to you.
>
> Thus they will speak. Sheathed in shade, for her they fell.
> And the rest shall be recounted in the annals of Israel.

Here we stand in silence in our shared pain, as today we join with our loved ones whose names are forever etched on this stone wall and in our hearts – generations of adults, children, and adolescents dripping with "Hebrew youths' dewdrops," all coming together in Heaven with the three boys. We can only imagine that encounter in the supernal realm, the sounds, the silence, the bowed heads of all those souls above with those of ours here below. For thousands of years we have invoked the image and protection of our ancestors, the fathers and mothers of our people, asking for mercy in their merit. We continue to ask for Heavenly mercy, confident in the Redemption of Israel, but now also in the merit of the holy, pure ones who gave their lives for the survival of our nation.

All of us standing here with a sense of shared fate, of pain and loss, must cope day by day, hour by hour, with the impossible. At the same time, fate is not all we have shared through the years – we also share a destiny. The hope for a better future, greater faith that *Am Yisrael Chai*, that this people still lives, that it has a role to play in this world, and that its hour upon the stage of all human history is not yet complete. As we stand here in pain, bleeding, crying out without words, we wish to strengthen the sense of shared fate and destiny of the Jewish People.

Our hearts are with the bereaved mothers, the pained widows, the crying orphans and parents. Our hearts are with the soldiers and civilians, the wounded and hurting, citizens who shielded others everywhere in the Land of Israel with their bodies, their lives.

Ribono Shel Olam, Master of the Universe, look how much good there is in Your world.

The positive traits You planted in humanity, created in Your image, will overcome the negative. Our loved ones who are no longer with us, who believed in humanity and the good within, tried to bring more love and kindness into Your world. Those who attack us and try to destroy us may have harmed the bodies of our loved ones, but their souls and the soul of the Jewish People will live forever.

Together, we can confront the challenges that await us as a people.

At the end of the ceremony at Mt. Herzl we drove to meet Gilad's friends from the yeshiva. These are meaningful, encouraging encounters that don't require us to muster very much speech – they, too, know pain and longing.

Gil-ad's friends had started the morning with a visit to his grave at the Modiin cemetery, and expressed their heartfelt feelings through stories and songs. One of his friends, for example, recalled that when Gil-ad saw him all alone or looking down, he would immediately come over and cheer him up. Similarly, the friend continued, that was his mode, whether on any old day or on the previous Purim: whereas most of the guys were already half-drunk, Gil-ad stayed sober and was able to recognize the friend's loneliness on his face – and then drew him back into the circle of friends. He didn't let him get away with withdrawing and didn't give up on him.

After the meeting, a quick trip back home to shower and get ready for another drive to Jerusalem.

A platter of hot falafel, *pitot* and fresh hummus with a salad on the side was waiting for us on the table, as if we'd ordered it. A dear neighbor thought of what I hadn't: we were hungry, and had to eat. We packed the platter with us in the car, grabbed sweaters, and drove back to Jerusalem.

The juxtaposition of Yom HaAtzmaut and Yom HaZikaron has attracted a great deal of discussion in our country.

For years I've felt the juxtaposition appropriate; it is neither contrived nor incongruous. For years I've believed that it makes a foundational statement, that it serves a constructive didactic purpose. I've supported the notion that a country grows out of a sense of yearning and purpose, but no less from pain and brokenness. Now I am at once the pain, the grief.

How will I feel about the combination this year? The juxtaposition? How will I cope with the sharp transition from commemoration of the dead and the unbearable void to the joy of Yom HaAtzmaut? From the outset I took care not to make assumptions or develop expectations about it. I told myself: let's just see what the day brings.

And now, at the end of Yom HaZikaron, I find the moment reflects the pattern of my life over the last year: my soul is buffeted by the daily transition from dealing with the grief to engaging in life, by the constant experience of simultaneous sadness and joy.

Sometimes, specifically after many hours of torturous pain, my troubled soul stands to face it and asks for a bit of rest. That's what became possible for me when Yom HaAtzmaut began.

That transition, which seems so impossible, gives me strength, gives me encouragement. Today provides depth and meaning to the loss of our son and allows us to recognize some order in the midst of the chaos that has become our lot. We again feel the sweetness of connecting to our people and country, and our national pride expands within us.

Yom HaAtzmaut Eve Official Torch-Lighting Ceremony at Mt. Herzl

What a ceremony, what a moving occasion, twenty-first-century Zionism at its best! My chest swells with pride, wishing life for this people...

And what a people.

As we're busy finding a place to sit, the people in front of us rush to set a table with cookies and a thermos of hot green tea, and those sitting next to us contribute Turkish coffee and snacks. "Just warm up and enjoy," our neighbors oblige from every direction. "We've been coming here ten years. Only here, on this mountain, can you feel Yom HaAtzmaut – the songs, the tunes, the marches, the dancing, the torches – just a huge production in good taste," they add with a smile.

My heart is awash with warmth and love for a nation that has seen so much. *L'chayim* to this people!

Friday, 4 Sivan, May 22

Shavuot Eve

The Karov Lalev organization distributes a booklet shortly before the holiday, containing explorations by ten people of the Ten Commandments. I ask to write about the ninth, "Thou shalt not bear false witness against thy neighbor." I chose to focus on the point that truthful testimony is an expression of reality, whereas false testimony is a betrayal of purpose, of the human mission.

> The attribute of truth in our sources is a basic foundation of the constructive development of the world. Thus in the book of Micha it says, "Give *truth* to Yaakov," and the Mishna in Avot states, "Upon three things the world stands: upon judgment, upon *truth*, and upon peace," among other sources. However, writes the Rambam in his *Guide for the Perplexed*, ideas have become muddled and there is no longer a sharp distinction in our perception between truth and falsehood. Such absolute definitions exist only in the World of Truth. In our limited world good and evil have become less distinct, subjective, relative. That generates uncertainty – how do we function?
> How can we identify what's good and what's evil? What's true and what's false?
> Uncertainty takes me straight back to those *chai* days: *chai* days of waiting, of uncertainty as to Gil-ad's fate, as to the fate of Eyal and Naftali. A powerful sense of inner truth enveloped me

at that time – a feeling I cannot explain in words. It seems this feeling was shared by all three families, whether individually at the start of that crazy period, or together, as it continued and we united. Many asked me at the time: "Who was your adviser? Who was it who wrote messages and composed them?" To the surprise of many, the answer was: the voice of the listening heart and that voice of healthy reason. The voice of inner truth that comes from a deep place.

That inner truth found faithful partnership at that time with positive thinking. I did not allow negative thoughts in where they would undermine me. I strove to remain optimistic and focus on positive scenarios. That positive thinking radiated out to others around me and influenced me as well – not merely in my thoughts about Gil-ad, but in displaying patience with the government, with the security forces, and with the media. Positive thinking is no small thing. It requires working on yourself, a moment-by-moment struggle with obstacles and the maelstrom of conflicting opinions. Still, when I realized the choice was to stay on my feet or fall, I remained steadfast.

It's important to clarify: positive thinking is neither daydreaming nor naïveté; it is hard work that pays off immediately. It's a way to train oneself to seize life and draw strength. I used it to focus on what's important and to ignore scenarios that under other circumstances would likely have caused me great discomfort: people coming into my house, doing laundry, cooking, and cleaning. On a more internal plane, such thinking helped us get up in the morning and confront a difficult reality that seemed nearly impossible. It was a coping strategy that enabled us to conserve our strength and maintain our sanity in proper measure.

In retrospect, one might think reality slapped us in the face. I need not describe how my soul deflated or the tremendous pain when the bitter truth became clear about the murder of Gil-ad, Eyal, and Naftali, may Hashem avenge their blood.

So was all that striving for naught?

Perhaps the greatest discovery about positive thinking is its capacity to construct a balanced view of reality. Positive thinking doesn't alter reality or determine it; it enables us to look at it head-on. To absorb the infinite possibilities embedded within that are activated by our supernal Partner.

We could have lived the same reality with broken hearts, frustration, and pulling out our hair. But so what? Would it have turned out any better? Or would we have disintegrated, broken, and lost all determination to continue?

You can't determine or change reality; the question is how we look at it, how we cope with it best. Focusing on the good during that time gave us strength and enabled us to cope with a complicated situation.

I still swear by positive thinking. It's a tool I need in coping with loss and bereavement, in handling the unbearable pain and daily void. Hour by hour I look for things that will give me strength to continue, to progress and not sink. Positive thinking fills me with strength and enables me to cope with the inconceivable finality of loss; to focus on the good that's washing over us, on our wonderful nation, and on the constant embrace we receive that gives us tremendous strength; to appreciate what we do have, to hug our five fantastic daughters and to think about good things. Positive thinking finds expression not only vis-à-vis the surrounding reality, but in how we treat others – focusing on the good in another, looking for what I like about each person, "baseless" love. Exactly as we were privileged to see the beauty and the good of our entire people last summer – overflowing goodness, helping others, concern for our fellows, abundant love and heartfelt good. Baseless love that's so plentiful among our people burst forth in all its power during those *chai* days, and continued through the Protective Edge war, when concern and mutual responsibility found daily, hourly expression. I think last summer subjective good became a public legacy, almost an absolute truth.

Sunday, 6 Sivan, May 24

Shavuot

Every holiday brings its own set of difficulties. Where will we spend it? How will we celebrate? I, who loves the holidays so much and am always checking the calendar to see when the next one will be, have suddenly become afraid of them. I'd rather they wait another moment before landing on us as I find myself deliberating about what to do.

The main thing is to do something different.

The most important thing, I tell myself, is to make sure the holiday in no way resembles the way we celebrated it last year.

The invitation to go to Tel Aviv read my mind. I check with the girls and determine they're also interested in a change, and then we accept the invitation and prepare to spend the holiday in Tel Aviv for the first time in our lives.

The all-night learning we attended took place at the Tzavta Club, a venue for other types of activities on other days. But for several years they have held an open learning venue for the diverse Tel Aviv public, and people fill the rooms all night.

MK Aliza Lavie facilitates the learning with aplomb. The Tzohar Rabbinical Association contributes. Lecturers adhering to various, even extreme, ideologies are invited to conduct a different kind of discourse. Diverse issues of great importance to Jewish identity are the subject of panel discussions: prayer without a *siddur*, a different view of Pirkei Avot, growth through crisis, et al.

I find myself on a fascinating panel about prayer without a *siddur*.

Four educated, well-read colleagues describe for the audience the difficulty in connecting to the traditional liturgy. One suggests adding modern poetry; another speaks about modern narcissism that does not allow a self-centered person to connect to prayer, and wonders whether the time for the authentic *siddur* has passed. Almost all who spoke before me convince the audience it's possible to throw away the *siddur* in our time.

I seem to be fighting this battle alone, but as someone who feels a powerful personal connection to G-d and His presence, I pray I'll succeed in conveying at least some of that sense to the audience, specifically using the *siddur*. I ask the attendees to open the *siddur* and listen to the words. The language is flowery, the texts not always understood, but look, wonder of wonders, I tell them, everything that occupies a person in all aspects of life, all his concerns, all his wishes, all the gratitude and other feelings from sadness to joy, from pain to recovery, from perplexity to the quest for the self – that's all in the *siddur*.

It seems to me the prevalent view these days, that the Creator is obligated to listen to prayer and answer it, distorts understanding of the essence of the need for prayer.

Of course it's hard to pray to someone you can't see and whose answer isn't always comprehensible, but nevertheless, prayer seeks a role in our souls. It's an inner, essential need we all have as humans. The soul in fact prays all the time. Sometimes a person praying puts his entire being into the prayer, as King David writes in Psalms: "I am prayer."

Prayer is not a means to obtain things. Prayer is an attachment to the most exalted plane. It refines our hopes and intentions. It teaches us what to strive for and marks our life's path with guideposts. Sometimes, as Abraham Joshua Heschel writes in his book on prayer – which was published only recently [in Hebrew] but describes my feelings well – "Prayer is more than something to light our way. It is a light within us."

According to him, "the spirit that settled upon a person the moment he sings G-d's praises does not flow from any desire for practical results... as the ultimate expression of speech... in the end the goal of prayer... is to translate the self... to discover the self."

Gil-ad, in his journal, talked about a time he served as the "community's emissary," the prayer leader.

I never heard him lead the services.

He would shrink away from being *chazzan* in Talmon.

People talked quite a bit about his prayer. His father, his friends, whoever stood near him. Prayer time is a kind of barometer for our connection with the Creator.

When my prayer is heartfelt, deep, flowing, my connection with the Creator is deep and flowing. When my prayers are recited distractedly, I know I have to improve my connection to G-d.

A kind of spiritual index, if you will.

Hannah Szenes in "Walking to Caesarea" also seeks to affirm the eternal nature of the act of prayer itself:

My G-d, my G-d
May these never end:
The sand and the sea,
Water's rushing,
The sky's lightning,
Human prayer.

I ask the audience to examine the *Shmoneh Esrei* liturgy. Such refined words, such implications – all issues are in there. "Listen to the words," I tell them. "What could be more relevant? Could we, today, compose such words and distill our thoughts so accurately? Can our capacities alone ever succeed in perfectly and completely covering all the existential needs and wants that prompt prayer, and not merely what bothers each of us individually?"

I continue: "If, for example, during the *chai* days I had chosen only to focus prayer on my son, in my language, the language of the heart, and reject the *siddur*'s formulation, would that not have had an adverse effect on livelihood, health, and security? We're so focused on ourselves, and here come our Sages with an inclusive, comprehensive formulation that leaves sufficient space for the individual, but places it in an enveloping framework."

I pressed my argument with a challenge to them: "How can we give up this *siddur*, this text that preserved us as a people for two thousand years? What will we pass on to subsequent generations?

Can we so cavalierly say we don't need the *siddur* anymore?"

It's true that at our accelerated pace we find it hard to concentrate during prayer and to focus on it. Prayer requires preparation and review beforehand. Sometimes we can't understand the lofty language. Sometimes we find it hard to connect to the daily prayer without it simply becoming routine.

So we have a challenge, but the distance between that and giving up the *siddur* is huge. "G-d hears not only prayer, but the desire to pray," writes Heschel, and adds, "holiness is a critical need in our lives, and that need births prayer."

From the looks on the faces in the audience I see my words have fallen on receptive ears. *Baruch Hashem.*

Tuesday, 15 Sivan, June 2

One Year since the Murder: A Memorial

As with everything else this past year, preparation is the hardest part. I feel I've really aged over these months.

At a Torah scroll inauguration ceremony in honor of Gil-ad at the Ramat Aviv Air Force Base, Rabbi Shmuel Meir Lau, the Chief Rabbi of Tel Aviv-Yafo, asked me, "How are you? Aging gracefully?" I thought to myself: Aging? Getting old, really getting old, and not so gracefully.

King Shlomo, the wisest of men, taught: "One who increases knowledge increases pain" (Ecclesiastes 1:18), and perhaps he also meant knowledge of death. It's always an unknown. It's something we come to know without preparation, without being able to learn about it from books. Death encounters us suddenly; you'll never be ready. Even people whose relatives or friends died after a protracted illness are almost always surprised by death. It's not expected. You don't believe it'll happen. How much more so your sudden death, Gil-ad.

That sharp transition between to be and not to be, that almost impossible transition, still inconceivable, from your being so alive, so present everywhere – to such a gaping absence. Of course a dead body is called a "void" in Hebrew. Your death created a gigantic empty space, and the only thing we can do is cope with the emptiness it created and try to fill the space.

We decided to hold a private commemoration ceremony, as you would have wanted, with attention to the little details – an evening wholly dedicated to you, all for you – really, all for us. All year we shared you with an entire nation, almost an entire world, and sometimes we didn't put you in the center. Our activities alternated among the templates "*Am Yisrael*," "the Three Boys," and "the boys," but what about Gil-ad? What about our Jilder?

It was therefore natural that we dedicate the commemoration on the first anniversary entirely to you – to focus on your personality and stories about you, to give prominence to your so-joyful, joyous character, as reflected in the photos we saw over the last year.

We asked the speakers to send their remarks to us in advance so we could prepare properly. Every letter is heart-rending; every communiqué intensifies the longing, and the tears flow. I usually let the pain and crying out only at home, while outside I try to channel the agony into meaningful activity. I've never liked being a crybaby, and I wonder whether this time, at the commemoration, that will work. I watched the presentations; I read the speeches. The tears have already had their say. Will I manage to hold back the tears inside? Then up jumps an challenging thought from the other direction: maybe I'm not supposed to choke back the pain this evening. Maybe it's not only permitted, but a natural obligation to release it.

But it's not only the crying I want to release. I want to set free all talk of you. I want to finally shine a huge light on your personality, to talk about what you were, to lament the greatness that was cut short, to give you your due, to be completely with you, as we really are, parents and sisters, all year long. But all year long we're only with you when we're alone. Tonight I hope to bring people to you, together with us. Experience has taught us to let things happen and flow with them, without planning how to feel or whether we'll cry.

Just be; just hurt.

We opened the event to the general public, but retained our personal touch. For that reason we didn't invite politicians or public figures, whose attendance would require security or media presence. We wanted to be with Gil-ad. To be with those who want to be only with him.

The event hall in Talmon was standing room only with hundreds of adults and youths; the silence was chilling and dignified. I began with the following words:

> My beloved, Gil-ad, we miss you so much.
> I opened a new folder on the computer – "Memorial for Gil-ad." I'm accustomed to starting new folders for Bar Mitzvahs or Bat Mitzvahs, and there was a celebratory air in the house when we organized previous occasions – now I find myself organizing a memorial ceremony for my son, for a kid who never reached the aged of seventeen.
> We put together a slide show; we set up boards with pictures of you; we're getting ready for the wrong event. My heart breaks and my eyes are tearing up. Exactly a year ago I started a folder called "Gil-adush Come Home."
> The folder has filled up since then, but our lives have in a sense become empty... You were born a little more than seventeen years ago, a cute, chubby baby – 4.28 kilos of sweetness. It wasn't an easy birth. Not just for me; for you too. I felt your soul had undergone trauma when it emerged into the air of this world. For three days I had you on my belly, hugging you, trying to calm you, promising you the world is beautiful, good, positive, that you had nothing to worry about. You nursed nonstop for three days, cradled in my arms. In the hospital we lay for hours at a time, belly to belly, skin to skin. I felt you weren't calm, as if you were trying to go back where you came from.

Only after three days did I sense you were ready to separate from Imma, to experience some distance, to cope with the world. I put you in the carriage and we went to Kfar Batya, where we lived as a young couple. Shirel welcomed you happily, as if she didn't know older siblings are supposed to be jealous when a new baby comes home. She was only two, but it was love at first sight between the two of you – a one-of-a-kind of friendship that would grow stronger and richer as time passed; friendship that would weather the stormy tension and anger of adolescence; a bond of deep, wonderful friendship.

Spending hours being held, you loved being pampered as a baby – gaining a kilo each month. You liked to sleep in the morning in the cool and noise of the air conditioner; if I turned it off you'd wake up immediately. You gave us such joy with your winning smile. People stopped me at the bank, in the supermarket, melting at the sight of your smile and your adorable face.

When you were eight months old we moved to Petach Tikva, to the Hadar Ganim neighborhood.

Your hair was as long as a girl's and we did a serious photo shoot before we said goodbye to your golden locks at the *upshirin*, leaving a lock in the album as a souvenir. We held the ceremony with Rabbi Mordechai Eliyahu, of blessed memory, in Jerusalem.

I look at your photo album and see a happy, contented childhood. Trips, poses, smiles – no sign that this life would end too early, with such cruel suddenness. You were a good kid, who did as he was told, loved by your preschool teachers. It would take several years until adolescence would show itself, when you would begin to construct and develop your personality, sometimes by rebelling against the adults around you.

Not relenting, not conceding, stubbornly adhering to your opinion.

When you were three, Tahel joined the family. You hugged her so much; you loved her so much. You helped calm her, skillfully putting in her pacifier.

I especially remember the bedtime routine – after the neverending stories and songs, you loved to recite the bedtime Shema and take your time with it. During the counting of the Omer, which we completed not long ago, you made sure to take that wheat kernel we picked especially for the purpose, and stick it to the right numbered day on the chart we made together. Each evening you'd slowly recite all the verses that went along with it. It might have been more than a desire not to go sleep yet that was behind that dedication and innocence.

Meitar joined us when you were five, and you welcomed her, as well, naturally and lovingly.

The start of first grade was so exciting. I remember like yesterday the *siddur* party at the Morasha school, how excited you were and how seriously you performed your part in the production. You were happy at every celebration, every occasion. Liked by the teachers, loved by your friends.

You expressed our desire for a brother while I was pregnant with Hallel, when you were eight. You really wanted a brother, and we made sure to prepare you for another sister. You were disappointed, but within months of her birth, as you were playing with her in the living room, I heard you remark to little

Hallel, "Can you believe I wanted you to be a boy? You're so amazingly cute."

When you were in fourth grade we moved to Talmon. You integrated into your class with characteristic speed and smoothness. You were a loyal and devoted friend who gave each individual connection special depth. You showed great humility with your friends, aware as you were of your amazing abilities. When I heard the story about the remedial education teacher, I wasn't surprised. Your sensitivity and concern for your friends, which were so characteristic of you, run like a thread through your whole short life.

As a child you loved to share your feelings, experiences, and misgivings.

Only in the last year did I sense you maturing in that you shared less, opened up less, finding other circles in which to find a sympathetic ear.

Memories of the preparations for your Bar Mitzvah bring a special smile to my face. You were so excited; you threw yourself into practicing and preparing. At the celebration you were really happy, and you had in you a great deal of appreciation and gratitude for everything being done for you. Maor joined the family just a few months before your Bar Mitzvah, Gil-ad. This time we decided not to reveal it would be another girl, preferring to broadcast that no matter what it was, the main thing is health and happiness. You were sure this time you'd get your wish and you'd have a brother. You were so sure that when you were told of Maor's birth you started crying and protesting. We tried to appease you by saying that if until now you'd been a prince, from now on you'd be a king. All your sisters, from youngest to oldest, felt and continue to feel your great love for them. They all feel, each of them, your absence every single day, every single hour.

The selection of Mekor Hayyim as your yeshiva came about with no small measure of divine assistance. It took you time to adapt to the depth and seriousness of the learning. But you quickly pinpointed the difficulty as stemming from grappling with the change inherent in the transition, and you transformed the integration into the yeshiva and its study methods into a challenge. Your constant desire to progress and produce good results characterized everything you did – both socially and academically. The depth and the thinking involving the small details of everything, your joie de vivre, and your enjoyment of the little things in life became indicators of your smiling personality, while your desire to be special, Gil-ad, was fulfilled in an extraordinary fashion.

Few people have managed to make an imprint on their environment during their lives as you did in your short time.

Over the last year we've come to know your friends, the kids you counseled, whom you loved so deeply, and to whom you were endlessly devoted. Your friends have become our friends. To those who didn't know you so well, I will say about you, my son, "Tell me who your friends are and I'll tell you who you are." I want to thank the friends and the community who came here today to be with us.

Thank you for today and in general, for the tremendous embrace each moment over this past year; thank you to our wonderful community and the good friends we're privileged to have here and there. Thank you for being you.

Shirel spoke after me:

> Sitting on the shore, facing the water
> Facing the foam forgotten in sand
> Still the rivers flow
> A beating heart's memory o'er all is spanned.
>
> What we had as children
> What we've now become
> The wind carried great hopes
> Now back as memory's leaves in autumn.
>
> – Idan Reichel, "Now Closely"

Shabbat is coming, and my mood's not so great. It's been a week of questions such as, "Can you believe it's been a year?" I believe it, I get it, but I can't digest it. I can't digest life without you. I've heard "I can't believe it's been a year" quite a bit this last week.

This year, twelve months of coping, of lack, of pain. Of trying to maintain my joy at life when I want to cry. I miss you every day. My friend, as we've said.

I miss sending you a text when I'm tired or hot, to ask how you are today, to tell you I miss you. I wish we could talk a little, so I could ask about where to spend Shabbat or what to prepare for Maor's birthday, so you can be the big brother your sisters wait to see each day. Who love to tell everyone about the love you show them. Whom you made feel you were all for them. So that Imma can tell you about how the house construction is going, and you can get excited and help her choose colors for the kitchen.

A lot has changed at home. Each of your sisters is trying to find her place without you. We all have one thing in common – we try, even when it's hard, to be happy. Your joie de vivre is something we all share; it's a strong element.

You had strong love. I still can't grasp that you were and are no more. You're intensely present in our lives, present but different. In *Lecha Dodi* we sing, "The final product was planned aforethought." This year has been full of thoughts. Thoughts about what will happen, what you were, and what you are for us now.

Over the last year I've spent a lot of time in the desert, a place of quiet power that forces one's thoughts forward, those thoughts about the past. Imma has always said that thinking creates reality, so we have to think positive.

How is it possible to think positively in all this? What's positive here? I'm looking for a little good in all this enormous difficulty. I was with you for a little more than sixteen years. It looked like I was guiding you from up ahead, older than you by two years, but really I was only learning from you. Relishing the moment you were helping Imma in the kitchen in my stead.

Now I have to learn to do things, to establish a new connection with sisters who are so much younger than me, whose connection with you was so natural and strong.

Yesterday I was at the hitchhiking post where your life's journey ended. There were two people standing there, waiting for a ride onward. Your journey onward has ended, but for me it continues, and I'm sure, I know, that for many like me, your journey in this world, of loving life, of laughter and joy, of powerful love – that path is growing and developing, paved through learning about the person you were, the caring friend, the loving brother, the admiring son, the special character only you had.

I hope we succeed in only growing and continuing onward.

One by one, close friends from different circles stand up to tell their story, your story, to share a memory or the great pain that accompanies them since your death. Daniel Almaliach, a childhood friend from Hadar Ganim in Petach Tikva, talked about the courage you showed even as a little kid. Oriah Guri, a member of the Ofarim chapter, spoke about the scar your death left on her heart, and how much she misses you. Yehonatan HaLevi, your roommate and classmate at yeshiva, tried to tell you about everything that's happened over the last year, about how well you accepted and included people, and he related that you taught him to miss who you were and what you did. Aryeh Berman, your study partner, talked of the search for truth that characterized you and which did not conflict with your innocence and faith.

I remember the song "I Adjure You, Daughters of Jerusalem," that I dedicated to you, Gil-ad, once you were kidnapped, and which touched me in a special way. "I adjure you, daughters of Jerusalem: if you see my beloved, what will you tell him? That I am lovesick." Yes, I, your mother, am lovesick, and if you find him, if you find my son, as I remember during the search period and now, tell him I am lovesick. During the second portion of the evening Elyada bar-Shaul spoke, a close friend. He chose to compare your character, Gil-ad, to other seventeen-year-olds who lost their loves walking the trails of Israel. Holy boys whose deaths sanctified Hashem's name and enabled us to walk freely along those paths. With his sensitivity Elyada explained the concept of "*tzaddik*" and "holy," terms now attached to you, Eyal, and Naftali, to the youth in attendance.

We concluded the evening with the words of your father Ofir:

Morning services, 4 Tammuz 5774.

I finish the Psalm of the Day and my eye suddenly catches the strange words in the *siddur*, "The mourners recite Kaddish." Me? The Orphan's Kaddish? During the *chai* days I stood at my place in the synagogue, just a few seats away from the mourners reciting Kaddish together. For *chai* days I stood, my lips full of prayer that Gil-adush return and I won't have to move seats to join that group. But G-d desired otherwise, and in our yard at home I began: **"May His great name be made majestic and sanctified."** A year has passed and G-d's name has been made so great, in your merit, Gil-adush, and in the merit of Eyal and Naftali. A year has passed and the three of you have been instrumental in so much sanctification of the *Ribono Shel Olam*'s name. How much sanctity and exaltation we have experienced alongside the inconceivable pain and sorrow!

"In the world He created as He willed it; in which He will establish His kingship; and sprout His deliverance; and bring close His anointed."

In the world You created as You desired we waited along with all of *Am Yisrael* for deliverance, to see you, Gil-adush, here in this event hall, at a thanksgiving feast. In our yard, representatives of polar opposites sat side by side, and they all wanted only for you to come back. We really though Mashiach was so close.

"In your lives, and in your days, and in the days of the whole house of Israel, speedily and soon; and say Amen."

Each day that passed in the hope you were alive added intensity to a life of unity and connection among the House of

Israel, who prayed to see you return home quickly and soon.

"Amen. May His great name be blessed forever and for all eternity."

Our Sages said: "At the moment when Israel enters the synagogues and study halls and responds 'May His great name be blessed,' G-d nods His head and says, 'Happy is the king who is thus praised in his house.'" Gil-adush, masses of Jews gathered here in the synagogue and in synagogues all over the world and answered, "May His great name be blessed," and the heavens themselves were broken open as barriers of the heart were broken down on earth. Our Sages have said that the recitation of "May His great name be blessed" out loud and with full focus and intensity tears apart any decree made against a person. Your decree was sealed, but that of so many others was undone in response to such mass prayer.

"May the name of G-d, blessed is He, be blessed, praised, glorified, exalted, elevated, made splendorous, uplifted, and lauded."

Since that day, for eleven months, three times a day, I bless, praise, glorify, and laud Your name, G-d, and in those moments I want to remember and hug you, Gil-adush.

"Beyond all blessing, song, praise, or consolation spoken in the world; and say Amen." We so wanted the prayers for your welfare to become blessings, songs, and praises, and all we are left with is prayers for consolation. A year has already passed without you, and all we are left with is the pictures, videos, stories, and moments seared into our hearts, forever.

"May great peace from heaven and good life be upon us and upon all of Israel; and say Amen."

Like an unending flow that began with a fine spray, great peace has begun to flow from heaven into all of our hearts. We've learned to appreciate and thank G-d for life, simple life, and with great humility to ask that it be a good life, and with amazing unity to ask it for ourselves and all of Israel.

Day follows day until eleven months pass; the third of Nisan arrives and my voice goes silent; my neighbors in the synagogue Yissachar and Betzalel continue to recite the Orphan's Kaddish, and I continue with them in my heart.

Gil-adush, you will rest in peace and we will continue to pray: **"He who makes peace in His supernal realm will in His mercy make peace upon us and upon all of His people Israel; and say Amen."**

And He who makes peace, bring peace mercifully among us all, with ourselves and our spouses, with our families and our neighbors. Watch over our Gil-adush, a boy full of youth, joy, and innocence.

I, who have finished reciting the *Kaddish Yatom*, Orphan's Kaddish, wonder to myself whether it makes more sense for it to be called *Kaddish HaTom* – the Kaddish of Innocence.

Morning: Visiting the Grave

We wanted to visit the grave with only the nuclear family: us and the girls. For the first time we also brought the younger ones.

The gravestones were placed on the date of the *yahrtzeit*. For an entire year, we went through a search process and thought about how to design and erect a monument that is at once both personal and national. Many good proposals came our way, proposals by extraordinarily talented, sensitive people. After a careful examination we selected the proposed design of our friend Moshe Shapira, an architect; we and the other families agreed it best expressed what was in our minds and hearts. Power and meaning radiate from the stones.

In another *chai* days, on the anniversary of the bodies being found, we'll hold a big public commemoration.

This year we'll move back and forth between two dates: the day of the murder and the day the boys were found. This year I again felt how long *chai* days can be.

From the cemetery we went to the yeshiva in Kfar Etzion, for a morning of memory with Gil-ad's friends. Avi Fraenkel and Ofir were incredibly moved. "Our heart is with you here, in the yeshiva," they would tell the friends. "Here is where the heart is; here is where the pain bursts out," they would both say, occasionally wiping a tear from their cheeks.

Wednesday, 16 Sivan, June 3

Unity Day

Unity Day is an initiative of Jerusalem Mayor Nir Barkat and the three families, run through the Gesher association. Through the day we receive reports of all the successful programs, about joint religious-secular projects, of young and old working together, left wing and right. Discussion circles are held at various locations, in addition to, of course, joint volunteer activities to distribute chocolate or cold drinks, all for the sake of unity.

The pain strikes deep in my chest, along with a feeling of exaltation that masses within me. "My heart is bursting" takes on physical meaning and form: a feeling of confusion, almost dizziness, the likes of which I never knew until a year ago. I feel like any second now my heart really will burst because it can't take the depth of the intensity, of the polarity, of the pain, and of the absence.

In the evening we gather at the President's House for a presentation of the first Jerusalem Unity Prizes. The idea for the prize first came up during the Shiva, during a visit by Nir Barkat to our house, when he came to offer condolences and find a way to memorialize the three boys in a meaningful way. The visit led to a strong friendship with a dear man working to advance unity in Israeli society.

We're happy and proud to have this privilege, and to be hosted at President Reuven Rivlin's official residence. We feel his embrace and his support for our efforts all the time, ever since his speech to the mass rally at Rabin Square a year ago.

The intensity increases, and we sense the divine presence has descended on the President's House, even if only for a moment.

Four institutions and private people working for unity with more than mere words have been selected to receive the first annual Jerusalem Unity Prize:
- Ram Shmueli and the Mit'chabrim organization, who have for a long time worked to deepen the sense of unity in society. Ram manages to bring together dozens of people for discussion circles, people who don't know one another – to talk in a civilized fashion about such issues as Jewish identity, the purpose of the Jewish State, and who is Israeli.
- Raya and Yosi Ofner, who lost a son in the 1997 helicopter collision, and who walk the Israel Trail with groups that bring together all the various shades of Israeli society.
- Rabbi David Menahem HaKohen, who uses song and creative discussion to rouse the hearts of the diverse crowd who comes to hear him every week.
- Nehemia and Nehami Wilhelm, Chabad emissaries, who in their patient and loving manner have woven in their Bangkok home into a single amazing fabric of Israelis and Jews who come to visit them each year.

Unity Day and the Jerusalem Unity Prize will become a tradition surrounding the boys' *yahrtzeit*, 15 Sivan, in Israel and abroad. It's a day that brings to a climax the meaningful work being done toward social unity, intensifies it, and attempts to give it prominence in public discourse and the media.

Saturday, Shabbat Parashat B'ha'alot'cha, 19 Sivan, June 6

It's been a year.

The town is organizing a communal Shabbat. Rabbi Yehoshua Shapira and his wife Naomi come to spend Shabbat with us, just like last year. The Third Meal is communal. We sing and talk. We sing and remember.

It's impossible not to recall these exact moments, right now, of that Shabbat a year ago. Those moments won't leave my heart – gathering in our garden, the singing, the prayer, and the hope. Today, looking back, when we're more experienced and battered by the year that's passed, I can say the hope infused us with strength, the oxygen we needed to survive the days of worry, of paralyzing fear; but the finality of it all is sometimes harder to handle.

Day by day the pain increases and the longing intensifies. This year, this Shabbat weighs more heavily on me.

A year. So long. So short.

Conflicting experiences have become a central motif in our lives over the last year, coloring so many moments with daily struggle. Still, we have chosen not to sink into the pain. We've chosen to take the pain in the direction of action and empowerment, to channel the longing into commemoration efforts.

This week we reached new heights. The whole week we've been moved by learning of all the wonderful activities by our people in Israel and the world; we've felt moments of exaltation, such as at the President's House, when we awarded the Jerusalem Unity Prize to people whose purpose is doing good things, to people who work for, and don't merely talk about, unity.

Nevertheless, it was impossible not to feel your absence in every cell of our bodies, Gil-ad. It was impossible not to remember what led us to these moments. My heart just breaks. Two conflicting emotions are trying to inhabit the same space, and my soul finds no rest; my body will explode any moment from the intensity. No outsider could understand.

So what is there in this unity? What have we found in it? How have we drawn so much power from it? Anyone who wants to taste the good inherent in *Am Yisrael*, anyone who wants a whiff of unbounded giving, of the bonds and connections among different streams in the Israeli milieu, should come and take a look at my cell phone for a short time, and be filled with positive energy.

It seems that an opening has been created. When the prize was awarded, about forty-five different places in Israel were holding discussion circles. Who'd have believed it? Last year I aimed to have three such circles take place, and the organizers thought I was too ambitious. We're progressing by leaps and bounds. The connections and huge embrace have expanded beyond Israel. From different places, the Jews of the Diaspora are saying to us, "We're with you; we might be far away physically, but in our hearts we're completely with you."

Last night I got a WhatsApp message from a precious Jew, a Lubavitcher from India. He wanted to share videos and photos of wonderful Chabad activities all over the world. I accepted gladly and the pictures flowed: separating challah in Manali, India; affixing a mezuzah in New Zealand in the boys' memory; studying *Chasidut* in Kfar Chabad; putting on *tefillin* in New Zealand; educational activities for children in Delhi; studying *mishnayot* in Rubana, Ukraine. Remembering and connecting. Remembering and embracing.

We get an especially large embrace from Rabbi Shai Shechter and his wife Rina, who live in New York. The whole year they've been calling, texting, and encouraging us. Each week we get a beautiful bouquet of flowers from them for Shabbat, with warm, touching words, as if they're trying with all their might to take away some of the pain that surrounds us. So much warmth, so much love.

Not only that: this wonderful couple came to Israel just to be with us during the week of the memorials, and they can't believe the wonder in our voices at their simple presence by our sides during such a meaningful week for us. "We're with you," they say, "all the Jews of America are with you." It's impossible not to think how much power is generated by that unity.

About six million Jews live in Israel, while another seven or eight million live in the Diaspora. If we internalize the fact that we're a nation of 13-14 million people, we'll understand we're a real force against those who seek to destroy us, and we'll progress to the next step, a crucial step in consolidating moral power: looking positively at others, recognizing that together we are a firm, solid foundation, realizing we have more in common than what divides us, and accepting one another as we are. What's more, we'll celebrate differences, complexity, and the special diversity that characterizes our people. Difference is constructive, formative, expansive, and challenging. Differences are real, and real pluralism means not trying to fit every Jew into a single template, but to accept each one as is.

During the Shiva the whole House of Israel crowded into ours. I was reminded of our Sages' statement in Tractate Nedarim: "Anyone who checks up on a sick person removes one sixtieth of his pain." I asked myself whether that applies to my situation. Could each visitor take away a sixtieth of the pain and make it easier to cope with? Reality, however, had its say, and the supply of pain is infinite. Despite the numerous visitors, the pain didn't lessen.

But the visitors did provide the strength and encouragement that enabled us to continue onward. We owe a special thank you to the amazing community of Talmon, who enveloped us from the first moment and has stayed with us through today. You can't face catastrophe alone, and we're full of gratitude for everyone's help and support.

Tuesday, 29 Sivan, June 16

For the last week and a half I haven't been able to function, to recover. Pain again floods over me, sticks its fangs into me and won't let go. I feel like it's the end of the world.

Yesterday we went to Hallel's clarinet recital, and today I'll be going to Maor's end-of-the-year party at preschool. I'm trying to be with them, for them, but not really succeeding.

My thoughts wander to this time last year – the height of the *chai* days. I dropped everything to be with Hallel for a short time, at her end-of-year recorder performance. I remember the strength I had to muster in order to leave my concern for you, Gil-ad, the search odyssey, the meetings, behind – or aside – and just be with Hallel. I remember how I willed myself to smile and put on a cheerful face for Maor's end-of-year preschool party so I could be with her as she celebrated, to clap and get excited at every song or dance, while inside my heart was being torn apart with worry, as I tried with all my might not to let disturbing thoughts control my emotions, but to direct them to the here and now – to be at the end-of-year party, for the girls. To be a mother.

It was so hard then, and it's so hard now. I feel like I'm not really succeeding at it right now. Maybe G-d gave us *chai* days of kindness last year so we could live through another set of *chai* days. I never thought for a moment, as I was with the girls at their end-of-year parties, that you were no longer alive; maybe we got those days as a gift so the girls could finish the school year and the celebrations before tremendous sadness would descend on the family, before the days of mourning would cross our threshold.

And now my heart is torn in two; I can't reconcile myself to being apart from you. I can't manage to stop crying; I can't stop wanting another hug from you, another touch, another moment with you.

It's true that living with constant uncertainty is impossible, but it turns out that living with the certainty of finality is also impossible. It's like cutting off air passages inside. It threatens to derail you from a normal life. That pain can't be taken away. The tears splash as I step over the threshold.

Tomorrow there will be a special event in Park Raanana called Sing Brothers – an evening of song for the sake of unity, inspired by the evening of song in Rabin Square last year the day before the boys were found. The tension described by the media – the social divisions, the lack of listening, and the unwillingness to affirm others – is intolerable. I'm supposed to speak there, but words won't come to me.

I feel so empty.

Ta-te, I'm tired. Can't You stop the train so I can get off?

Apparently not...

The Omnipresent has many paths available.

My eyes catch a piece of mail from this morning: a letter from someone I don't know. I thought it was just another of the thousands of letters that came to us over the last year. Each with something to contribute, each with its own sweetness.

> Now that a year has passed since that horrific night, and in honor of the Unity Day in the memory of the three boys, I want to write down my feelings, an anonymous guy who knows none of the families. I was a yeshiva student (I've since married)

from abroad (New York), studying at a yeshiva in Jerusalem.

The sense of "Israel camped [singular case] facing the mountain" – as one man, we all felt. The concern, the recitation of Psalms, the prayer assemblies, the pain, your faith, and the grief.

After I came back from the funeral I spoke to a (Haredi) *mashgiach* at a yeshiva, whom I saw there, and asked why he went. He answered, "For three weeks I've lived with these boys – how could I not attend their funeral? It's like the funeral of a family member!" That really was how we all felt.

But I wanted to add a story the likes of which you may not have heard.

My grandfather (who passed away two weeks ago) suffered from dementia for years. He had almost no short-term memory. What he had for breakfast, what day of the week it was, what holiday starts tomorrow – he knew none of those things. He didn't know his own physiotherapist's name. But when the therapist came in, he asked, "What's with the boys?" He remembered them as if they were his own family; it just entered his soul. The love and unity at that time crossed all boundaries and broke through all barriers, and I pray that spirit continues and grows, and in its merit we meet deliverance.

May their memory be a blessing.

Air is starting to return to my lungs. I take a few deep breaths. My energy is getting slowly restored. What an amazing people we have, I muse, and I already have an idea about what to speak about tomorrow.

How will I say it? G-d knows – "Hashem, open my lips and my mouth will relate Your praises."

319

Friday, 2 Tammuz, June 19

We visit the grave again, this time with friends and extended family, to mark a year since the bodies were found.

Rani Sagi, our dear friend, chooses to dedicate his illuminating words to the link between the name Gil-ad and the *gal-ed*, the monument that our father Yaakov erected, and proceeded to explore the multiple meanings and interpretations of the term "monument": a parting command to continue on our path; the soul itself, since a person's soul remains intact even after his passing, and since it demands of us the power of the soul for life, to provide strength, to create souls. Hillel Darshan, a study partner of Gil-ad's from the yeshiva, recalled how he learned from Gil-ad how to pray, and how the ability to pray became accessible to the whole nation as a result of the kidnapping.

Revital, Ofir's sister and Gil-ad's aunt, read a poem she wrote. I also spoke:

> A year...
> So little time, it seems like only yesterday. And yet so much time... it feels like I haven't seen you in years.
> So much sadness and grief; so much life.
> So much pain and longing; so many moments of spiritual exaltation.
> Everything is still so delicate and fragile. There's so much activity and yearning for stability.
> So inconceivable, so palpable, So little and so much.

The extremes that have become a central motif of our lives this past year characterize many of the moments in the daily struggle that's been forced upon us.

My Gil-adush, so beloved, you left so suddenly and I didn't have a chance to say goodbye. In my last text message to you I wrote, three days before you died, "I miss you... we want you home..." You wanted to go to a friend's house for Shabbat, and I uncharacteristically asked you not to: "Definitely not..." You asked why and I answered, "I miss you... we want you home..." How little I understood what missing you is, what wanting you home is.

"I'll be there some other time," were you last written words to me.

I came to understand many things this year that I never understood before. Perhaps I even learned what the "knowledge" is of which King Shlomo speaks when he says, "One who adds knowledge adds pain." And maybe I also learned what humility is – the ability to live without understanding, to accept reality with all its difficulty, with the fact that it's sometimes unbearable, seemingly impossible.

What is it about death that breaks us down, that crushes us to pieces?

What is it about death that draws us so far downward? What is it about death that gradually squeezes away all my strength? That breaks, that closes in. Endless longing that throws everything off kilter. Pain that exhausts me, that makes me so tired, that pushes us down, down, that floods me with tears and powerlessness, with burning in my heart. It just hurts and hurts. "Rachel weeps for her children, refusing to be consoled."

What is it about life that makes you want to keep living?
What is it about life that makes us want to get everything out of each moment? What is it about life that moves the soul within? That encourages us to do, to achieve, to advance, that pushes us forward to get involved? That it's important to us to leverage life, to give it meaning, to keep going even when we're tired? Some internal power, some unexplainable drive – to live, to be happy, to smile.

To keep your smile going, Gil-ad.

You left so suddenly, without warning. You left us a goal, a path. In your death you commanded us to live.

The soul always seeks respite, serenity. "*Ribono Shel Olam*, Master of the World, provide proper respite." What is that "respite," that rest? Perhaps the feeling of fatigue that fills us after our daily attempts to cope, a respite from pain, from the fears that dog us, that are with me all the time along with the burden and pain that have been with me for a year already. A desire for rest.

And what's "proper" rest? The word *nachon* also means prepared, ready for action. The departed soul is ready to accomplish things with power it never had in this world, but perhaps will find up there, close to the divine presence. Proper rest.

"Avraham will rejoice, Yitzchak will sing out, Yaakov and his children will rest on it" – even the fathers of the nation came to their rest with a smile.

"A rest of love and of generosity; a rest of truth and of faith; a rest of peace and calm, of quiet and security." It's been a year of increasing our unconditional love, the generosity among our people. Truth and faith lead us on our path. We seek peace and calm even in this turbulent world.

"A complete rest that You desire; may Your children recognize and know that from You comes their rest, and in their rest they will sanctify Your name.
"You are one and Your name is one."
We lack the capacity to understand.
May your soul be bound up in the bond of eternal life.

We etched on the stone: "Is Efraim a precious son to me; is he a playful child, that when I speak of him I remember him more and more?"

It's interesting that among the thousands of letters we got, I found a treatment of that verse from an interesting personal angle. Carmela Amitai Yechezkel is one of the outstanding women of our generation. From the address on her envelope I saw she lives in Jerusalem. I don't know how old she is. In the months following the murder she wrote me some pearls from time to time. I saved all her letters. Her words are precious, valuable. Nobody writes that way anymore. Her style is eloquent and one of a kind, woven with references from classic Jewish texts, attesting to an extraordinary breadth of horizons. She admits she doesn't handle typing so well and loves penmanship's authenticity. Her handwriting is so artistic, and her writing style indicates tremendous knowledge of Tanakh and Jewish philosophy.

Before Rosh HaShanah I received New Year's greetings from her on a nostalgic postcard. Without intending to, by referring to a verse in the Haftarah for the second day of Rosh HaShanah, she gave her own interpretation to the words we chose for the gravestone.

> It seems to me each bereaved family that has experienced the loss of a child feels like a limb has been severed from the body. Each family has its Efraim, its playful child, but what's special about this verse is its emphasis on the memory of our Father

in heaven. He's the one who remembers, who talks about it. Many *mitzvot* were given to us involving our remembering, but here, G-d shows us the value of memory even beyond the communal: when a person talks to or about someone, it means he remembers him, but here memory stands out on another level. *Zikaron*, memory, from the world *zach*, pure. Memory isn't passive; it changes reality and consciousness in a person. It's a kind of soul connection not with what was, but what is eternally present. This divine memory illuminates human memory and moves it.

I hold the deep hope that here, too, He who illuminates your steps on this odyssey also recharge you using the batteries of memory unique to Him. By the way, when the word *od*, more, appears at the end of a verse, it means something completely different from when it is in the middle. In the middle of a verse it is understood as a neutral linking word, whereas at the end of a verse it is infinitely magnified, to the utmost, as when Yosef meets his father Yaakov again: "He cried on his neck *od*." There is nothing deeper or higher than that.

I met her not long ago. An amazing woman. The written encounter has grown into meaningful meetings that fill my soul.

Monday, 5 Tammuz, June 22

The phone rings. On the line is a dear woman from Ramat Aviv:

> Dear Bat-Galim, I just got back from the U.S. and I have to share this with you. I was at the graduation ceremony for my granddaughter's Jewish school in Manhattan. The rabbi of the school got up to bless the students, and told them a story you have to hear. A few weeks ago he went shopping at a local supermarket. Ahead of him in line at the checkout stood an old man who took out a credit card to pay. When he took it out, a piece of paper fell out of his wallet, with the names of the three boys.
> The rabbi told his students that he was quite moved. In the middle of New York, there's a Jew who knows the boys? He asked him if he knew them. The man answered he didn't know them personally, but put their names in his wallet with his credit card to remind himself every time he pays with the card, that these boys paid with their lives for being Jewish.

Chills.

"And that's the message I'm bringing back to you," she concluded, emotional.

Indeed, I think to myself, that's the story of our people.

Wednesday, 7 Tammuz, June 24

A year and a day.

The pain exposes new frequencies of intensity at different moments.

A year and a day. For several moments the longing increases, enveloping my soul. For a few moments it lets go a bit.

A year and a day. The word "coping" has taken on a practical, exhausting meaning; it's the most routine word out of our mouths now.

A year and a day. I can answer, "How are you?" with "Everything's fine," without my stomach contracting.

A year and a day. People have gone back to their daily routines.

A year and a day. The commemoration efforts are taking on unparalleled dimensions.

A year and a day. The lessening pain looks for its place.

A year and a day. Tremendous uncertainty about the second year.

Thursday, 8 Tammuz, June 25

Edges

People don't like being on the edge.

It sounds unpleasant. We usually prefer to belong to the mainstream, the center. The extreme is threatening, stressful. Even in the physical sense the edge implies something sharp, easily falling, unbalanced, unstable, limited. In the human sense as well – it's not easy to be at an extreme. A person at an extreme is outside the consensus, expressing thoughts outside the acceptable range.

This year we encountered two human extremes: the height of evil and the height of goodness. It's shocking how evil people can be, taking their free will and directing it toward the worst possible ends. Murder, hurting, violence, and on the same plane – insensitivity, emotional attack, numbness, neglect of commitments, to the point of causing great harm to others.

Until the murder I was sure my greatest trial was in having our house built. We've been doing it for six years already. After Gil-ad was kidnapped a contractor from a neighboring town came and promised to finish it properly and quickly. We were supposed to move in by Pesach. But promises and deeds are separate things.

We went through so many contractors, so many upheavals, encountering so many professionals who didn't finish their work on time and kept demanding more money. Major grief. And in fact, when the summer came, when we were supposed to move out of our current residence, the house wasn't ready.

Ta-te, we can't handle any more trials now. Your hug is too tight; please let go a little.

Monday, 12 Tammz, June 29

Everyday banal struggles bother most of us. Who will pick up the kid from preschool; when will we get a new car; when's our next vacation. Suddenly the Angel of Death appears at the door, and opens a new, unfamiliar one. He presents a fait accompli that requires grappling with a new conceptual world with scenarios we've never experienced: grief, loss, gaping lack, a void that can't be filled.

I'm learning to cherish the moment. I'm trying not to turn into a panicky mother, to let my daughters go where they want. It's not fair that my personal pain and agitation limit them, I murmur to myself occasionally. Still, something in my basic trust in life has been damaged. The instinctive initial assumption for most people, that we'll live a long life, isn't so steady now.

Death suddenly becomes possible. It's part of our discourse. It's with the girls from such a young age. Nothing can be taken for granted.

I register the girls for summer camp. They should be busy, enjoy themselves. My summer will no longer be like previous ones. The vacations I loved will likely also change. Summer camps remind me of you, Gil-ad, an admired counselor.

At one of the discussions I had with teens, some Talmon youth were also present. I told them about your special quality of responsibility that showed itself in so many realms. Never, for example, did I have to remind you to study for a test. I never had to tell you to do homework. Your responsibility showed in social contexts, as well. You always said if yeshiva were fun, everyone would learn better.

You participated in organizing activities in yeshiva and the local youth chapter. You always took care of birthday parties for all your friends. You remembered everyone; you knew how to make everyone feel special. To give the proper attention to each person. You outdid yourself as a counselor.

And yes, even your last telephone call, the moment you realized you'd been kidnapped, was an act of responsibility. What can I do? Call the police. Wait for a moment of the captors' inattention and make a call without their noticing. Responsibility.

Immediately after my talk a girl comes up and tells me she didn't know Gil-ad personally, since the activities in their chapter aren't coed, but continued: at a scouting camp that took place two years ago, after ninth grade, the whole grade went to camp together. One evening the friends were sitting around joking to pass the time, chucking and telling stories that echoed in the air. At one point the group dispersed; most of them went to walk around the camp, to meet new people, to find members of the opposite sex.

Out of the corner of her eye she noticed Gil-ad staying where he was. He took out a book and started learning. "It's so much like the Gil-ad you talked about," she said with a half-smile.

I was so moved to hear the story. That's what you were like, Gil-ad; you knew how to integrate and precisely balance joking and seriousness, frivolity and depth. As if you insisted on living King Shlomo's statement: "There is a time for everything, and a moment for each purpose under Heaven."

And another story from that same camp, a camp known for gatherings beloved by the campers: challenging discussions, new friendships, and inter-chapter connections. Everyone wanted to be known, to stand out, to be in the center. It's natural.

One camper, less accepted by the others, kept mostly to himself the first few days. Gil-ad spotted him by chance. From that moment he stayed with him and encouraged him. After a few days the girls asked: who's the camper walking around with that cute counselor?

Tuesday, 20 Tammuz, July 7

Today began at Oz Vegaon Hill at a meeting with the commanders and scouts who participated in the search.

The hill, which overlooks Gush Etzion Junction, became a tourist site the day the boys were found, and was named after them: the *gimmel* of Gaon for Gil-ad; *alef* for Eyal; and *nun* for Naftali. Some of the participants recalled for us the decision-making process and the searches themselves. Some told of the soldiers' enthusiasm and their refusal to go home before the boys were found.

A convoy of armored military vehicles escorts the families to Hurvat Arnav, the second stop on our tour. I hadn't considered the military logistics necessary to reach the place where the boys' bodies were found. A hail of stones greets us, to remind us the breathtaking view is a profound illusion that masks a protracted ideological conflict between two nations over the land of Hevron.

The army embraces the families warmly today also.

It's clear to the commanders that we have to be here, and they do everything to make the tour go as smoothly as possible.

A small group of friends and close relatives arrive. They hear things directly from the people who found the boys, recite Kaddish and Psalms and hug one another while singing quietly and powerfully, with songs which absorbs the salty tears falling down everyone's faces.

Gil-adush, in this place I feel you so close. I stand on the land of Hevron, where the awful murderers buried your body and the bodies of Eyal and

Naftali. I feel it's the closing of a circle. The thought that I won't be able to come here whenever I feel like it, makes it very hard to leave. I hug you tight in my heart and refuse to go. Just a little longer. A little more.

The clock is ticking. The brigade commander announces the end of the meeting. With a heavy heart I take one last look at the dry ground, the quiet ground that miraculously told its story and revealed its secrets.

The scale of the miracle becomes larger considering the huge territory spread out before us. The expression "finding a needle in a haystack" takes on special relevance when we look around and wonder how they managed to find the boys.

I suddenly realize how relative everything is. I thought eighteen days was a long time, excessive, unending. Suddenly I realize how little it is. So confusing. The time could have been doubled or tripled without the manifest intervention of Divine Providence.

It simply couldn't be taken for granted that our sons would be found.

Monday, 11 Av, July 27

Packing

They say new troubles make you forget old ones. Is that so?

In the last two months construction of our new home has inexorably become the main pursuit in our lives. The fact that we'll have to move out of our current place by the end of the year forces us to go on despite all the difficulties. We have to do everything to avoid suffering an additional move. From here, I thought, the only place we're moving is our new home.

Thus I found myself skipping from a commemoration to the ceramics store (to choose wall coverings). From an exciting meeting with the architect to choosing a gravestone for my precious son. From choosing interior doors to planning another memorial event. Harsh transitions of body and soul have become our daily routine over the last year.

And here the Creator reminds us who's in charge. A person can and must plan, can and must try, but in the end we depend on His will. It seems that in terms of the house, our clocks aren't synchronized with G-d's. We have to move out and our new place isn't ready. Our efforts didn't help in this case, and not only in this case.

I'm on the brink of collapse.

Ta-te, I need strength to handle the big things.

We pack, we clear shelves, organize drawers. Too bad you can't just pack up your thoughts in a box. We've learned that with hard work you can control them, but sometimes all I want to do is pack them away on the side somewhere.

The Drawer System of organization teaches that an organized drawer means an organized soul. So true; so searing. I've spent a lot of time this year organizing my thoughts, my soul, my character traits. Grappling with grief means an opportunity to encounter myself, my husband, my children, and reorganize stuck relationships. Unfortunately, at the same time grief also summons mistakes and rough spots in relationships that used to flow smoothly.

Time won't let me do a thorough sifting and filtering of the clothes and papers in the house, but I do snatch a few hours of this compressed time to do some organizing. Proper packing will make this temporary transition much easier.

I leave your closet for last. There are still a few drawers waiting for me to take care of them. Most of my time is spent deciphering your journal, commemorating, participating in public unity initiatives, building, and now moving.

I come upon a winter undershirt you were saving for the day you'd be drafted. Many times this year I imagined you in uniform. I was full of anticipation for the moment I'd fill with maternal pride at my only son – handsome, tanned, with your eternal smile, resplendent in uniform. Contributing your brains and brawn to the IDF and Israel.

Your handwriting peeks out at me from an end-of-year activity you had, evidently in third grade. I always wondered why we save all the kid's drawings from preschool. Why do we collect all those certificates? Who even looks at them? Binders and folders gather mounds of dust until a lazy eye decides to brush them off before Pesach, if at all. But now I'm leafing curiously through your binder of certificates – hungrily reviewing your early grade school teachers' praise for your goodness of heart, overflowing with constant desire to help teachers and friends. I hold in my trembling hand a certificate you drew up for yourself at about age eight:

Name: Gil-ad Michael Shaer Born on: 19 Tevet

My parents named me this because: they want me to have joy forever

Place of birth: Kfar Batya

My hobby: going to the Beit Midrash

My favorite color: yellow

My favorite song: *Shir HaKavod*

What I want to do when I grow up: be a famous researcher

My favorite book: *The Secret Septet*

If I were granted three wishes I would ask for:

1. To be prime minister

2. To be part of the secret septet

3. To get everything I ask for

So much innocence, so much purity.

How I love you and miss you, my beloved son.

Sunday, 17 Av, August 2

One Summer Later

Hot. It looks like global warming. Summer 2015 has been unusually hot in Israel, in social terms as well.

There's an emotional tempest following the murder of Shira Banki at the Jerusalem Pride Parade. A girl of good character and ethics, salt of the earth, who participated because she wanted to support those who are different, the "other." Her death leaves a void not just in her family but in society as a whole.

The earth is burning; the land is scorched; the atmosphere is heating up.

The editors of *Yediot Aharonot* ask me to write a few words.

I write in hopes that my words will help cool down and calm the flames. I write that we have to cool the air from the same exalted place we reached as a society and as a people last summer. It's our nation's natural and proper place. Even if some individuals fail, that does not characterize its attitudes and leadership. We must adhere to positive thinking and remain coolheaded. Behind every incident is a family with faces and names, and we have to realize there's no room for stigmas and generalizations. We need inclusiveness, not stereotypes. I call on the people to take responsibility and silence the violence, but not the pain.

To silence the attempts at coercion but not the demand to examine the root causes. Let's consider: how and why did we get where we are? Let's explore in detail the ways we can implement suitable improvements, repairs, and mend the rifts and ills in society for the sake of a better future for our children, in every sense, and so we can feel whole with ourselves, whole but growing, marching forward in hope.

Let's imagine what we need to do to repair and improve so tomorrow our children will wake up to a better, more loving, more welcoming future; so that life will be better; so that we will feel at peace with ourselves, knowing we're moving forward.

Monday, 25 Av, August 10

I come back from the police station, from the ongoing work on your journals, Gil-adush. I'm tired, drained, emotional. The journey into your heart isn't easy.

Your writing is concise and direct. I'm reminded of your organized notebooks, which attested to the high level at which you understood the material. I think about the years in which I would examine my better students' notebooks to determine whether the material was comprehensible, whether my explanations and lessons were conveyed properly to the students, and where to improve my teaching.

There's no doubt a notebook reflects the student's understanding of the material. Your notebooks are like that, Gil-ad. Exemplary. Organized. Demonstrating an advanced ability to express yourself. Each sentence adds to the previous. Precise. Not too long or too short. It's so hard to get students to write things so briefly, so clearly. You had that, Gil-ad, and you excelled at leveraging it.

I peek into your inner thoughts with some worry. I'm almost unsurprised by what I read. I'm happy to discover I understood what was on your mind. The innocence of youth. The innocence of a boy writing something, certain that's where it will remain. A boy in adolescence who experienced highs and lows, a storm of feelings and deliberations. The writing of a smart, skeptical child-teen. Making demands of himself. Looking for happiness, goodness, joy.

A boy who senses he's in the middle, in a process, and doesn't imagine for a moment his life is going to be cut short physically and that the song of his life will continue long after he's gone.

These pages seem to contain it all.

Your last year opened with months of uncertainty, which later settled into the contentment of joy and satisfaction. It seems you went whole to your death. It's so sad, yet so reassuring and moving to know that so soon before your departure from us you felt good about yourself and your surroundings.

Moral questions poke at my brain unceasingly: should I publish your secrets? If so, when? And how?

At the laboratory I put on the white gloves and feel like I'm in a Sherlock Holmes movie. The story of this journal seems unreal, as if the story of your kidnap and murder were more realistic. I feel tremendous heavenly assistance that the journal was found, and what's more – that through manifest divine intervention, you wrote only on one side of each page, with wide margins, so that the parts that were burned or soaked were relatively small. Still, the writing needs to be deciphered.

At the lab they photographed the journal and gave it to us. Most of it is readable. Now we're going through it a page at a time, trying to understand what's smudged, what's been erased. It's a fascinating, long, and deep process. It takes me to you again and again.

The forensic staff shows extraordinary sensitivity, dedication, and loyalty. S. stays with me the whole time, apologizing to me that she's seeing your hidden thoughts. Hugging me when necessary. Making a latte for each meeting; maybe the coffee will provide the oomph I need to face this task. I remember the ambulance they brought to our house when they first told me they'd found the diary. We read line after line and type what we can decipher. When we can't read it with the naked eye, we use the computer's electronic eye, replacing the visible spectrum. What one wavelength can't show, another can. We use tweezers, a magnifying glass – the simplest accessories and the most advanced computers. The Israel Museum also contributes its experience and knowledge in preserving burned, soaked materials. We're making slow progress, but managing to decode most of the writing.

It's good that in my work as a teacher, after checking hundreds of tests, I've become an expert in deciphering handwriting. Suddenly another fruit of years of exhausting labor. Who'd have thought I'd need that skill, and for such a purpose...

S. shows me a copy of Ilan Ramon's diary that they decoded in this lab.

The comparison to Ilan Ramon's diary makes me tremble.

The notebooks are the same size. The spiral binding is identical.

In both cases it failed to fulfill its intended purpose and only part of it was found. The pages of Ilan Ramon's diary were soaked, but they still managed to recover a large portion of them. Your diary's pages were also soaked. Some were burned; they don't know if this is the whole thing.

Ilan became a national figure. You, Eyal, and Naftali became national figures.

But your diary is so personal, so innocent. It's not the diary of a soldier going out to battle, knowing that untold eyes would see the journal if he doesn't return.

It's the diary of a boy with no pretense, a boy at the start of forging his own clear self.

A boy who looked for the goodness, the happiness, who wanted to live up to his name – eternal joy – and succeeded.

Sunday, Rosh Chodesh Elul, 1 Elul, August 16

For several weeks I've been going to the police lab to decode your diary. One day one of the senior commanders comes in to ask how I was.

At first I don't understand. But then it comes out that they'd found another bunch of papers from Gil-ad's bag.

I can't absorb it. Another greeting from you? What will it be? Is there more stuff that hasn't reached us? I ask to go in person to the station in Hevron to check. The department head promises to go himself to make sure there's no more relevant material.

I leaf carefully through the new pages in front of me. Some of his schoolbooks and a pre-matriculation test on which he scored 98. I remember his history teacher describing how he couldn't understand why Gil-ad was waiting in line to challenge his grade. It turned out he didn't want to dispute the grade, but to understand what he needed to improve in order to score 100.

That's what you were like, always trying to do the best possible. If you're going to do something, do it well, and nothing can withstand such will.

Gil-ad's image was etched in that history teacher's heart. Two years later, he would name his newborn son Gil-ad.

Sunday, 1 Elul, August 16

Switzerland

The vacation to Switzerland caught us at a busy, tumultuous time. We seized it with both hands. We saw it as an opportunity to take a break, to refresh ourselves, and just be together.

We wanted a respite from the daily intensity, from the social tension here in Israel, and from the emotional stress around the house construction.

With all that swirling around in our heads, we landed in Switzerland. The invitation came to us just in time. An outsider would have a hard time understanding that no luxury, no trip, can reduce or decrease the loss even a bit. The opposite – a vacation can sometimes even underline the gaping void.

It doesn't matter what we do; we'll never be whole with what's missing.

For three days I practiced setting my thoughts aside and just enjoying the place. We spent a week with just the family, with our main worry being where to go in the morning and how to spend the day. The calm, the green, the grazing cows at the side of the road – all that made me think of the giant gaps separating Swiss society from Israeli.

An entire people in Israel wakes up each morning to a tense reality, facing livelihood issues and security uncertainty. An entire people is trying to live a life of meaning, of giving, of accomplishment, and of mission. An entire people is coping with terrorism, with wounds, with almost-daily loss of life.

It's so hard to put my thoughts aside.

I can do it, I tell myself. I proved to myself I can control my thoughts, but it's still hard to do.

Your absence, Gil-ad, grows in intensity on this trip. You loved to travel, to hike, in Israel or abroad; to see the world, to discover cultures, to behold vistas, to get intoxicated by the beauty of Creation and to connect with G-d through nature.

Gil-adush, the pain of your absence, in a place where nature's beauty reaches the sky, becomes unbearable. I have to work on my thoughts again – what I took from there I brought here.

I try to give myself some air to breathe, to get attached to the beauty of Creation – to the mountains rising to incredible heights, to the green expanses merging with one another to form gorgeous shades. Snowcapped mountaintops touch white clouds as the azure lakes meet the blue heavens at the horizon.

Everywhere, wherever you look, nature's beauty bursts out in inconceivable amounts. Pain and beauty flood over me, and I guess will never be separate for me ever again.

Monday, 1 Tishrei 5776, September 14

Rosh HaShanah: Crowning Hashem King over the World
G-d's presence was noticeable during the *chai* days and afterward during Protective Edge. My heart burst with worry and powerlessness, but at the same time our house experienced an elevation of spirit. The Divine Presence hovered there.

The fact that the boys were murdered right away, a few minutes after getting in the car, makes me realize that nothing would have helped. It's a decree – it hurts; it's incomprehensible; it's hard to accept – but it's a given.

It wouldn't have helped to get to the car sooner; more prayers wouldn't have helped; more good deeds wouldn't have done it. It was a decree not contingent on us and our behavior. There's Someone who governs the world in a way we don't understand, with which we often disagree, but He runs the world and we don't.

You need a lot of humility in grief.

In an opinionated generation, of knowledge and understanding of so many things, it's hard for us to accept there are things we can't understand or control.

In a generation that can find liquid on Mars, travel through space, and find natural gas under the endless sea floor, we're also trying to understand the Creator, interpreting every event, trying to explain G-d's workings with our intellect – diminishing G-d more and more, and then, when we don't like what's happening, refusing to connect. We disengage. We stop praying.

Our connection with G-d has to be completely different. I want to believe in something big, something I can't explain or fully understand. In Someone of whose thoughts my thoughts can't conceive the full breadth or depth.

I feel G-d's embrace. Even if it's too tight. Even if it's painful. Very painful.

Friday, 12 Tishrei, September 25

Second Year

They promised us the second year would be easier. So they promised.

In truth? I don't recommend it. Maybe we were in shock last year; maybe we got a huge embrace from all of *Am Yisrael*; maybe people are getting on with their lives and display less patience and sensitivity after a year. Maybe the desire to be strong and show the girls that life goes on has helped us. Maybe these are just some additional challenges that have become our lot this past year and make everything else difficult.

Maybe I don't remember anymore, and maybe that's just the way it is. It just hurts.

We've already learned you don't compare your pain to others'. There's no competition, and unfortunately, there's no shortage. There's more than enough pain to go around. It just hurts.

Friday; Shabbat is coming. A red-orange sun in the sky.

Only in Talmon can you see such noble beauty. I try so hard to bring in Shabbat with serenity. I know many people who try to bring in Shabbat serenely; it sometimes looks like a life's mission.

What I wouldn't give to have a window open in the supernal heavens and be shown a moment's peek at your Shabbat and how you, my precious son, prepare for it. But even if a window doesn't open, I believe, I know, you're happy there. Sometimes that gives me strength; after all, every parent wants the best for their children. Usually that's not enough. I want you here, close to me. I miss you. I miss you so much.

Do you miss me too? What happens to the emotions when body and soul separate? You were such a sensitive child – you always wanted the best for everyone. What happens to that up there? You're definitely not sitting still. We need a lot of prayers down here. For us, who have been left with the unfinished tasks, challenges, and fixing.

What a group has joined you, Eyal, and Naftali recently. Rabbi Aharon Lichtenstein, Uri Orbach (who asked to be buried near you and your two friends), and a long roster of terror victims over the last year. Isn't it crowded up there in that special section?

Shabbat is almost here, and soon I'll again pray with you during the Chazzan's repetition, during the part that connects the souls up there with the souls down here: "A crown they will give You, the masses of supernal angels, with Your people Israel, assembled below..."

Every time I'm in the synagogue for that prayer I think about the amazing bond between the precious souls on high with the precious souls down here, all seeking one thing – a crown they will give You, the King of all kings.

Monday, 29 Shevat, February 8, 2016

44th Birthday

My birthday prompts deep existential thoughts.

I remember the words of Yaakov: "Few and evil have been the days of my life." If that's how Yaakov summed up his life, what can I say, little old me?

Like Yaakov, my life is split in two, with the dividing line your death, Gil-ad. Times are tough. My soul has been tried by horrors and upheaval I'd never known and which threatened to subdue me. I needed special emergency reserves to draw from my life the strength and lessons that were totally unnecessary during the first part of my life.

So many fronts on which to cope. Even if it looks like I wrote about it all, what I didn't write dwarfs it.

I'm forty-four, and I feel like I've crossed oceans and deserts of emotional upheaval, that I've lived through so much. Sometimes I feel the exhaustion of a sixty-year-old.

After a talk I gave, a woman came over to me and said, "You're a blessed woman."

The words left me in shock. How can there be such a gap in perception, I wondered. How can how I feel be such a polar opposite to what this woman is saying to me. I have to change something about my attitude, I told myself. I have to talk about what I have.

Nothing can be taken for granted.

It's daily work.

We get drawn so easily into what we lack. Grief can suck you in. Tremendous pain always waits in ambush around the corner, waiting for the right moment, a moment of weakness and distraction, and then it pounces on you with all its power.

So yes, I can try to feel blessed even after the enormous blow that's landed on me, but it's a challenge.

You gave me a lot of strength, dear lady.

It's all a matter of perspective, of where you look at life from.

That's what makes all the difference.

Wednesday, 10 Iyyar, May 18

People ask me if I've changed.

I hope so.

We all need to change all the time. Change is embedded in us.

Every year during the Tishrei holidays I pray and hope that the coming year be better than the last. A year of greater clarity regarding my existence in this world. A year with less pain. A year with the strength to properly fulfill my mission in this world.

Each birthday I stand in front of the mirror, examining the person reflected in it, looking inside and hoping I'm better, truer, more worthy. I hope I'm progressing and developing.

All the more so after such a traumatic event, an event that prompts deep introspection, deeper examination of things, and changes you in so many ways.

Still, a friend who hadn't seen me in twenty years said to me with a smile, "The same Bat-Galim. The same smile. The same look in your eyes."

Of course deep internal changes don't make me somebody else. The deep internal work is supposed to make me more Bat-Galim. More myself.

For example, I discovered I don't breathe. I remember my students complaining there was never a dull moment in class. I would load them up with material in history or civics at a dizzying pace, trying to meet the objectives I'd set for myself and for them, and I did it.

But now I realize I wasn't breathing, and not only during class.

My life is a chain of uninterrupted races.

In my weekly radio program on the Moreshet network I hear myself – talking fast, not breathing.

Long moments pass without regular breathing. Breathe slowly... I even have to work on that.

I'm learning to run long distances; I'm learning to organize my soul; I hope I'm on the right path.

Sunday, 17 Av, August 21

Shirel and Itamar's Wedding Day

How do you marry off a daughter after such a loss?

Shirel, our oldest daughter, so beloved – how will I escort her to the *chuppah* with a broken heart? A month before the wedding my soul found no rest. The event seemed impossible to me. The young couple's engagement, in Sivan, was very close to Gil-ad's memorial service, and the preparations for the celebration were mixed with immense pain.

I remind myself again and again of what I have.

The young groom, Itamar, brings so much happiness and joy. The goodness flooding over us with the new family joining our ranks is almost unbelievable. Relatives who are also good friends – neighbors from Talmon – even before they were upgraded to the status of one family – is a rare, great privilege. Not to be taken for granted.

A week before the wedding I collect myself. My daughter's getting married!

I learn again that life's complexity makes it possible to feel tremendous joy alongside the existing void. The joy is manifest at higher and higher levels the closer the wedding gets, managing to fill up my existence, almost. Happiness and gratitude to the Creator for finding a husband in such a pleasant manner. Happiness from knowing that my daughter has found her other half, that she's satisfied and happy, that she's content.

I'm reminded of something Rabbi Singer said about the intensity of pain, which creates a depth that can then hold tremendous joy.

In my head echo the words of the poem "Pain's Precision, Joy's Blur," by Yehudah Amichai,* which describes my feelings exactly:

> Pain's precision and joy's blur.
> I consider the precision
> With which people describe their pain
> At the doctor's office.
> Even those who never learned to read and write
> Specify:
> This is a pulling pain; this one tears; this one's like a saw
> This burns; this is a sharp pain, that one dull.
> This one's over here, right here
> Yes, yes. But joy blurs everything.
> I've heard people say
> After nights of life and celebrations
> It was wonderful,
> I felt like I was in Heaven.
> And even the spaceman floating in space
> Connected to his spacecraft could only cry:
> Wonderful, fantastic, I have no words.
> Joy's blur and pain's precision
> But I also want to describe with the precision of a sharp pain
> The vague joy and happiness.
> I was taught to speak by pain.

And again brilliant Maor with her innocent questions, asks me, "Imma, so will Itamar be instead of Gil-ad?"

---

* Yehudah Amichai, "Pain's Precision, Joy's Blur," from *Open Closed Open*, Schocken Publishers, Jerusalem and Tel Aviv, 1998, p. 108.

"Itamar is like Gil-ad," I answer her. "Not instead. No one could be instead of Gil-ad, but Itamar is dear and loved like a son to us, like Gil-ad."

The feeling that our family is expanding fills me up. This is exactly what we need.

Friday, 15 Sivan 5777, June 9, 2017

Third Year
Missing a child.
There are days I can answer the question, "How are you?" with "Great," and I actually feel that way.

Shirel married Itamar, they finally moved into their new home, and routine is gradually resettling into daily life. What's changed is the understanding that the depth of joy can be manifest with the same intensity as of the pain.

A third year.
The pictures in the slide show don't change; what changes is the melody.

I've learned that my reservoir of tears is infinite – they always taste the same. What changes is the intensity of their flow.

A third year.
I think I've internalized the fact that Gil-ad won't come back; what changes our daily reality is our perspective.

Like a baby or a wounded person, we're learning to walk from the beginning. What changes is our perseverance and my patience for all this.

A third year.
Time sometimes loses some of the meaning it once had. What changes is the content, the language, the words we find to express ourselves.

Grief and loss are with me every day with every step, every pace. What changes is the realization that it's possible to live a full life nevertheless, along with that.

A third year.

My sensitivity has increased; sometimes I feel like my nerves are exposed and I'm impatient with trivialities. What changes is my realization that you don't have to be afraid of it.

I try to breathe slowly; what changes every now and then is my rate of breathing.

A third year.

The masseuse trying to loosen my tense muscles asks what I have in my diaphragm.

What doesn't change is the pit that refuses to be filled. What doesn't change is the soul that refuses to be consoled.

I'm more connected to myself.

Life's complexity allows pain and joy to exist within me side by side.

What doesn't change is the longing that has no end. I still cry during prayer. I still cry.

A third year.

Still missing a child.

Concluding Moments

How do you end an unending story?

So we had an inspiring summer and discovered what our nation is capable of.

We saw we have tremendous powers of unbounded love, mutual responsibility, dedication, and care. All for one and one for all.

The big question bothering me is what to do with that. Do we put Summer 2014 onto the bookshelf, the shelf of history, and learn about it in a few years with pathos and longing? Will we yearn for past moments and stay there?

Or will we do what's so expected, necessary, and demanded of us: take that destabilizing summer and make it part of our daily life, internalizing and instilling it in ourselves so that in our everyday we won't see such a huge national gap between then and now. The image of G-d that's in us will continue to grow. It's a personal responsibility each and every one of us carries.

Let's stop for moment the unceasing race to be in the changing headlines and seek the essential headline: how did connection sprout amid a people that seemed so divided? Was it a one-time thing, forced by emergency circumstances, or is that our true nature and those divisions are just a shell we have to remove with the right work?

It's amazing...

What made all those precious people feel so connected to this story?

Rabbi Druckman wrote at the time: "We looked for the boys and found ourselves."

What was it that we looked for and found in ourselves?

I think the answer lies first of all, simply in the solidarity of each person with the other's pain and distress. Indeed how could anyone not feel our pain, our inhuman situation into which we were thrust with no preparation? Anyone with humanity can feel solidarity naturally and humanly with our situation then. Still, I think there's another, deeper, more Israeli, more Jewish, level: we feel the connection between hearts because we know deep inside we're part of something big. The realization that there's something basic, a deep common denominator connecting everyone; the sense that we share more than we differ; the recognition that we're one people, with a shared past and future – these bond all segments of the population in Israel and the Diaspora.

Something in our identity has sharpened, clarified, as we remember we're brothers – "Return, Brothers."

Return, brothers; return, boys, and not just the boys – we're returning to ourselves, to the essential goodness in us. Each of us connected to the goodness inside by searching for the boys, and that made people connect to our story in a meaningful way. People felt the need to be better, each in his own way.

Senior IDF officials, such as Lt. Gen. (Res.) Benny Ganz and Col. (Res.) Eliezer Shkedi, are talking about the strength of the society and the disunity in it as Israel's next existential threat. Wow.

It's in our hands. It's our responsibility.

Each of us must ask himself: "Where was I during that meaningful summer? How much goodness did I see in myself, in the people around me, in this nation? What am I doing with that goodness? Where am I taking it?"

It's our responsibility to take that goodness further, without waiting for times of crisis or difficulty. A taxi driver who came to console us during the Shiva said, "People on the roads are driving differently now."

A different wind was blowing here among us; there was a joining of hands; we saw ourselves and others in a positive light.

That's the goodness stored within us. That's the true capability we have as a people.

When you repeat something again and again to remember it, there's a chance you'll internalize it.

Another bond, and another,
    And the multipliers of love are revealed in our society.
    And when we multiply love,
    With care that we can see here
    (In Israeli society and among the Jews of the Diaspora)
    We'll find our strengths together; we'll discover how being together strengthens us
    Because we don't have the option to be divided; quarrels weaken us.
    And we have to make space for everyone,
    Without changing ourselves, without leaving anyone out.
    Because that absence diminishes the whole, whereas connection augments it.
    And maybe one plus one isn't two,
    But an even bigger, more meaningful one, And it's worth investing in that unity,
    Because we can't live with the invisible and with the unknown.

Today we can no longer suffice with "Return, Brothers"; the winning combination is "We're All Brothers!"

Gil-ad's Diaries

The following are sections of Gil-ad's journal.
This is the original text.
I've inserted ellipses where we could not decipher the text.
I've added comments and explanations in square brackets to
help make the text more comprehensible.

BS"D

Tuesday, 7 Shevat 5774

[...]

I jogged with Fischer this evening. After not having run since the end of ninth grade...

It's satisfying.

BS"D

Thursday, 8 Shevat 5774

Tonight I'm doing the Lamed-Heh trail* with Id, Uri, Kfir, Hen and Yair. I hope and pray it turns out well. Not just firecrackers and girls, but also values and other more important things. We'll see if
I succeed in giving over some of the guidance that Rabbi Osher [of Yeshivat Mekor Hayyim] gave us this afternoon.

BS"D

[...]

Everyone has the "drugs" that calm him and make him feel good. For me it's sugar and math. Yup, I like eating sugar. But it's very bad for me. Oysh. Sometimes I control myself. Sometimes not. And... yes, mathematics – there's nothing more fun and relaxing
than doing a good math exercise.

---

* The Lamed-Heh trail is the path taken by 35 soldiers in May 1948 in their hope to assist in the battle for the besieged Kfar Etzion. They were discovered and killed before reaching their destination.

[...]
I have a very powerful dream. I want so much to make it come true but inside
something's keeping it from me.
To play music.
A dream to express myself. To find myself [with an instrument...] connected to it. So why don't I do it...
[...]
to start. I know I won't succeed. I don't [just] know. I feel it.
A bitter feeling of failure inside. I'm filled with envy every time I see someone playing. If I could have a wish fulfilled, I'd
ask immediately to know how to play. Something inside me loves every instrument. Drums,
guitar, piano, the standard instruments, but so special, each one expressing itself. And something that's choking me is keeping it from me.
To play.
A dream.

BS"D
Monday, 17 Adar I 5774
Just last Monday I served as *chazzan* at yeshiva
for Shacharit and Mincha. Shacharit was one of
my strongest prayers ever. Before the prayers I prepared myself to serve

as an emissary. For the prayers to go from the community to G-d through me.
It was an empowering, special experience.
I was so moved during the prayer. I worked to focus and purify

my prayer and I felt amazing.
Now I pray that many more of my prayers will be
like that. Because right after my prayers I fall.
I'm late to prayers and sometimes even miss them.
But today I decided I'm going to stop falling.
Falling into s[in]. Falling into despair. I won't let it
take control of me.
I hope to succeed. With G-d's help
[...]
This evening we came back from a gathering with Rabbi Yitzchak Ginsburg
at the Shvut Yisrael yeshiva in Efrat. It was very special.
The Rabbi blessed me to learn Halacha and Hassidut. Mostly Hassidut.

There's been a lot of talk in my grade recently about how bad people have it
[no one's] into it, and everything's a "waste of time." But things are like that **only because** of that talk!
The general [atmosphere] is what sets the tone. If people start saying everything's great,
and the atmosphere['s good, there]'s strength and desire, people want to accomplish stuff, to learn and receive, then
we can rise to higher levels.
[Bottom li]ne, it all depends on the atmosphere. Each one of us has an impact.

BS"D
Thursday, 20 Adar I 5774
I'm happy now because now I'm doing work
with Amichai [Krakover] on Megilat Esther
and we've started to develop an idea.
It makes me happy because it's something I've done,
and it gives me a feeling of satisfaction [...]

It makes me happy to have people close
[to] me who are happy. When I'm satisfied. Someone
[...arouses] joy in me. Also when there's a happy occasion [...]

BS"D
Thursday, 27 Adar I 5774
I'm sitting with the essay in front of me, "Greater Was the Removal of the Ring," that I wrote
together with Amichai over the last week in our Tanakh track.
It's an incredible feeling to produce a novel Torah thought. Joy floods me. While I was writing we suddenly felt
a sort of "mini-divine-presence coming to rest upon us." I was so, so happy!
I'm very proud of this essay. My *chiddush* in Torah.
With Hashem's help I want to experience that again in my life [and] many more times.
Thank You, G-d!

BS"D
Tuesday, 9 Adar II 5774
Yesterday it was "Adar Day" in Jerusalem.
What joy there was! I haven't been that happy in a long
time. I like being happy. My name is Gil-ad, after all.
And I've decided I'm going to live up to my name my whole life –
Gil-ad: happy always.
I've also noticed a change happening in me. I used to really want
to be where it's happiest and full of the most laughter. Now I'm
the one who makes
that happen. I felt amazing.
[...]

BS"D
Sunday, 21 Adar II 5774
I ran an amazing program. Thank You, Hashem!
After having it ready for two months I finally got to run it.
Like aged wine, it sat in my head well and came out exactly the
right way.
It's been a long time since they [the kids] sat there so quietly and
seriously.
It's also helping me with the same subject; I'm getting better at it.
[...]
Modesty.
A person's characteristics when he's by himself – does he live a life
of internals or externals, that sanctifies only his life
within himself – even when no one's looking.

A person doesn't share and call attention to everything about himself.

There are things that belong only to him: basic characteristics, thoughts.

When you bring it out, it becomes the property of others; it's not personally yours anymore.

The soul is a part of the supernal G-d [– Tanya]. The body is the soul's container. The body is holy.

Modesty [externality and internality] = humility. A person recognizes his own value [including beauty] But knows his inborn Characteristics and talents aren't his doing.

What does Judaism have against the physical?

Judaism doesn't oppose the material; the opposite, but one who stresses the external

over the internal can't avoid sinning.

Spirituality is the highest thing, but by nature it's hidden; if we stress the external –

[...] body – over the internal, we're likely to forget the internal.

[Fr]iends, products, and other things we choose based on their quality, not their appearance.

A friend, you don't just replace him cause he's less attractive.

[...] the internal bond is much stronger than some fleeting externality!!

[There's] a place for beauty, but modestly. Modesty doesn't smother beauty, but to [...]

[it has to be] strong, not connected only to the external, but mainly to the soul and strong emotion.

Modesty – to stress the internal, and through that, the external is revealed.

[...]
The words *ish* and *isha* – man and woman – contain [the letters of *esh*, fire]
Love between man and woman is full of energy like [fire].

"Fire – if handled properly – also creates [light]
and electricity, warming things and doing everything: cooking, operating the
refrigerator, the oven, the air conditioner, the washing machine, the [iron, etc.].
But if handled wrong – it can bu[rn, electrocute]
and cause burns; it can burn down the house, and even [kill].

Electrical wires are always covered. You ca[n't] touch them, [and for greater]
safety they're covered. They're always parallel, and only
when you need to use them do they connect and work ingeniously.
[Is it even] possible to ask why you're not allowed to touch wires?
Why they can't be
exposed? Why they're concealed in a house? Why we don't let them [come into contact]
with water?

You can say you're not allowed to do anything with fire, no, no, [no,] bu[t] the tru[th]
is [that if you take proper precautions] with f[ire it] makes life [easier and happi]er. [Whe]n does trouble happen[? When you're not careful!]

You don't have to get burned in order to learn that fire [burns] Both because not all burns heal, and there might [remain a scar] for the rest of your life, and also because it's possible to learn from the experiences [of others]."
[A quote from *The Revealed within the Concealed*, a booklet on modesty put out by Bnei Akiva]

This week I had fantasies about physical contact with girls, second thoughts about modesty
with unprecedented force.
After I read that passage I relaxed.
[...]
I feel so good about myself! I'm so happy!
Have a good week.

BS"D
Monday, 7 Nisan 5774
There's something special about me!
I felt I've finally found something I'm good at.
My life force.
That's what I call it.
I feel I have tremendous vitality.
It's manifest in the great joy I try to have
(Gil-ad... it's not just my name),
It's manifest in the powerful love I have: love of my family,
of friends. I have the infinite power of love that wants
the best for those I love and are close to me, that wants to be close to them.
It makes me happy.

[...]
I've decided I'm sick of sliding back during vacation. I'm done with getting up late
in the morning, barely praying, skipping prayers and not doing anything meaningful. For the time being, *Baruch Hashem*, I'm succeeding!
It feels good. All the prayers. Watching [my]self
Using my time really well. Working. *Baruch Hashem!*
Thank You, G-d! And help me maintain[n]...

BS"D
Friday, 16 Iyyar 5774
Use of time is something everyone wants to be good at.
This week was amazing.
3 pretests and a matriculation exam, and that definitely shows I'm deep in
my eleventh-grade studies.
Laying the cornerstone for the youth chapter. To tell you the truth, I was moved. Till now
I've had hesitations about my being a counselor. Yes, I'm a little worn down. But it's
dependent on my will. And I'm not yet totally set on that decision with myself.
As with any decision, in this case,
I have to be whole with myself. Otherwise I've lost out in every direction.
[...]
When we came back from Pesach break and we started this part of the year, I decided

I'm going to give everything my all. To push myself to produce not as much as I can –
but more. To integrate. With my family and the chapter it's been hard to invest
recently. But *Baruch Hashem* I felt I'm integrating splendidly among Torah, classes, friends. During all the sessions I'm learning fantastically with
amazing partners. I'm putting a lot into my classes, hoping to do well, and *Baruch Hashem* I
feel like overall it's going very well. And with friends, I'm deepening bonds
and friendships. We go out to have a good time, to enjoy, because it's so important right now.

This Shabbat – it's a Shabbat Yeshiva, but half the class isn't around. It's a downer.
Every decision you make you go all the way. So with Hashem's help it'll be an [amazing Sha]bbat
and thank You for everything, Abba in Heaven!

BS"D
Monday, 19 Iyyar 5774
Our Sages have said: "Anyone whose fear of sin precedes his wisdom, his wisdom lasts,
and anyone whose fear of sin does not precede his wisdom, his wisdom does not last."
There doesn't seem to be a connection between the two!
Let's try to think, What is one's fear of sin? How is it so special?
Fear of sin, I think, is a trait of someone considered, who weighs

his steps, a person who pays attention not just to what he's doing, but also thinks
about the outcome. A person who's not like that, who only acts according to the drives
within him, who lives by his urges, and automatically gives them precedence over wisdom,
hasn't earned the retention of his wisdom. Wisdom is the asset of a person
of consideration, not of impulsivity. Such a person is certainly worthy of having his wisdom
endure, as it comes from a deeper, more thoughtful place. All of his wisdom
is true, deliberate, considered wisdom. Not fickle, momentary.
I hope I'm worthy to [have] fear of sin that precedes my wisdom.

Thanks

Thanks to the Creator of the World who privileged me to write these things down and bind them in a book.

A special thank you to my husband Ofir, who always supports, accompanies, and empowers me. Thank you to my five beloved daughters – Shirel, Tahel, Meitar, Hallel, and Maor – who have been joined this year by our new son-in-law, the refined and good-looking Itamar. They all give me the boost I need to choose life, and teach me what coping is.

Thank you to my wonderful neighbors and friends, who are there for me.

Thank you to my neighbors on the synagogue bench on Shabbat, who bear my pain and tears.

Thank you to Roni Arazi, president of Mashrokit, for the idea for the book's title.

Thank you to David Swidler for his professional translation of the book, to Hila Ratzabi on the meticulous editing. A special thank you to Nir Zigdon and Odelia Orbach owners of eCommunity, to their entire team and especially to Shimon Finkelstein for taking on the task of publishing the book on Amazon, which finally brought the book into your hands, the reader.

A big, special thank you to Carmela Amitai-Yechezkel, whom I got to know after she sent us a condolence letter during our first year of mourning; the bond with her continues to deepen. Carmela was with us in her love and solidarity through the writing of this book, and served as an interlocutor for forging ideas, infused me with the strength to finish it, and diligently devoted herself to its final formulation.

Thank you very much to dear Barbara Freedman, who accompanies me through the challenges of the English language, and from an English teacher became a teacher and friend for life.

Many thanks to Sharon Brown, Marisa Stadtmauer, and Terri Henrenstein for their help and assistance in publishing the book in English. You understood how important it is that this story be translated into a language that is spoken by many, encouraged and helped me bring this vision to life.

I owe a thank you to many other good people – some of whom we've been privileged to know over the last three years, and from whom we've received tremendous support. Their names and places have been omitted from the book, but are etched deep in my heart, with love and infinite appreciation.